New Models for American Education

Edited by

JAMES W. GUTHRIE
EDWARD WYNNE

Prentice-Hall, Inc., Englewood Cliffs, New Jersey

P: 13-615120-5
C: 13-615146-9

Library of Congress Catalog Card Number: 73:135410

Printed in the United States of America

Current printing (last digit):

10 9 8 7 6 5 4 3 2 1

PRENTICE-HALL INTERNATIONAL, INC., *London*
PRENTICE-HALL OF AUSTRALIA, PTY. LTD., *Sydney*
PRENTICE-HALL OF CANADA, LTD., *Toronto*
PRENTICE-HALL OF INDIA (PRIVATE) LIMITED, *New Delhi*
PRENTICE-HALL OF JAPAN, INC., *Tokyo*

This book is dedicated to the memory of
Robert F. Kennedy,
his ideas and ideals.

*"Some men see things as they are and say, 'Why?'
I dream things that never were and say, 'Why not?'"*

Contents

Foreword

Nothing could be more appropriate for public education today—particularly for urban education—but by no means exclusively so—than the consideration of new models to replace the old, or new ways of implementation of those sound and traditional models which simply have been permitted to fail among lower status children in American cities.

The contributors to this book have been selected purposely to reflect divergent experiences and perspectives and have been urged to express their views with candor. All, however, are concerned with the ineffectiveness of public education, especially as it affects the poor and the minority group student, and the differential quality of education available to the affluent. All are concerned to confront this problem by presenting constructive alternatives. All assume that it is the responsibility of the schools to achieve at least minimum goals of student performance. The effect, in general, is to shift the focus of public school education from the presentation of alibis to the establishment of performance objectives for schools as well as students. The shift means that allegedly inferior student inputs, such as inadequate family background, do not excuse the school from achieving at least minimum performance objectives among all the children they serve. The premise for the shift is that, despite student diversity, the vast majority of children in schools are normal and, therefore, these children can, if properly taught, achieve and surpass national standards in basic skills.

Various devices for improving school performance are offered. Some emphasize diagnosis and assessment of student problems, performance incentives, and other measures of accountability within and without the system. Others emphasize basic organizational changes, such as the reallocation of power via decentralization and community control or alternative school systems.

I do not agree with all of the prescriptions—and indeed the range itself precludes consensus. However, I do agree strongly that the public school in America is presently unresponsive to contemporary educational needs. The institution must be reorganized in fundamental ways if the objectives of academic achievement are to be met for all children. The school, as it stands, has become a pawn in a power struggle among conflicting interest groups. The interest of the child himself is often incidental to other priorities. The institution has come to reflect and reinforce—when it should serve to transcend—the differences of race and class in American life. The needs of the child, which are the needs of society and the justification for public support of schools, must once again be made central to the educational process.

Past experience has made clear that no one answer or gimmick can solve the deeply rooted and wide-ranging problems of public school education. The solution lies only, in my view, in a total approach. Such a total approach involves the establishment of clear and specific objectives, high teacher expectations for student performance, a network of supports for teachers and supervisors, and a consistent and rigorous system of assessment of performance.

But even the most innovative and daring of models can be distorted, diluted, or diverted. We have learned this from our experience with anti-poverty programs and compensatory education experiments. The forces of reaction are entrenched and determined. They are quite capable of embracing reform only to corrupt it. So the exploration and the adoption of new models, however promising, is the beginning and not the end of the journey. Nevertheless, it is time that journey got underway.

KENNETH B. CLARK

Preface

Education, or at least formal education, at the time of our nation's founding was viewed as having only limited practical value. Extended schooling was a luxury reserved to an elite few. In the period between then and now, economic and social developments have transformed education into an enterprise which is estimated presently to involve one out of every three individuals in our population. From a time when almost no one went to school, we have evolved to a point where almost everyone goes to school.

Despite the vast expansion of the functions schools are expected to perform and the awesome changes in the numbers and characteristics of students, the basic model for education is that which characterized schools in the 17th and 18th centuries. The traditional practice of grouping students within four walls to listen to a teacher has persisted; while we have undergone revolutions in fundamental endeavors such as manufacturing, agriculture, transportation, and communication, the process of schooling has remained remarkably stable.

The fact that other institutions and practices have changed over time is not in itself a particularly persuasive argument that schools should also change. However, education has expanded to become an integral part of our social fabric; as such, it now is tied tightly to our other institutions, the economy, the family, the military, and so on. As a consequence of this linkage, when the other institutions change, and schools remain the same, tensions are provoked. Such tensions may only be visible at first around the periphery, at points where the educational system is in contact with other systems. Difficulty for certain groups in locating employment, increased crime, rising levels of social conflict may all be consequences of the friction which occurs when schools and the other social institutions with which they come into contact do not move in harmony. In time, however, this tension moves from the periphery and begins to characterize the educational system itself.

It is the contention of the editors and contributors to this book that it is time to reexamine the basic educational model in the United States. We may well have reached the point at which we cannot tolerate further discrepancy between what schools do and what their clients and surrounding institutions expect them to do. The evidence and expression of dissatisfaction are increasing.

But what changes should be made? If it is clear that our educational model is in need of reform, it is not so clear as to what direction such reform should take. Only a charlatan can claim to have a final answer, and certainly this book is not meant to convey a simple solution. We do not endorse or recommend the adoption of any one model or any combination of models. Rather, our hope is that the presentation of this array of possible changes will provoke informed discussion. It is our intent that professional educators take part in the discussion, and we would look for them to be among the best sources of additional information about any of the new models presented here. However, ultimately we hope the forum will be enlarged to encompass interested laymen. It is our premise that significant educational reform will occur only when the larger society begins to desire change and participates in discussions about it. This book is directed toward that end.

As with any authors and editors, we were assisted greatly by other people in our efforts to assemble this volume. Our heaviest debt of gratitude is owed Marion L. Crowley who typed and assisted in editing the final manuscript. We are grateful to Ramona Fellom and Jackie Janzen for their work on earlier versions. Also we wish to acknowledge the contributions and constructive criticisms of our colleagues and students in the Division of Policy Planning and Administration, School of Education, University of California, Berkeley. Particularly in this regard we wish to thank Charles S. Benson, Guy Benveniste, G. B. Kleindorfer, Rodney J. Reed, and J. Chester Swanson.

Finally, we would like to say that a great deal of the energy for this book stems from the idealism which was imparted to our society by Robert F. Kennedy. This book is dedicated to his memory and the proceeds from its sale are used for the support of fellowships for minority group graduate students at the University of California.

JAMES W. GUTHRIE
EDWARD WYNNE

THE CONTRIBUTORS

DWIGHT W. ALLEN, School of Education, University of Massachusetts, Amherst, Massachusetts.

WILLIAM H. CLUNE, III, Counsel and Research Associate, Illinois Institute for Social Policy, Chicago, Illinois.

JAMES S. COLEMAN, Professor, Department of Social Relations, Johns Hopkins University, Baltimore, Maryland.

JOHN E. COONS, School of Law, University of California, Berkeley, California.

ANDREW EFFRAT, Department of Sociology, The Ontario Institute for Educational Studies, Toronto, Ontario.

FREDERICK DAVID ERICKSON, College of Education, University of Illinois, Chicago Circle Campus, Chicago, Illinois.

WILLIAM V. FANSLOW, School of Education, University of Massachusetts, Amherst, Massachusetts.

ROY E. FELDMAN, Department of Political Science, Massachusetts Institute of Technology, Cambridge, Massachusetts.

GEORGE B. KLEINDORFER, Department of Education and School of Business Administration, University of California, Berkeley, California.

ELIEZER KRUMBEIN, College of Education, University of Illinois, Chicago Circle Campus, Chicago, Illinois.

HENRY M. LEVIN, School of Education and Department of Economics, Stanford University, Stanford, California.

RALPH J. MELARAGNO, Senior Research Scientist, System Development Corporation, Santa Monica, California, and Co-Director, Tutorial Community Project, Pacoima, California.

GERALD NEWMARK, Senior Research Scientist, System Development Corporation, Santa Monica, California, and Co-Director Tutorial Community Project, Pacoima, California.

THOMAS F. PETTIGREW, Department of Social Relations, Harvard University, Cambridge, Massachusetts.

WILSON C. RILES, Superintendent of Public Instruction, California State Department of Education.

HARVEY M. SAPOLSKY, Department of Political Science, Massachusetts Institute of Technology, Cambridge, Massachusetts.

ROBERT T. STOUT, Claremont Graduate School, Claremont, California.

STEPHEN D. SUGARMAN, attorney with O'Melveny & Myers, Los Angeles, California.

RALPH W. TYLER, formerly Director of the Center for Advanced Study in the Behavioral Sciences, Stanford, California, now with Science Research Associates, Chicago, Illinois.

one

Introduction

NEW MODELS: THE NEED FOR SCHOOL REFORM

James W. Guthrie

> Let us begin by perfecting the system of education as the proper foundation whereon to erect a temple to liberty, and to establish a wise, equitable, and durable policy, that our country may become indeed an asylum to the distressed of every clime—the abode of liberty, peace, virtue, and happiness. . . .—Robert Coram, 1791[1]

Robert Coram was a Revolutionary period journalist who, shortly after the founding of this nation, took up his pen to advocate the establishment of an extensive and effective system of public education. Like many patriots, he was remarkably idealistic, and, as the above quotation suggests, his expectations were by no means modest. Nevertheless, over the years, much of Coram's plea has been translated into practice, and a substantial portion of his hopes have been realized.

However, there is still work to be done. We have increasing and persuasive evidence to the effect that large segments of the public are dissatisfied with the performance of our educational system. And, as a nation propelled by a tradition of educational idealism, and relatively unencumbered by material scarcity, we are under a strong compulsion to

1 Robert Coram, "A Plan for the General Establishment of Schools Throughout the United States," reprinted in Frederick Rudolph, ed., *Essays on Education in the Early Republic* (Cambridge: Harvard University Press, 1965), p. 145.

fulfill the goals stated by Coram; our national conscience will be haunted by anything less than perfection of our educational system.

It is not at all clear, however, that we can achieve the needed improvements by retaining intact our present model for elementary and secondary education. Human aspirations are partly a product of instruction, as well as innate desires. Thus, if important educational changes are needed, society may only move toward those changes if new or improved models are proposed to whet its appetite for change. Consequently, our main purpose in this book is to introduce and examine several alternative educational models. Some of the alternatives are founded on premises which conflict with current practices and, thus, the likelihood is that they would have to be adopted altogether and to the exclusion of the present system. Other suggestions for improvement are in fact "modules" and may be combined with existing schools or school districts in varying ways. Hopefully, the models will serve as foci for public and professional debate, and as stimulants for change. Because we believe public intervention in policy making to be an essential component of change, we have attempted to develop a collection of articles that can be read by the concerned layman, as well as the professional educator. However, before turning to these new ideas, let us first survey some of the past successes of our educational system, attempt to assess present public opinion about it, and analyze some possible explanations for its apparent inability to perform satisfactorily.

THE GREAT EXPERIMENT IN PERSPECTIVE

In the early portion of the 19th century, America began to provide more people with more education than any other society had ever done before. In other cultures and at other times, schooling was a scarce commodity, available only to a wealthy few. Retaining education as the preserve of an elite was justified by the belief that only a small minority of persons was intellectually able to benefit from schooling. Thus, to many observers, America's efforts at mass education took on the color and tone of a radical venture. Even a number of the most generous persons looked upon it as the "Great Experiment." Could it work? Could everyone benefit from schooling? What would happen to the talented few when an effort was made to dispense education to the many? Moreover, could a nation survive such a siphoning of resources as would be necessary to provide schooling for everyone?

Today, almost two centuries later, these questions appear to have been answered. Obviously, our economy has not been warped by any disproportionate expenditure of resources in the education sector. On the contrary, economists now contend that a significant portion of our remarkable economic development would never have occurred if we had not tried our "Great Experiment."[2] It appears, moreover, that large numbers of individuals, the "common masses" if you like, can profit from schooling. Our literacy rate is high, as a people we read more than most any other nation, our workers are productive at tasks requiring the ability to interpret complex technical instructions, and we support orchestras, museums, poets, and art galleries in an unmatched manner.

The state and ability of our populace on all these dimensions may not meet the criteria of a connoisseur, but taken as a whole, no large nation has ever before reached such a high level of overall sophistication. And, for the die-hard skeptic who asserts that there still remain many thousands of adults who read "comic books," we can reply, "At least they can read, and that is probably more than their social and economic peers in most other places and times have achieved. Finally, fears about stifled genius appear to be unfounded. America seems to have produced her share, and perhaps more than her share, of the world's great artists, scientists, inventors, statesmen, and, yes, even military commanders.

Thus, to those who inquire as to whether or not the "Great Experiment" has succeeded, the general reply most assuredly must be a firm "yes." Consequently, those who advocate altering the educational system in a drastic fashion should proceed with some caution. A system which has produced with such relative success should not be discarded lightly or rapidly. The evangelistic proponents of educational change and prophets of societal doom would do well to view themselves within the perspective of this successful history before so roundly condemning the entirety of America's educational efforts.

However, to answer the general question about the effectiveness of our educational system in the affirmative is to oversimplify the situation on at least two dimensions. First, the system has not been consistently successful. From time to time, it has been held to be ineffective, and only a major reassessment of its purpose and redefinition of its operation enabled it to reassume a successful posture. Second, to affirm its past successes should not blind us to the possibility of present shortcomings. Indeed, there is a mounting outcry to the effect that our "Great Experiment" may presently be in the throes of one of its most serious failures and badly in need of reform.

In the Epilogue to this book, we discuss some previous school reform efforts, and attempt to identify the social and political dynamics which appear to influence large-scale educational change. However, the burden of *this* chapter rests not so much upon history as it does with contemporary conditions. We sense a growing public dissatisfaction with the

[2] See Theodore W. Schultz, "The Rate of Return in Allocating Investment Resources to Education," *The Journal of Human Resources,* Vol. 2, No. 3 (Summer 1967), 293-309.

American educational system. Increasing numbers of people are coming to view the schools' efforts as, at best, inappropriate and, quite possibly, harmful for many of the children they serve. Moreover, there is a growing public feeling that schools may not only be failing students as individuals, but also failing our total society in the process.

WHO'S DISSATISFIED?

Whether you take as your source the rising tide of complaints on the part of parents and citizen groups, the unrest of students, the increasing number of popular novels describing failures of our schools, or the heightened level of governmental concern over education, the evidence is mounting that significant numbers of Americans either already have made or are about to make a very serious reassessment of the entire educational system.

It is difficult to identify the roots of this movement in time. There have always been dissatisfied elements in our population who have voiced criticism of the schools. In the 1950s, Admiral Rickover and the historian, Arthur Bestor, complained bitterly that schools were academically inadequate and lacked the intellectual rigor necessary to prepare our nation's leaders. At the time of World War I, and on into the 1920s, Congress and businessmen complained that the schools were remiss in not preparing more technicians and skilled workers to meet the needs of our increasingly technical industrial machine. Prior to that, at the turn of the century, critics raked the schools for their scholastic sterility and asked that the curriculum be altered so as to place students more closely in touch with reality. We could continue to enumerate complaints and to trace them all the way back to the time of our nation's founding. No institution as visible and pervasive as the schools can hope to meet successfully the expectations of all the people at all times. The sources of dissatisfaction and suggestions for alleviating problems will vary with the group and issue at hand, but at any one time we can almost always find dissidents who desire educational reforms.

Thus, our message is *not* that the phenomenon of public dissatisfaction is unique; such is not the case. Rather, the point we wish to convey is that criticism about American education appears to be rapidly reaching a significant threshold of intensity.

PARENTS AND CITIZENS

The growing concern for change is expressed in a variety of ways. Parents of under-educated children are becoming increasingly vocal in their criticism of school systems. Take, for example, the boycott actions of Harlem residents when their suggestions for the operation of I.S. 201 were not heeded; or, the photographs of angry black mothers stalking the picket lines and admonishing striking New York City teachers whom they viewed as depriving students of a much needed education; or, the growing demand for community control of schools by ghetto parents who hope somehow to establish educational organizations responsive to the needs of their children.

The educational impotence to which these citizens are objecting is most obvious in our large cities. However, these same distressing circumstances also exist in many of our rural areas. A difference in rural areas is that lower population densities and extremely debilitating poverty (concern for their children's stomachs may come first in parents' minds) have served to inhibit the organized outrage exhibited frequently by parents in city ghettos. In time, however—and probably in a very short time—we will hear from rural groups also. The growing realization of their plight by American Indians and Mexican-Americans is already a harbinger of complaints to come. A great deal of our rural poverty is experienced by these two groups, and one of their most intense demands is likely to be for more effective schools. Similar pleas from rural whites will not be far behind. Even now, there is evidence from Chicago of the beginning of an unseemly coalition. Newly arrived whites from the poverty pockets of Appalachia sometimes seek organizational advice from militants in nearby black ghettos.

STUDENTS

The cry for change comes not only from parents but also from their children. Student protest is not an entirely new phenomenon in our history: we have experienced and survived student riots before. What is different today is the deep-seated nature of the conflict and the degree to which it pervades not only colleges but lower education as well. Student protest is attributed to a large number of factors. However, we must distinguish between underlying causes and temporary triggering incidents. Some of the alleged "causes"—the war in Vietnam, the conspiracy of the so-called military-industrial complex, the empty ring of the war on poverty—could clearly be the subject of understandable dissatisfaction. However, it may also be that such social defects are esentially stimulants which are triggering a more basic predisposition toward student dissent. For instance, is the current increase in youthful drug abuse all the result of large and demoralizing ideological issues?

While the protests have typically tended to involve more college than high school students, all the protestants are products of a common secondary education, and the seeds of their dissatisfaction may well have been sown at that time. Why has their school experience left them so alienated from the larger society? What do they mean by their demands for "relevant education"? In what ways have some of even our most "exemplary" suburban schools failed? Finally, at what point will these student dissatisfactions inspire new patterns of demands on schools from their parents?

WRITERS

Holden Caulfield, in J. D. Salinger's *Catcher in the Rye,* was a product of a private school and a well-to-do family. Yet his feelings about the insignificance of his schooling and his teachers enabled thousands of adolescents to identify with him, and, simultaneously, gain insights into their own disappointment and frustration with school. The film version of *Blackboard Jungle* became popular with teenagers as much for introducing the pulsating song, "Rock Around the Clock," as for anything else; however, it also dramatically informed their parents of the dreadful conditions in some big city high schools. Bel Kaufman, in *Up the Down Staircase,* used humor to describe the organizational rigidities which stifled her as a teacher, but her sharp wit did not disguise the pathetic fashion in which overadherence to centrally issued regulations hindered the most persistent efforts of teachers and students to work productively.

We could continue by analyzing many more such works: *The Vanishing Adolescent, Death at an Early Age, Thirty-Six Children, Growing Up Absurd, How Children Fail,* and so on. On occasion, even a renowned scholar enters the act as was the case with James Bryant Conant's *Slums and Suburbs.* In some instances, these writers have treated the subject in an overly polemical and romantic fashion, and reality becomes distorted. Sometimes the author's own problems of psychological adjustment or, more accurately, maladjustment are as much a cause of the student ills he describes as are the school systems with which he is finding fault. However, these works in their aggregate have hastened the growth of public concern for educational reform.

PUBLIC OFFICIALS

A significant era of judicial dissatisfaction with school performance was begun by the famous 1954 United States Supreme Court decision in *Brown* v. *Board of Education.* In this and a number of later cases, the courts made plain their views that racially segregated schools are detrimental to those children who are discriminated against. These cases may have triggered more debate and delay than desegregation, but this should not deceive us into devaluating their contributions altogether. The desegregation cases place the weight of the law behind the dissatisfied and lend a great deal of moral suasion in their behalf. Also, the cases served to bring the dismal school conditions of minority group children before the general public—an important step in the reform process.

In an indirect fashion, the factors which triggered judicial dissatisfaction with existing educational practices have also stimulated congressional action. Approval of the anti-poverty bill, the 1964 Economic Opportunity Act, was in part fostered by congressional skepticism about the effectiveness of public schools for all poor children. Headstart, Upward Bound, and the Job Corps were all originally designed to operate outside the boundaries of the "educational establishment." In time, the politically powerful forces of the established system won a piece of the action and obtained passage of the 1965 Elementary and Secondary Education Act. Under Title I of this law, over $1 billion is annually available to schools with poverty students. Still later, the establishment successfully co-opted the operation of almost all the educational programs administered by the Office of Economic Opportunity. Although most congressional legislation now places federal education funds in regular school channels, there is a large body of testimony to the effect that, when forced to rely solely upon their own devices, public schools had failed to cope successfully with the problems of educating a significant portion of the student population.

Congressional concern for schools is also evident in the 1964 authorization for the Equality of Educational Opportunity Survey. The results of this survey, the so-called Coleman Report, document dramatically the schools' failure to reach poor and minority group children. Critics of the Report argue vehemently that its findings regarding the causes of school effectiveness are flawed due to the application of inappropriate statistical procedures. However, there is little disagreement concerning the Report's finding about the under-educated condition of large groups of American children—a finding which has done much to refocus the attention of the public and government officials upon the need for school reform.

In many ways, the executive branch of the government is more sensitive to urban problems than either of its two structural peers. Thus, it is not surprising that a number of pronouncements about weaknesses of public schools and proposals for reform have flowed from this source. The major initiatives for both the 1964 anti-poverty bill and the 1965 Elementary and Secondary Education Act arose from the president's office. In addition to promoting legislation, the executive branch has called attention to the schools' plight by holding White House Conferences, establishing presidential commissions devoted to education, and by publishing volumes such as *Racial Isolation in the Public Schools.* This latter document was prepared in 1967 by the Civil Rights Commission and provides additional evidence about the educational inequalities presently burdening minority groups. Similarly, though not directed at the ills of education exclusively, the more recent *Report of the National Advisory Commission on Civil Disorders* (the Kerner Commission Report) devotes almost half of its pages to recommendations regarding needed educational reforms.

While constructive state action has not occurred with the same intensity as at the national and municipal level, there are signs of movement. In New York, the state commissioner of education actively intervened on behalf of school change in situations involving *de facto* segregation and school decentralization, and the state legislature has authorized extra appropriations for urban school problems. Moreover, in the hope of finding solutions for a growing number of educational problems, the governor and state board of regents recently established the New York State Education Commission. In California the State Committee on Public Education made far-reaching proposals regarding elimination of *de facto* racial segregation, establishment of experimental schools in central cities, and reform of fiscal conditions hampering local school systems. The Massachusetts legislature enacted a bill mandating abolition of *de facto* racial segregation in the schools. (It appears, however, to be enforcing the law with more concern for its opponents than for the oppressed.)

Of course, until change pressure reaches the state locus of power, reform is likely to be hampered. The hope in this respect is threefold. One possibility is that the redrawing of state political district boundaries, as required by Supreme Court decisions in *Baker* v. *Carr* and subsequent reapportionment cases, will help shift the attention of state legislatures from their past predilection for rural concerns to a more sympathetic attitude to urban problems. Second, a new series of court cases alleging discrimination in state arrangements for governing and financing public schools may be successful. To date, two of these cases have been tried, one in Chicago and one in Bath County, Virginia. In each instance the judge ruled that the mere existence of disparities in educational resources did not of itself suffice to constitute an injustice under the law. However, in other states, approximately 20 similar cases are pending. Even if the courts continue to rule against plaintiffs and in favor of the present system, it may be that attendant publicity will stimulate state action. And, third, a combination of local pressures and federal incentives may, in time, trigger reform at the state level.

BUT WHAT'S WRONG WITH THE SCHOOLS?

What is it what has moved parents, students, writers, government officials, and citizens in increasing numbers to register dissatisfaction over the schools? Just what is it that renders the educational system incapable of meeting the needs of a significant segment of the population? The answer to these questions varies depending upon your perspective. Some blame the schools' failure on a generation of lazy, inept, and strike-prone teachers. Others lay the problem at the doorstep of the larger community for being miserly with the money schools desire so much. Still others accuse educational administrators of failing to exert leadership and possessing a rigid outlook. The indictments tumble on and on; some are rooted only in emotions, others have a base in reality. The author, Jonathan Kozol, has one answer; the teacher union president, Albert Shanker, another; and the conservative state school superintendent, Max Rafferty, yet another. Is there a way to get at the roots of all their complaints? Are there common cords which pull together the perceptions of all these elements? We think so, and in this section we attempt to provide an overall view of the causes of dissatisfaction.

The schools' ills appear to be a consequence of two fundamental causes. One has to do with the generation and distribution of resources; the other is connected with the schools' inability as an institution to sense and service the demands of its clients. We turn first to the dimension dealing with resources.

INADEQUATE RESOURCES

A central problem in the realm of resources is that a child's social class greatly influences the quality of school services he will receive.[3] Children of wealthy parents typically have access to the best schools, and conversely, the children of the poor have the worst schools. As a tendency, this holds true almost regardless of the educational unit we are examining, individual classrooms, entire schools, school districts, states, or the nation. Children from slums, and rural areas, too, typically go to school in the oldest and most outmoded buildings located on the smallest school sites. Their teachers are frequently the least experienced and most poorly prepared. Moreover, until recent assistance from federal programs, they almost always had the oldest and most worn-out instructional materials.

These inequities in school services result from the general condition that a poor child tends to have fewer, perhaps only half as many, dollars spent on his education as does his more fortunate peer. One might ask with some puzzlement: "How can such disparities occur?" Moreover, in the face of all the widely publicized efforts to eradicate poverty, how can such disparities persist? These disparities exist and persist because the structures of our public institutions tend to direct resources toward those who participate most actively in political decisions. The parents of the poor, until recently at least, do not participate in such decisions;

3 For added evidence on this point, see James Guthrie *et al., Schools and Inequality* (Cambridge: M.I.T. Press, 1971).

consequently, they tend to be discriminated against. This is a simple explanation, but the institutional devices by which this discrimination occurs are not simple.

BUREAUCRATIC MALAISE

As we implied in the preceding section, even in the event of more and more equitably distributed funds, the ills of the schools probably would not vanish. There exists another and, in some ways, a deeper problem. Our schools have accrued a system of organizational patterns and incentives which render them increasingly insensitive to the needs of the children within them. In the last 70 years, school districts, particularly large city school districts, have evolved from fragmented organizations administered and structured on the basis of political wards to highly centralized bureaucracies in which policy making takes place only at the upper end of a multilayered hierarchy.

When the schools were organized around wards, they tended to mirror the needs of the neighborhood they served. However, they frequently were so tangled in the webs of political machines that they were seldom efficient in educating children. Today, these systems have been politically sanitized, at least, as far as conventional patterns of partisan politics go. However, in this effort to make the schools apolitical, the pendulum of reform appears to have swung too far. In an effort to overcome capricious and corrupt decisions, regulation after regulation was promulgated. It has come to be that the safe path for an administrator is to follow these regulations, even if they were written in another era for another school population, even if they obviously stifle the idealism of teachers, even if they obviously stand in the way of children learning. And, for the most part, what is safe for administrators is safe, and therefore good, for teachers. The entire system has become drowned in its concern for stability. Christopher Jencks refers to this problem as "organizational sclerosis" and describes the attributes of the disease in this fashion:

> In such a system everyone gets along by going along with the man over him. Most come to see themselves as play actors. The student tries to dope out what the teacher wants, and give it to him. Usually all he wants is a reasonable amount of quiet in class and some appearance of docility in doing assignments. The teachers, in turn, try to figure out what the principal wants. That usually means filing grades and attendance records promptly, keeping trouble over discipline to a minimum, and avoiding complaints from parents or students. The principal, in turn, tries to keep the central administration happy (and the administration tries to keep the school board happy) by not sticking his neck out and by damping down "trouble" before it gets "out of hand." [4]

[4] Christopher Jencks, "Is the Public School Obsolete?" *The Public Interest,* No. 2 (Winter 1966), 23.

The fundamental reasons for this lack of concern on the part of public school personnel are difficult to identify precisely. It may be, however, that sheer organizational size is a root cause. Many of today's schools contain hundreds and, in some cases, thousands of students, and some school districts contain tens of thousands. Instructional staff, supervisors, and administrators are all employed on a matching scale. Such arrangements militate against close personal knowledge. For example, a secondary school teacher with from 100 to 200 students simply cannot know each of them intimately. For the teacher to know each student's parents in addition is almost unthinkable. Similarly, a principal responsible for 100 or 200 teachers, or a busy superintendent responsible for 100 or more principals, simply cannot know all his subordinates well. This span of control may be too extensive to affect accountability by personal contact. From top to bottom, from superintendent to teachers, down the entire organizational hierarchy, the face-to-face relationships which appear to be necesary to elicit and sustain personal commitment are absent.

Nor does the situation appear any less pessimistic when one looks up the organization. Students in large groups may feel little pressure as individuals to perform for a single teacher. The same may be true for groups of teachers with regard to their principal, and so on until one reaches the top of the school organizational pyramid. Those who doubt that the aggregation of people into large clusters can act to drain individuals of a sense of obligation to participate or perform should recall the times, not just in school but in other places as well, when they did not know an answer, had not prepared their homework as requested, or otherwise were not working or able to perform as expected. Under such circumstances one can frequently take comfort and refuge in the fact that the large classes reduce the chance of being called upon personally to such a low level as to eliminate a concern for participation. There are those who claim that the one-room school of yesteryear had many educational advantages, and one of them may have been a sense of personal intimacy which generated a commitment to perform as expected. If nothing else, at least a parent did not have to obtain written permission from a "downtown" bureaucrat to talk to his or her child's teacher.

Bureaucratic rigidity and pursuit of the *status quo,* however, are not the only organizational malfunctions which presently hamper schools in their efforts to educate children. For example, as administrators constructed bureaucracies to make decisions about schools, teachers were pushed further and further from formal centers of power. Consequently, in a more predictable fashion, teachers have sought means by which they can reassert influence over the policy decisions which affect their work. They have succeeded in this effort by establishing tightly knit, militant teacher organizations, which frequently are fashioned after the union model. In the bargaining process, these organizations have pursuaded school boards to agree to literally volumes of additional regulations. These new rules specify salaries, fringe benefits, and working conditions. Moreover, they frequently prescribe rather narrowly the tasks a teacher can be called upon to perform and the reasons for which a teacher can be transferred or dismissed. The end result is to insulate the teacher from any effective process of evaluation. This is not to imply that such evaluation processes took place prior to the advent of rigid contracts; they seldom did, and even if they did they were seldom taken seriously. Our point is that, as researchers develop ways to assess objectively some dimensions of effectiveness for a teacher, a school, or a school district, our freedom to employ such assessment techniques is becoming more and more curtailed.

Militant teacher organizations arose first in the big cities, and this probably is no mere coincidence. The flow of middle class parents from the cities frequently created a power vacuum with regard to education. The remaining parents often did not pay close attention to the operation of the schools. Consequently, as the teacher militancy movement gained momentum, there was little countervailing political force to hold it in check. Now many of our big city systems appear to drift almost helplessly, buffeted by self-seeking demands from powerful teacher organizations and unable to require greater productivity for the outlay of additional pay.

Our separation of the schools' ills into two categories is in many ways an oversimplification. We do not wish to imply by this division that the categories are disconnected. In fact, the problems of resource allocation and organizational insensitivity and inertia are tightly coupled and reinforce each other at a number of points. Moreover, it is precisely this complexity which renders it difficult to find an adequate solution. This is in no way to imply, however, that a solution is impossible. We believe it is possible, and we move now to a preliminary description of the proposed solutions which are taken up in detail in subsequent chapters.

WHAT THE MODELS PROPOSE

The following collection can be divided into two classes of articles. The first category illustrates what current school effectiveness research can tell us about the performance of schools and how the scope of this research is enlarging. The second group suggests new ways in which schools can be organized and managed in order to improve their performance. The designers of these models outline for us the research and rationale supporting their approaches and discuss the manner in which the approaches might be applied or sold to a community.

If schooling is to be improved, whether we keep the present educational system or substitute some new model or models for it, we will need to know what it is that we expect the schools to do and how they can do it. This concern for specifying and measuring student performance is one of the foundations upon which reform efforts must be built. Consequently, in Chapter Two, Ralph Tyler, one of the principal proponents of behavioral objectives in education and the measurement of academic achievement, describes current efforts to assess the performance of our nation's schools and school children. Schools and school personnel have been remarkably sensitive about such efforts, and this sensitivity has handicapped past attempts at evaluation and assessment. The chapter by Tyler describes previous efforts at assessment and concludes with a detailed explanation of the genesis, rationale, and evolution of the present nationwide project to be conducted under the auspices of the Education Commission of the States. The discussion makes clear that the assessment project will apply unique tools in unique ways to measure educational outcomes, and that the course of its development has not been an easy one. This assessment is now in operation, and periodic reports and findings will be forthcoming. The history and analysis offer important insights to all citizens who will be concerned with interrelations between these findings and developments at the local school level.

In Chapter Three, "From Information to Reformation," Edward Wynne attempts to build on the perspectives offered by Tyler. He contends that more routine and public use of educational output measures may alter the goal structure of schools in important and constructive ways. The chapter explains the rationale for his proposal, offers suggestions as to how the change might be put into operation, and attempts to forecast some of its effects.

Compensatory education is one of the important techniques proposed to assist children from low income families. Such programs assume these children need specially designed and improved instruction to overcome the handicaps they face in a traditional school environment. Typically, compensatory education programs use special funds that have been set aside for that purpose. Integrating such programs into the existing school process, and ensuring that they achieve the desired effect, is not always simple. There is also the larger question of whether such an "add-on" approach is the answer to special learning needs. In Chapter Four, Wilson Riles, formerly Director of Compensatory Education and Deputy Superintendent of Education of the California State Department of Education, discusses these questions in the light of his personal experience in managing such programs.

In Chapter Five, James Coleman applies his knowledge as a sociologist to describe present performance incentives for school administrators, teachers, and students. His themes are that human beings react to the true goals that are before them, as opposed to those proffered by organizational ritual and liturgy, and that the present incentive structure of schools discourages learning. Once the "real" goals have been frankly identified, we can consider more seriously how and why the current system goes wrong, and what kinds of goal changes could make a difference. The analysis considers not only performance incentives for school staffs, but also for the students.

The authors of Chapter Six consider the problem of student incentives and motivation from a different perspective than that of Coleman. Andrew Effrat, Roy Feldman, and Harvey Sapolsky contend that school has no innate appeal for many poor children and, consequently, steps must be taken to induce them to learn by means somewhat extraneous to the learning process. The instrument they select is financial; children are to be paid in accord with their performance—the hope being that at least the child may be stimulated to learn the minimum amount needed to function in today's world, and, under ideal conditions, he may come subsequently to view schooling as being of sufficient value by itself that he engages in it regardless of the money.

In Chapter Seven, Ralph Melaragno and Gerald Newmark describe their efforts to assist a California elementary school to install a tutorial school model designed by them and their associates in the System Development Corporation. The model assumes that most of the teaching in the school will be done by students, either within grades, or across grades, and that teachers will be used primarily to diagnose problems, advise tutors, meet with parents, and otherwise act as consultants. Since it aims to affect the total educational environment, it also pays particular attention to the matter of involving parents and the community in the learning process. Because of difficulties that have been traditionally associated with gaining educational reform, implementation of the models pays careful attention to the problems of staff and institutional adaptation, and advocates measures such as encounter groups in order to facilitate change.

Frederick Erickson and Eliezer Krumbein have been providing consulting services to a number of small, private, reform-oriented schools in Chicago, schools which are attended principally by low income students. From this work and their own analyses, they have evolved a theory about the kinds of forces that cause schools to use the resources available to them productively. The theory suggests that it is not only "how much you have," but also "from where you get it" that makes for a good school. This theory and the facts supporting it are translated into a new ecological model for schools which is described in Chapter Eight.

In Chapter Nine, Henry Levin analyzes the justifications offered in behalf of community control by school decentralization proponents. He relates these contentions to other current themes motivating black activism within America, as well as to the shortcomings that are peculiar to existing urban schools. The analysis argues that decentralization, keyed to community control, is a necessary precondition for improved schooling in urban areas.

In Chapter Ten, Dwight Allen and William Fanslow confront us with a reality that is all too frequently overlooked, the fact that many students, especially in high school, consider their schooling as a form of incarceration. In effect, the students are the real disadvantaged in America. You do not need to be poor to be neglected or deprived. Once this premise is accepted, the stage is set for a radical reconsideration of current education practices, including those followed within what are presently considered our "better schools." The authors specify some of the changes that might logically flow from such a reconsideration.

Thomas Pettigrew is a social psychologist who has studied the effect of personal interaction on human attitudes and learning. In Chapter Eleven, he focuses his attention on the subject of overcoming effects of racial segregation upon black students. His detailed analysis of research findings discloses the complexity of the issue. As a result of his analysis, he proposes educational parks as an important part of the solution to the challenge of desegregation. He explains how they might be implemented and operated.

In Chapter Twelve, Henry Levin and James Guthrie, with co-author George Kleindorfer and Robert Stout, explain a new economic concept and its relevance for the reform of schools. The concept is known as "capital embodiment," and it serves as an intellectual tool for planning the degree of financial investment which should be made in the education of an individual child, a state, or a nation. By using this "tool," decisions about the allocation of funds and other resources can be made much more rationally than is presently the case. The authors conclude by demonstrating its utility in planning the education of poor children. Also, they offer more general comments regarding the financing and administration of schools.

John Coons, Stephen Sugarman, and William Clune are lawyers by training, and they approach problems of education from a far different perspective than that of the tradition-oriented educator. Rather than suggest means by which the present system of public schools might be improved, they pose the prior question: "Should we retain public schools or not?" The genius of their thesis is that they themselves are not so presumptuous as to attempt to answer the question for all men for all time. Rather they suggest a mechanism which would enable each family unit to answer the question for itself. Their arguments, as set forth in Chapter Thirteen, contend that education can be improved if we once more imbue it with healthy elements of individual choice and competition.

In Chapter Fourteen on "Mentorship," Edward Wynne directs himself to the implications of America's educational revolution, the fact that never before in world history has a nation kept such a large proportion of its youth in school for such long periods of time. He contends this prolonged formal education is a major cause of much of the youthful dissatisfaction we see about us and recommends that the external adult society must reassume its traditional responsibilities for conducting the vital task of informal education. The chapter explains a means and describes a model by which this might be done.

Finally, in the Epilogue, we make an effort to place the proposed new models in the overall perspective of educational reform in the United States. As we stated earlier in this chapter, schools have undergone changes before, and there is no reason to believe that they cannot undergo constructive changes again. In the Epilogue we attempt to describe the societal conditions which must underlie such changes.

two

How Well Does the Present Model Work?

All right! So the schools should be changed. Few seem to disagree that change is needed. But what change? What is it that schools should do that they currently are not doing? What should students know that they do not know? In fact, what do students know now? What do schools do now? All of these questions, and hundreds of others we could pose, frame the fact that productive change is at best difficult and probably impossible unless it is rather firmly guided by accurate information.

Surprisingly enough, however, there presently is a great paucity of relevant information about many important facets of school operation. One of the most important areas of ignorance is about the "outputs" of schools—exactly what effects do schools have on their students? The word "outputs" may have provocative overtones to some, but it is a useful analytic concept. It assumes that any organization aimed at accomplishing tasks can be viewed as a system for receiving resources, or "inputs," and processing them into "outputs."

Of course, these concepts are not self-defining; we would all agree that textbooks and teachers are inputs, but different persons may well disagree as to whether or not the home background of a student (which can affect his learning capabilities) is an input. Similar differences in opinion arise over the concept of output. At one time, we considered output to be the number or proportion of graduates or the number of student days in attendance. We have moved from these definitions, and now school output is typically seen as the amount and type of learning exhibited by students. To the degree possible, we need to refine this definition further and, for obvious reasons, subdivide it into school-induced learning and out-of-school learning (via parents, TV, friends, and so on). But such precision may be beyond our methodology at this moment. In any case, there is wide agreement that discovering the amount of knowledge acquired by students under varying circumstances is essential to achieving important educational improvement.

However, in general, we do not know what or how much American children learn. We have some measures, for some subjects, for some types of students, in some sections of the country. We know a small amount about levels of student reading and mathematics ability, but even this knowledge is grossly insufficient. We know almost nothing about history, languages, literature, the social and physical sciences, and so on. Of course, even if we had such knowledge, we would not necessarily know how they learned, or how to help them learn better, but we could at least begin to explore these questions more profitably.

Our ignorance about outputs is the consequence of a number of factors. First, there are complex conceptual questions involved in devising measurements that can answer the questions we would like to have answered. Second, there are the administrative problems of applying such measurements to schools widely scattered throughout our country. The enterprise also must be financed. Finally, and perhaps most importantly, educators and many other Americans have demonstrated rather persistent hostility to the concepts implicit in this approach. The motives for this resistance are complex and cover a wide spectrum, from a fear that the very process of evaluation may encourage excessive emphasis on more easily measured (but less important) objectives, to a desire to escape from public criticism for failing to manage effective schools.

The national assessment project is an effort to develop a system to overcome this medley of obstacles and put in operation an effective, nationwide output measurement system. The experiences and plans of the assessment effort are significant in themselves and also offer important clues concerning change strategies and tactics to other persons who hope to produce school reforms.

It is perhaps significant that Ralph Tyler, at the age of 60, after already having had one illustrious career in research and teaching concerned with education, committed himself to assisting the assessment effort. At the outset, he was Director of the Center for Advanced Study in the Behavioral Sciences and former Dean of the School of Education of the University of Chicago. Perhaps only his persistence and prestige could have organized a project that involved such numerous political and intellectual questions. Still, six years elapsed between Tyler's first assignment and the administration of the first instruments. What happened in between is important and revealing, and we turn now to that narrative.

NATIONAL ASSESSMENT: A HISTORY AND SOCIOLOGY

Ralph W. Tyler

It may seem strange that schools have existed for millennia and yet, until recently, no sustained systematic effort has been mounted to appraise their educational effectiveness. Over the years, schools have been judged by the characteristics of their teachers, by their facilities, by certain features of their programs, and by their financial support. Only briefly in periods during the past 125 years have attempts been made to obtain and use information about the educational achievements of pupils as a major basis for assessing school performance. In this chapter an effort is made to depict past attempts to measure the performance of schools, to analyze the causes of their failure, and to describe the background and plan of operation of the present national assessment project. The rationale underlying this description is that no effort to restructure American education can be entirely successful which lacks an accurate understanding of the successes and failures of the present system.

ASSESSMENT EFFORTS BEFORE 1960

In the middle of the nineteenth century, Horace Mann debated vigorously with Boston schoolmasters over the quality of education provided in their schools. He persuaded local school committees to administer uniform written examinations to a sample of students from the Boston public schools. The results corroborated most of Mann's criticisms regarding the inadequacy of the schooling obtained by Boston students. However, in spite of the fact that it illustrated the benefits of using examinations as a basis for assessing school performance, this initial effort was not sustained.

The Reverend George Fisher, an English schoolmaster, produced in 1864 a "scale book," which was intended to furnish standards of pupil achievement against which schools could compare themselves. But this innovation was not widely adopted and interest in it quickly diminished. Thirty years later, the work of J. M. Rice in the United States also produced only a passing reaction. Rice was appalled by his observation of the extended, seemingly meaningless, spelling drills in American schools, and he sought to show school leaders that these lessons were mechanical and relatively futile. He succeeded in persuading a large number of schools to administer a set of spelling tests he had constructed to 16,000 students in the years 1895–97. Test results did not reveal a correlation between the time schools devoted to spelling lessons and the achievement of their pupils. However, Leonard Ayres reported, "The presentation of these results brought upon the investigator almost unlimited attack. The educators . . . united in denouncing as foolish, reprehensible, and from every point of view indefensible, the effort to discover anything about the value of the teaching of spelling by finding out whether or not the children could spell."[1] Although Rice was a member of the National Education Association, he was a pediatrician, not a schoolmaster, and, consequently, he was viewed as an outsider attacking the profession. His use of tests was rejected by school leaders, and the idea did not become part of the developing practice of the schools.

However, in the twenty years following Rice's spelling investigation, standard tests of achievement were constructed for most school subjects. In the 1918 Yearbook of the National Society for the Study of Education, *The Measurement of Educational Products,* Walter S. Monroe[2] described more than one hundred standardized tests of pupil performance. But these tests were developed to measure the achievement of individual students, not to assess the effectiveness of the school. Their design and the means used to establish scores, scales, and norms were based on theories of individual differences in achievement, not on principles involved in describing or measuring what pupils have learned. The distinction between measuring individual differences and appraising school performance is not only one regarding the procedures followed in designing and calibrating the instruments, but also one regarding emphasis. Traditional standardized achievement tests seek answers to questions such as: "How does this pupil compare with other pupils? How does the mean or median of this pupil group compare with the mean or median of the normative population?" Whereas the question to be answered in assessing school performance is "How much have the students in this school learned?" I shall comment later in more detail on this difference.

[1] Leonard P. Ayres, "History and Present Status of Educational Measurements," in Guy Montrose Whipple, ed., *The Measurement of Educational Products,* Seventeenth Yearbook, National Society for the Study of Education, Part II (Bloomington, Ill.: Public School Publishing, 1918), p. 11.

[2] Walter S. Monroe, "Existing Tests and Standards," in Guy Montrose Whipple, ed., *The Measurement of Educational Products,* pp. 71-104.

The accreditation movement in the United States began as a concerted effort to distinguish "good" schools from "poor" ones. In 1872 the University of Michigan established a plan for accrediting secondary schools whose graduates would be admissable to the University on the basis of transcripts evidencing completion of college entrance requirements. In 1873 the Indiana State Department of Public Instruction developed an accreditation plan for its public high schools. The North Central Association of Colleges and Secondary Schools established in 1902 the first regional standards for accrediting secondary schools, and other regional bodies at later dates adopted somewhat similar plans. Over the past fifty years, accrediting has become a widely used means for cooperative study of institutional structures, staffs, processes, and finances both of high schools and of colleges. By developing self-conscious inquiry into the structure and functioning of an educational institution, accrediting agencies have probably influenced improvements in the quality of educational performance, but there is no available evidence of this fact in the form of data on the educational achievement of students. By and large, the standards adopted for accreditation represent the judgments of leaders in the field and desirable features of the instructional process. These judgments, no doubt, are frequently sound, but they do reflect past experience, and may be inappropriate for present or changing conditions. It is also true that most of us are unable to separate our acceptance of features which we have found common in schools for which we have a high regard, from our judgment of the value of these features and their actual contribution to the effectiveness of the school.

Many analyses of schools, for example the Coleman Report, have been unable to demonstrate significant correlations between achievement test scores of children and ratings of school quality. This suggests that current judgments about the essential features of a "good" school may be in error. In 1934 a comprehensive examination in the subject fields of mathematics, science, English, and history was given to sophomores in fifty randomly selected colleges in the area accredited by the North Central Association. The correlation between mean student test scores and ratings by an accrediting committee was less than .25, which further suggests the limitations of present accrediting processes as a basis for assessing performance.

School surveys in the United States have also dealt with the quality of schools. In 1915–16, a massive survey of the public schools of Cleveland was undertaken by a score of well-known educators, mostly university professors, under the leadership of Leonard P. Ayres. This was the first large school survey in which standard tests were used as part of the effort to assess the strengths and weaknesses of the educational system. Because of the newness of the procedure, the surveyors were not aware of some of the major pitfalls. They assumed that schools in which mean test scores in every grade were markedly above the norms must be excellent ones, that schools in which mean test scores in every grade were markedly below the norms must be ineffective ones, and that schools in which mean test scores were close to the norms must be average. No efforts were made at that time to allow for different promotion policies so as to relate grade placement to years in school, nor to deal with differences in socioeconomic levels of the families from which pupils came. In later surveys, group intelligence tests were used to establish "performance expectancies" against which to compare achievement scores. When this was done, most of the children in the big cities were "achieving about as expected," so that there seemed to be little new information furnished by the administration of a battery of standard tests. Later testing specialists, such as Truman Kelly, pointed out the fallacy of using intelligence tests as though they were independent measures of a child's potential. (Both achievement tests and intelligence tests are measures of pupil achievement and the overlap between a typical student's scores on achievement and intelligence tests is represented by a correlation between .80 and .90.) By 1940 it had become clear to most persons conducting school surveys that there was very limited value in using standardized tests as a major yardstick for assessing school performance, because of the difficulty of separating the complex factors in the educational situation when using instruments designed for a different purpose. Cremin explains the decline as follows:

> The overenthusiastic educational scientism of the 1920's invited a negative reaction. Teachers felt threatened when standard tests were applied to their classes on an administrator's order. Administrators were threatened by external comparisons of one school with another on the basis of tests and cost statistics. Those who realized that a liberal education could not be captured in a net of true-false questions accused the testers of acknowledging only such educational values as their tests could measure. The reviewers of the scientific movement writing for the landmark yearbook of the NSSE in 1938 pointed to disappointing limitations that had been discovered in the research approach, limitations that restricted the significance of many findings.[3]

The failure, at least until recently, to develop tests designed specifically to assess school performance is not due entirely to the difficulty of developing the instruments and designing methods for estimating the influence of various important factors on pupil achievement. Part of the delay has resulted from the fact that schools have been viewed to a considerable extent as societal sorting mechanisms rather than educational institutions. Tests are employed to sort people for courses, curricular tracks, admission to college, and the like. They are designed to measure indi-

[3] Lee J. Cronbach and Patrick Suppes, eds., *Research for Tomorrow's Schools* (New York: Macmillan, 1969), pp. 63-64.

vidual differences and relative performance of groups, not to appraise the extent to which the schools are facilitating learning.

One hundred years ago, three-fourths of the U.S. labor force was engaged in agriculture and in nonfarm, unskilled labor. Less than 10 percent of all youth attended secondary school, and less than 2 percent were enrolled in college. At the turn of the century, 38 percent of the U.S. labor force was engaged in agriculture and another 23 percent in nonfarm, unskilled labor. Children were leaving school in increasing numbers after reaching the age of twelve. There were then many opportunities for the unskilled to be employed as well as for the semiskilled and skilled. Our farms, factories, mines, and business firms needed a labor supply and there were only limited opportunities for employment in professional and managerial positions. A school was considered a "good" school if it failed to promote a considerable fraction of its pupils each year. A high school's quality was judged by the proportion who failed to graduate. A famous professor of law at Harvard was reputed to say to each incoming freshman class, "Gentlemen, look at the man to the right of you, then look at the one to your left. Neither of them will still be with us next year." Schools and colleges gained reputations for selecting people, not for helping them to learn.

This notion of testing only to skim the cream has been applied by other scholastically oriented societies, such as the Chinese mandarin class, and still pervades the operations of many of our schools and colleges.[4] In effect, the traditions of the past still confuse the schoolmasters of the present. We still aim chiefly to identify the scholarship winners, the college bound, the top quarter of the class. In this effort to single out the high performers, we have accepted practices in the construction and use of tests that seek to separate individuals on a linear scale and do not serve effectively to demonstrate the extent to which all of our pupils are learning.

Now, however, our society has become one which is so-called "post-industrial." Only 5 percent of the labor force is unskilled. Opportunities for employment in technical, professional, managerial, and service occupations have increased more than 300 percent in one generation. Our society is now seeking to identify potential talents of many sorts and to furnish opportunities for these talents to reach fruition through education. Research on the brain and in behavioral genetics indicates that the learning requirements in our schools and colleges place no strain on the basic potential of the vast majority of human beings. Schools can be encouraged to help all students learn rather than to serve primarily in screening and sorting. From the standpoint of an individual student, the

[4] Philip H. Dubois, "A Test-Dominated Society: China 1115 B.C.—1905 A.D.," *Proceedings of the 1964 Invitational Conference on Testing Problems,* Educational Testing Service, 1965, pp. 3-11.

criterion of an educational institution is one in which the student gains a wider range of alternatives in his life choices with each increment of education. He is aided to find new doors of opportunity rather than being trained ever more narrowly to fit into a specific societal niche. It is against this background that new efforts to assess school performance must be viewed.

RECENT ASSESSMENT DEVELOPMENTS

Within state and local school systems there are several notable assessment programs presently in operation or being developed. For more than a decade, the state education department in New York has conducted, in cooperation with many of the local districts, a testing program that relates average scores on educational achievement tests to average scores on aptitude tests, to levels of financial support, and the like. The information obtained in this program is employed by schools in guiding their development efforts. It has the limitations inherent in the design of current tests, which focus on the "average" achiever and which produce inadequate data on the educational achievements of the more advanced and the less advanced students.

The Department of Public Instruction of the Commonwealth of Pennsylvania, stimulated by the state legislature and board of education, has designed a plan for continuous appraisal of the quality of education in that state. Requirements in several of the federal education acts that educational programs supported under this legislation be evaluated in terms of their effectiveness has led to establishment of a consortium of state departments of education, supported by the Office of Education, to construct new evaluation instruments. A number of city school systems have been designing their own procedures for appraising the effectiveness of their educational efforts. Pittsburgh, for example, under the leadership of Malcolm Provus, director of research for the city schools, developed an evaluation system called a discrepancy model, which is used there and is being adopted by some other school systems.

Increasingly, the public is asking for evidence of educational attainments and school people are recognizing what they term "accountability" for the performance of the schools (see Chapter Three). Hence, it seems inevitable that educational assessment of various types and for various purposes will be developing widely in the next decade.

These developments in education are part of a larger movement to obtain relevant and dependable information about the performance of our society. As the nation has grown and become increasingly complex, it is no longer possible through individual observation or informal procedures to assess our progress and problems. The Full Employment

Act of 1948 established a Council of Economic Advisors which accelerated collection and use of data regarding our economic development. Later, the National Manpower Act accelerated establishment of machinery for collecting data on manpower needs, training requirements, and other factors not previously covered by the census of employment and unemployment. John W. Gardner, while Secretary of HEW, convened a panel of advisors to outline a publication that would serve as a social report to the nation and include information on progress and problems relative to such significant phases of modern life as health, longevity, safety, individual opportunity, housing, and culture, as well as education. The pioneering work of this panel combined with the efforts of others in universities, research centers, foundations, and public agencies, should result in important additions to our knowledge about our national development.[5] Dependable information is essential to intelligent planning and wise action to improve our national life.

THE NATIONAL EDUCATIONAL ASSESSMENT

The following, somewhat detailed description of the development of the current national educational assessment is intended to serve two purposes: (1) to provide information about this important endeavor, and (2) to furnish suggestions about the problems as well as opportunities that face all efforts to promote comprehensive appraisals of educational achievement.

In July, 1963, United States Commissioner of Education Francis Keppel assembled a group of educators and laymen to discuss the need for dependable information about the educational attainments of our people. After discussion of the problem, I was asked to prepare a memorandum outlining procedures by which necessary information might be periodically collected to furnish a basis for public discussion and broader understanding of our educational progress and problems.

Returning to the Center for Advanced Study in the Behavioral Sciences, I prepared a draft of a plan for the proposed assessment program. Three Fellows who were then in residence at the Center, Clyde Coombs, psychometrician from the University of Michigan, Fred Mosteller, head of the Department of Statistics at Harvard, and John Tukey, head of the Department of Statistics at Princeton, were asked for their criticism of the plan. With the help of their comments, the plan was revised and sent to Commissioner Keppel and John Gardner. The latter was then President of the Carnegie Corporation of New York. After they

[5] U. S. Department of Health, Education, and Welfare, *Toward a Social Report* (Washington, D. C.: U. S. Government Printing Office, 1968).

discussed the memorandum with colleagues, Gardner convened a conference in December, 1963, of some of the leading people in the field of educational testing to discuss the memorandum in terms of the present state of the testing art. He queried conference members as to whether or not we were at a point when such a plan could actually be implemented. The conference demonstrated that new instruments and new procedures were necessary, but it was the consensus of the participants that the plan could be implemented.

In January, 1964, Gardner assembled another group of leaders in educational organizations including the NEA, the AFT, the American Council on Education, the National Association of Land Grant Colleges and State Universities, the National Catholic Education Association, and the Council of Chief State School Officers. The questions posed to this group were, "Is this proposal a good idea? Should the project be attempted?" The discussion was an extended one. Some of the dangers of irresponsible use of achievement data were suggested, but also comments were made regarding the increasing demand for achievement information and the fact that schools should be accountable to their supporters for results. Finally, there appeared to be agreement that the project should be tried, but that great care should be taken to avoid any dangers to the schools and communities involved.

Following these two conferences, the Carnegie Corporation employed Dr. John Corson, then professor in the Woodrow Wilson School of Public Administration at Princeton, to outline an orderly procedure for the conduct of the assessment. He proposed that the project be divided into two phases, an exploratory or trial period and the actual assessment program. In the exploratory phase, three tasks would be undertaken: (1) conversations would be held with school people and interested laymen for the purpose of explaining the assessment and discovering problems likely to be encountered; (2) the instruments required for the initial assessment would be constructed; and (3) the plan for using the instruments in obtaining data for the national assessment would be constructed. This recommendation was accepted, and in August, 1964, the Carnegie Corporation granted funds for the first phase of the project and appointed the Exploratory Committee on Assessing the Progress of Education (ECAPE). The committee's charge was to conduct the exploratory phase of the project.

During the academic year 1964–65, seven major conferences and many smaller meetings were held with teachers, curriculum specialists, administrators, and school board members. Participants in these meetings, while recognizing the need for comprehensive information on the progress of education, were nevertheless remarkably sensitive to the dangers of a poorly developed program and the possible misuse of information obtained from it. School administrators were particularly concerned about the possibility of a school system being criticized or condemned if assessment results showed low achievement by students in that school system. To protect schools from attack, administrators strongly recommended that assessment results be reported in a fashion which would prevent the identification of local school districts and state systems. This proposal was adopted as a policy of the project. They further recommended that assessment instruments be developed in cooperation with teachers and tried on a pilot basis in the schools. If schools found the assessment meaningful and helpful, then it would be appropriate to recommend its use on a nationwide scale.

Among hundreds of school administrators present in these conferences, only three expressed strong opposition. One took the view that the assessment was a first step toward federal control of education. Another contended that he was sure that, in spite of all efforts to prevent it, results would be used for odious interschool comparisons. The third stated a position opposed to any external testing because he saw this as a means by which the local curriculum would be distorted in order for the school to perform well on the test.

Unexpected opposition arose from a strange coincidence which took place near the end of 1965. The late Harold Hand, then professor of education at the University of South Florida, had reviewed the Office of Education budget presented to Congress and found a large item there for "Achievement Studies." This was the appropriation for the Coleman Study of Equality of Education Opportunity, but Hand incorrectly concluded that this money was to support the national assessment. It was therefore a "project of the federal government" and not a study sponsored by a private foundation. He gave a ringing denunciation of the whole enterprise at the March meeting of the Association for Supervision and Curriculum Development, picturing the tentacles of the federal government wrapping themselves around the independent efforts of local school districts. This speech and many others he made later on the same theme, I believe, strongly influenced some of the leaders in ASCD, for it was the only national educational organization to adopt a resolution opposing the assessment.

Another apparent coincidence affecting public attitudes toward the assessment project occurred in California. In that state, the legislature had previously enacted legislation requiring schools to test students in certain grades. There was a proviso that the results were not to be released to the public. Nevertheless, 1966 test results were leaked to the press, and San Francisco newspapers carried a story about the "poor showing" of the San Francisco public schools. At that time, Harold Spears was Superintendent of the San Francisco Schools and, coincidentally, President of the American Association of School Administrators (AASA). It seems likely that this unpleasant experience with the California state testing program led to the AASA Executive Committee sending, on January 9, 1967, a letter to all its members requesting them not to cooperate with the assessment project, not even to permit the pilot testing of assessment exercises in their schools. The letter explained the opposition of the Executive Committee in these words:

> At its 1966 convention in Atlantic City, the American Association of School Administrators took a firm stand against a national testing program. Its resolution on "National Testing and National Curriculum" stated:
>
> "The AASA opposes any act which would, in effect, establish a national testing system or a national curriculum. Not only does such a high degree of centralization infringe upon the legal responsibilities of the state and the school system and the professional responsibilities of the individual teachers, but we believe it inevitably defeats the declared aim of American education—the individual development of each child. Attempts to evaluate or compare all systems through prescribed national tests will result in a curricular structure which will vitiate attempts of local schools to serve individual pupils.
>
> "The AASA believes that the voluntary cooperation of local school districts, education associations, foundations, state departments of education, and regional agencies is capable of producing sufficient data for research, evaluation, or assessment purposes and as much standardization of curriculum as is consistent with the maximum quality desired.
>
> "Mandated by this resolution of the membership, your Executive Committee has been examining continuously and in detail the development of the national achievement testing aspects of the National Assessment of Educational Progress (NAEP), a project of the Carnegie Foundation's Exploratory Committee on Assessing the Progress of Education.
>
> "The timetable for this project, according to Dr. Ralph W. Tyler, its chairman, provides that tryouts in private and public schools of tests for the proposed national assessment of education will take place this winter and in the spring of 1967. The testing instruments are being developed under contract by four leading test development agencies and will assess learning in reading and language arts, science, mathematics, social studies, citizenship, fine arts, and vocational education. As stated by Dr. Tyler and Jack Merwin, staff director, '. . . the assessment will include not only objective questions, but opportunities for the demonstration of performance skills, essay questions, and interview information.'
>
> "The Executive Committee of AASA, after examining as thoroughly as possible the pros and the cons of the NAEP project, finds the arguments *against* this program the more persuasive. *It, therefore, recommends to its members and the educational institutions which they serve that they refuse to participate in the tryouts of these tests and in the eventual testing program—presently slated for the fall of 1967.*"

The letter then continues for several more pages describing the objectives of the AASA Executive Committee.

This letter created considerable controversy in the association. I am myself a life member of the AASA and have been since 1931. Hence, I wrote the executive secretary protesting an action upon which I had no opportunity to comment nor to present relevant information. Telegrams of protest were sent the AASA from faculty groups at Harvard, Chicago, and Stanford and from the executive board of the American Educational Research Association. The president of Teachers College, Columbia, and the state commissioner of education in New York forwarded vigorous letters of objection. Newspapers including the *Wall Street Journal* and the *Houston Post* criticized the action as indicating a fear of facts on the part of school administrators. The National Congress of Parents and Teachers and the National School Boards Association issued statements that they had not given support to the action taken in the letter. Other efforts were being made behind the scenes to modify the position expressed in the letter. Under these circumstances, the annual meeting of AASA in February, 1967, provided an opportunity for its resolutions committee to review the issue, reverse the flow of AASA opinion, and prepare a favorable resolution, which was then adopted by members of the association.

The wording of the AASA resolution provided solace for various segments of the membership and prevented an extended conflict. Following the recommendation, an AASA committee, chaired by George B. Brain, Dean of the College of Education of Washington State University, formerly president of AASA, began meetings with a subcommittee of the Assessment Committee to learn more about the project and the AASA criticism. The major conclusions of this committee were:

1. There is a public demand for an appraisal of the product of the schools.
2. If this demand is not met by a carefully planned and conducted effort, it will be met by an ill-advised, hastily concocted attempt.
3. The ECAPE project appears to have been carefully planned and well designed.
4. This project is one that AASA should endorse if it were to be administered by a public or quasi-public body.

The Exploratory Committee undertook a number of steps to meet these conditions, and, as the eventual outcome of these steps, the management of the national assessment (designed by the Exploratory Committee) was transferred to the Education Commission of the States on July 1, 1969. The commission is a public body, chartered by Congress and financed by state legislatures. Its membership is composed of official representatives of the forty-five or so states that are members. It is, in effect, the primary organization for communicating among the states about education policies. The Committee on Assessing the Progress of Education, which carries forward the technical work commenced by the Exploratory Committee, is the major advisory group for the assessment efforts of the Education Commission. Thus, it appears to me that the assessment is developing under auspices that assure constructive cooperation in carrying it on. The initial concerns and fears seem to have been resolved through efforts to explain the project more fully and to dispel the misunderstanding that resulted through confusing this assessment with a nationwide individual testing program.

But the apparent success in allaying these apprehensions was not simply a matter of salesmanship. From the outset, the design and the development of the project have taken seriously the problems and dangers that are involved. The discussions with administrators, curriculum specialists, teachers, and school board members recommended that the initial assessment include more than the three R's and that it ultimately cover the range of important educational tasks of the modern school. In harmony with this suggestion, instruments were constructed by four leading test development agencies,[6] in the fields of reading and the language arts, science, mathematics, social studies, citizenship, fine arts, and vocational education. In subsequent years, other important areas will be included. Each assessment requires three years to complete, with three fields included in the first year, three in the second, and four in the third.

In each of these fields, scholars, teachers, and curriculum specialists formulated statements of the objectives which they believe faithfully reflect the contribution of that field and which the schools are seriously seeking to attain. For each major objective, prototype exercises were constructed which, in the opinion of scholars and teachers, give students an opportunity to demonstrate the behavior implied by the objective. These lists of objectives, and prototype exercises which help to define them, were then reviewed by panels of public-spirited citizens in various parts of the country. Each panel spent two days reviewing the material and making a judgment about each objective in terms of the questions: "Is this something important for people to learn today? Is it something I would like to have my children learn?" This process resulted in some revisions of the original listing of objectives and a few eliminations. The procedure was designed to ensure that every objective being assessed is: (1) considered important by scholars, (2) accepted as an educational task by the school, and (3) deemed desirable by leading lay citizens.

A national assessment to identify kinds of progress being made in education, and problems and difficulties arising, will not be very meaningful unless separate measures are obtained for populations within the total country which vary among themselves and thus present different degrees and kinds of progress and different problems to be solved. The particular populations that need to be treated separately may change over the years ahead, but for some time, age, sex, socioeconomic status, geographic location, and rural-urban-suburban differences will probably

[6] American Institute of Research, Educational Testing Service, Psychological Corporation, and Science Research Associates.

be significant. Hence, the present plan involves assessing a probability sample for each of 256 populations defined by the following subdivisions: boys and girls, four geographic regions, four age groups (nine, thirteen, seventeen, and adult), four divisions by large city, small city, suburban, and rural classifications, and two socioeconomic levels.

Many earlier investigations indicate that pupil achievement is likely to vary most in terms of socioeconomic level of the family and in terms of the kind of community setting in which the student resides; urban-rural differences and suburban-inner city differences have often been found. However, the national assessment project has encountered difficulty in obtaining dependable information about the socioeconomic level of students. In California, for example, state legislation prohibits asking school children questions about the home, although such questions are commonly used in surveys to indicate socioeconomic level. The legislation's purpose is the laudable one of protecting children from invasion of privacy, but it appears to prevent obtaining information that would never be traced to an individual child and would help the public to understand an important dimension of educational achievement. This law is an example of difficulties likely to arise in identifying characteristics that may be important in reporting and interpreting assessment data.

The fact that populations are to be assessed, rather than individuals, makes it possible to extend the sampling of exercises far beyond that of an individual test in which the subject is required to respond to the entire battery of items. This comprehensive assessment requires for the three fields in the first year so many exercises that if one person were to take them, he would need some fourteen hours to complete them. By comparison, with a population sample, fourteen persons, each spending one hour, can complete all the exercises. In this case, 7000 persons can serve as a sample of 500 for each of the assessment exercises, and no one will have to devote more than one hour of his time. Although the assessment will be made every three to five years in order to ascertain the kinds of progress taking place, it is very unlikely that many of the individuals who participate in one phase of the assessment will be involved in any subsequent phase. Hence, no serious demand will be made on one individual's time. Furthermore, it is unlikely that children taking exercises in later years will be drawn from the same classrooms as earlier ones. Therefore, demands made upon a teacher in releasing a child for an hour will be minimal.

Since assessment does not require all participants to be in classes, the exercises being used are not limited to usual test items. Interviews, questionnaires, performance tests, and observational procedures are also employed to furnish information about interest, habits, skills, and practices that have been learned. Because school objectives commonly include these areas, it is necessary to see that some assessment is made as to their levels of attainment.

Assessment exercises will differ from current achievement tests in another important respect. Most group achievement tests are used to establish reliable average scores for grades or schools; hence, tests are concentrated on items which are typical of average performance. Exercises which all or nearly all can do, as well as those which only a very few can do, are eliminated. But, for purposes of assessing the progress of education, we need to know the progress being made by the disadvantaged or "slow" learners, and by the most advanced, as well as finding out what is being learned by middle or "average" children. Formulating exercises of this sort has been a new venture for test constructors. They were required to develop exercises at each level in which approximately one-third represent achievements characteristic of the lower third at that age level, one-third represent achievements characteristic of the middle third at that age level, and one-third represent the achievements of the top third at that age level.

Test making contractors were not able to meet this requirement in the first set of exercises they submitted to the committee. Experiments with these items indicated that only a very few were appropriate for the lower third. In many cases, test directions were not understood so that the children did not know what they were being asked to do. It was necessary to obtain assistance from teachers who work with disadvantaged children in order to identify the kinds of learning tasks which these children are mastering and the language for directions that is understandable to them. The development and pilot testing of appropriate exercises delayed the project nearly a year.

To summarize the educational attainments of the 256 populations that are being assessed, no test scores will be computed; in fact, no meaningful scores can be obtained. Instead the following sorts of data will be reported:

> For the sample of seventeen-year-old boys of higher socioeconomic status from rural and small-town areas of the Midwest region, it was found that:
>
> 93 percent can read a typical newspaper paragraph such as the following;
> 76 percent can write an acceptable letter ordering several items from a store such as the following;
> 52 percent take a responsible part in working with other youth in playground and community activities such as the following;
> 24 percent have occupational skills required for initial employment.

Staff members of the Education Commission of the States will prepare reports of assessment findings, much as we now obtain reports of the findings every ten years of the decennial census. These reports would be available to all people interested in education and would provide them with significant and helpful information as to what has been learned by each of the 256 populations. In subsequent years, the progress made by each of these populations since the preceding assessment will also be reported.

It has taken nearly six years for national assessment to move from an idea into a functioning activity. Thus, mature development of the national assessment of education is, in many senses, just beginning. All problems have not been, nor can they ever be, permanently solved. But the outline has been drawn, and we are on our way. The assessment will furnish background information against which the progress and problems of states and local schools can be projected and better understood. States and local districts will increasingly be concerned with assessment of their own achievements. The shortcomings of appraisals based on current educational tests have been mentioned earlier. State and local efforts are needed to develop appropriate assessment programs and instruments. The contractors working on the national assessment and other competent test constructors will need to work with state and local school people and laymen in developing the means for intradistrict, intraschool, and intrastate appraisals of educational progress and problems. The experience of the national assessment project furnishes a model that will be useful in guiding state and local efforts. Moreover, this model soon will provide background information which will be extraordinarily helpful in assisting us as a nation in making choices as to the future direction of our educational system.

three

New Models and Accountability

If the national assessment effort, or similar endeavors, are able to provide us with substantially more complete information about the nature and effectiveness of our present educational system, then how can that information assist in the reform process? That is, once knowing what the schools do and assuming we still desire reform, what good is all the new information? In Chapter Three Edward Wynne addresses himself to this question. His concern is with the processes by which information about schools can be packaged and utilized to promote change. However, his desire is not only to develop means for promoting short-run change, but also to demonstrate the manner in which an effective information system can be used as an accountability instrument capable of stimulating long-range school effectiveness.

Edward Wynne is a former labor lawyer and has worked in union organizing campaigns. He has also administered antipoverty programs which attempted to promote school change. These experiences have heightened his sensitivity to the role of communications in promoting change movements. Also it has persuaded him of the necessity to perceive successful school innovation as the product of discussion, controversy, and perhaps even conflict. These perspectives also suggest that successful educational reform may hinge on the development of new semipolitical alliances. Consequently, the change model he describes presents a new mode for school-community relations.

Such a perspective is rather long range, but Wynne's experience has persuaded him that short-range plans produce short-range results. He has attempted to identify and isolate the most sensitive focal points in the school-community relationship, what happens to children in school.

He then suggests how leverage might be exerted at that point to mobilize school improvement proponents (outside and inside of school). Like some of the other models in this book, Wynne's article on "output measures" does not describe exactly what different activities should take place in the classroom. Rather he proposes the steps that might be taken to translate information about schools into a force for change, a force which could then restructure what goes on in the classroom.

FROM INFORMATION TO REFORMATION

Edward Wynne

Any prescription for school improvement must first concern itself with the characteristics of the school as an institution. I contend that such an analysis will permit us to comprehend better the obstacles to reform that exist within schools and possibly to design improvements that may diminish or overcome these barriers. As an institution, the school fits the classic bureaucratic model described by the German sociologist, Max Weber,[1] over fifty years ago. Weber observed that bureaucracies had certain common features: carefully structured and restricted distributions of authority, formal criteria for employment and promotion, emphasis on written rules and procedures, the professionalization of the job task, and an established routine for the determination of leadership. Weber did not assert that bureaucracy was automatically bad, but simply that it is the means by which complex societies ensure the accomplishment of important but semirepetitious jobs.

However, both Weber and later writers saw that the bureaucratic model had certain potential shortcomings that required, at least, periodic examination and adjustment. For instance, the organizational sociologist, Michael Crozier, observes that:

> It is clear that in any kind of organization there is a constant pressure to escape from reality. This tendency corresponds to what popular sentiment calls bureaucratic tendencies. Generalization is one way to achieve it; completely impersonal rules are another. Both permit escape from an otherwise necessary adjustment. . . . We shall describe as a "bureaucratic system or organization" a system where feedback process, error-information-correction, does not function well.[2]

From the history of school performance evaluation, we can see that the feedback process does not appear to be functioning well for our

1 Max Weber, *On Charisma and Institution Building,* S. N. Eisenstadt, ed. (Chicago: University of Chicago Press, 1968).

2 Michel Crozier, *The Bureaucratic Phenomenon* (Chicago: University of Chicago Press, 1964), p. 186.

modern school structure. Ralph Tyler's history of the national assessment effort (see Chapter Two) should make clear to us the intense suspicion that some educators have developed toward such evaluation techniques. For instance, Tyler documents the case that a component among school administrators felt the assessment effort to be potentially "dangerous." Dangerous to whom?

There was never any suggestion that the names of particular children might be tied to the results. As far as the tests affecting or scarring children, students are already being extensively tested in programs promoted by the schools themselves. The major new feature of efforts such as national assessment is that the data might be used to measure schools, just as schools now measure children. Need I suggest more about the "dangers" of assessment? Up until this moment, I know of no significant instance of superintendent, principal, or other administrator being evaluated, promoted, or rebuked by a school system because of a school's measured performance as a learning institution. It appears the schools are attempting to escape from the possibility of feedback.

The results of the output assessments published to date support this analysis (and suggest precisely how the assessments are "dangerous"). None of these assessments, so far, have been able to demonstrate precisely how much existing school practices aid pupil learning. It is correct that the research does not suggest, with any precision, what might be better; however, lack of support for the established wisdom is a powerful argument for diverse experimentation.

Experiments, however, run afoul of Crozier's no-feedback rule. The rule is generated because members of an operating bureaucracy have gained their status by satisfying established wisdom—taking courses and acquiring skills in the rituals prescribed by existing practice. Any radical change in these practices is a threat to the "investment" they have already made in their "profession." Indeed, some new criteria might make them less qualified for promotion or pay increases than current outsiders. Who knows, some research might argue for pay cuts for teachers with excessive experience. While we may be upset at the idea of personal considerations affecting any person's professional opinion for or against change, we are first dealing with human beings, who have mortgages to pay, kids to send to college, and seniority they have accrued. How would we act if a change were proposed in our business or profession that threatened these aspects of our own lives?

POSSIBLE PRESCRIPTIONS

This analysis suggests that schools are resistant to radical efforts to promote change or objective evaluation because such efforts are a threat to the status of the professional involved. Such a diagnosis does help to explain why innovations such as attempts to bring schools closer to their lower-class clients have frequently resulted in strongly defensive, near-hysterical resistance.[3] At the same time, the diagnosis is profoundly discouraging. On one hand, output research suggests that radical experimentation is warranted, and perhaps prescribed; on the other hand, such efforts are very likely to be met by intense hostility from the very persons who must carry out these efforts. Remember, key officials of the American Association of School Administrators threatened to frustrate the national assessment program until a former president of their association became chairman of the guiding committee. The administrators called this making assessment "representative." We might inquire, "representative" of whom? Moreover, members of the AASA appear to have dissuaded the assessment program from making public the performance of any individual school, school district, or state. After all, who does the public think schools belong to anyway, taxpayers or their professional staffs?

Some change proponents have suggested that the barriers to innovation may be removed by forms of school decentralization, contractual systems, or private schools. However, there are evident drawbacks to these alternatives. Only a few of the independent schools existing today have been shown to be more innovative than public schools. For instance, consider the following appraisal of the Job Corps urban center program, which was organized and conducted by private contractors, and was supposed to develop innovative programs.

> . . . the centers did not always adhere to the criteria [for graduation] established and in some instances did not maintain the records necessary to determine whether Corps members had met the criteria. Consequently, a number of Corps members were classified as graduates, although it did not appear that they had developed the necessary attributes required for employment in the area of their vocational training.
>
> The academic programs of the centers were structured to provide the Corps members with the reading and mathematical skills necessary for employment in the area of vocational training. In recognition that certain levels of academic achievement were essential to successful performance in various occupational areas, the centers generally established minimum academic requirements that were to be attained either prior to entering a specific vocational program or by the time of completion of that program. Most of the centers we reviewed generally did not enforce the requirements however, and, as a result, many Corps members had not reached these academic levels by the time they had graduated. . . .[4]

[3] George Brazer, "Influencing Institutional Change Through a Demonstration Project: The Case of the Schools," mimeographed (Paper prepared for Columbia University and Mobilization for Youth Training Institute Program, April 1964).

[4] U. S. Congress, Senate Committee on Labor and Public Welfare, House Committee on Education and Labor, by the Controller General of the United States, "Review of Economic Opportunity Programs," 91st Congress, 1st Session (Washington, D. C.: U. S. Government Printing Office, 1969), p. 59.

It is true that some private schools have better staffs, but this may simply be attributed to their (sometimes) better pay and the fact that some teachers may find their more intimate and less rigid environment more attractive. But since we are looking for innovations that will have applicability for approximately 50 million school children, we had better not assume that we can easily offer large-scale pay increases for their 2 million teachers, nor that we can be interested in reforms that persist only in an intimate environment. Finally, even if our newly created independent schools did display better ideas, how do we think we would bring about their adoption by public schools? There are many interesting ideas available now, and yet little that is new seems to be happening.

For instance, there is the old proposal to pay teachers with relatively scarce skills (usually in the sciences) higher salaries. Seems simple, doesn't it, yet the idea is making almost no headway. Why don't we enlarge evaluation so we can find out what's working; but, wait, that's "dangerous"! Some researchers have suggested that teachers' verbal ability may be powerfully related to their teaching effectiveness [5]—this seems on its face to make sense. Since a good teacher should be good at explaining things, why don't we try to relate teachers' pay to their verbal facility test ratings rather than the education courses they have taken; or can you already guess the resistance that such an effort would face?

In sum, the crucial barrier is not that we lack worthwhile (and perhaps even probable) ideas, but rather, that such ideas are usually "fattening or unhealthy," and are not "acceptable" to schools. It is true that such ideas may involve changes in the structural character of schools, but such changes may be just the ones that are needed. One observer, surveying school innovation in New York, said that while much change "appeared" to be happening, "few innovations took place in the kind of people employed, in the way they were organized to work together, in the types of instructional materials they used, or in the times and places at which they taught. In short, schools, as structured institutions remained the same." [6] In the face of this pattern, one could be pessimistic about important ideas ever being adopted as long as the determination of innovation policy is in the hands of schoolmen.

A TOOL FOR PUBLIC INTERVENTION

The term "public schools" can be seen as having two meanings: (1) *run for the public,* and (2) *run by the public.* Lately, we seem to have

[5] Samuel Bowles and Henry Levin, "The Determinants of Scholastic Achievements: An Appraisal of Some Recent Evidence," *The Journal of Human Resources,* Vol. 3 (Winter, 1968), 3-24.

[6] Henry M. Brickell, *Organizing New York State for Educational Change* (Albany: University of the State of New York, 1962), p. 19.

forgotten an important historical lesson: namely, that the major characteristics of public school systems have been designed, not by educators, but by laymen. The concept of a public school, a school common to all citizens, was articulated and popularized in the early 19th century by workingmen's groups, lawyers, reformers, and politicians such as Horace Mann, New York's Governor De Witt Clinton, and Thaddeus Stevens in the Pennsylvania State Legislature.[7] Later school reform and redesign efforts, such as the progressive education movement,[8] the post-sputnik curriculum reforms,[9] school desegregation, and our own poverty education efforts have been triggered and guided by laymen. Imaginative educators have made important contributions, but lay energy appears to have been the critical component. Perhaps lay intervention must again save the day.

However, one cannot realistically expect school decisions to be examined, evaluated, and made by laymen. How can lay vision promote a will for experimentation? What is the machinery for delegation and accountability? I propose that the appropriate role for lay intervention is in the establishment of a new motivation system for schools, a motivation system that will enable feedback channels to form. Laymen must compel school districts to use technicians to establish honest public output evaluation systems so that a community can determine whether schools are being efficiently run.[10] Such systems will specify objective goals for school performance. This, in turn, will permit communities to see what their children are learning, and to know in what ways their schools are falling short of desired goals. The systems will be designed to permit comparisons of the effectiveness of schools with equivalent staffs and equivalent educational challenges. They clearly will not produce accurate and perfect data all at once, but such systems can suggest a framework within which data collection can be improved.

Information feedback systems will permit the public and schoolmen to revise many of the current dysfunctional criteria that are now applied to schools; for example, age of school buildings, number of certified teachers, class size, length of principal's experience. At the same time, they will stimulate administrators to identify the characteristics associated with real school and teacher productivity. Persons with innovative and adaptive temperaments will be seen by administrators as tools to help them win promotions, and means to pay the mortgage, rather

7 Elwood P. Cubberley, *Public Education in the United States* (Boston: Houghton Mifflin, 1934); and David B. Tyack, *Turning Points in American Educational History* (Waltham, Mass.: Blaisdell, 1967).

8 Lawrence H. Cremin, *The Transformation of the School* (New York: Random House—Vintage Books, 1961).

9 Paul E. Marsh and Ross A. Gartner, *Federal Aid to Science Education* (Syracuse: Syracuse University Press, 1963).

10 Edward Wynne, "How to Measure a School's Performance," *American School Board Journal,* Vol. 156, No. 2 (August 1968).

than as potential troublemakers. Since there are signs that parent–school interaction accelerates student learning, we may expect administrators aggressively to seek parent engagement. All persons with worthwhile school improvements to promote will find their situation enhanced. Assuming that they can produce evidence to the effect that their scheme will assist learning, they will be sought out, just as sophisticated buyers today seek out better products on the market. By using an information system properly, we perhaps can avoid embroiling ourselves in the complex (and not necessarily productive) task of creating substitutes for public schools, with all the divisive implications this suggests. Rather, we can use our energies to release the productive capabilities that are inherent in the present system.

You may say, "OK, it's appropriate for laymen to tell the public schools how to conduct the public's business, and, if there should be such intervention, promotion of output accountability seems to be a logical strategy. But why should such an effort progress any farther against school resistance than the many other lay-promoted innovations that have been frustrated, such as school decentralization, school desegregation, or national assessment? Why is this strategy better than other strategies?"

In part, because there appears to be a fascination among people with the first product of output measures: numbers. In his book, *Technology and Change,*[11] Schon concludes that the adoption of numerical controls is one of the most important forces for change that can be imposed upon an institution. On one hand, numbers help us to distill and manage large abstractions. On the other hand, numbers permit us to suggest shades of distinction and fine gradations that must often be made in life. For reasons such as these, society is inherently interested in numerical estimates of performance. Take the weather report. Rather than being told rain is probable or unlikely, we are now given the percentage chance of rain. We respond to this because it is a more meaningful communication. (Incidentally, it gives us a better check on the weather bureaus—how well do their percentage estimates agree with the weather that actually occurs?) So an output measure strategy may win public interest.

Again, the public, on the whole, believes that parents are entitled to receive performance data from bureaucrats. They are not sure that schools should be desegregated, that private corporations should run schools, or that parents should hire teachers. Nevertheless, even a number of persons of a conservative persuasion will agree that parents are entitled to see honest and meaningful numbers. Indeed, the demand

[11] Donald A. Schon, *Technology and Change* (New York: Delacorte Press, 1967), p. 39.

for honest numbers might conceivably serve as a base for new citizen education coalitions, with interracial and interclass composition. Rather than having one neighborhood or group fighting against another for dollars or other benefits (and the bureaucracy safely standing aside from the fray), we may able to unite all citizens under the banner of "Give us the facts."

We can also draw support from the output evaluation efforts that are underway. For example, New York,[12] Pennsylvania,[13] and California [14] have programs at different stages of development; many local school districts release test data, and the school evaluations done for Title I ESEA are public records.[15] There are serious shortcomings to most of these activities; generally, inadequate data are collected or released, the focus of the tests is often excessively narrow, the honesty of the testing program is often suspect, and many of the operations are insensitive to the need for public participation.[16] However, the efforts are susceptible to improvement and enlargement, if there are purposeful public demands. I suspect that the individual school district is the best base for the utterance of such demands. The most accurate data can be developed first upon an intradistrict base, and the citizens (and school board) of an individual district form a natural unit for articulating educational objectives and data demands. At later stages, local citizens can progress to promoting data banks which permit interdistrict comparisons, but perhaps the best initial building block is the district. Since all these accountability efforts are reinforcing, however, there is no need to disparage diverse efforts.

One might inquire as to whether or not output data will be too complex for the public effectively to comprehend. To which a response might be: "You mean that it's more complicated than the Gross National Product; remember, John F. Kennedy made the decline of the GNP an important issue in his 1960 Presidential campaign. Please tell me how GNP is calculated? What items are in the 'package' employed in determining changes in the cost-of-living index? How is a pitcher's earned run average calculated? What stocks are used in determining the Dow-Jones price average? How is the unemployment rate measured? How is a random, stratified sample selected by pollsters for political

[12] New York State, *Pupil Evaluation Program* (Albany: University of the State of New York, State Education Department, 1966).

[13] Pennsylvania State Department of Public Instruction, *Phase I Findings* (Harrisburg: Pennsylvania State Department of Public Instruction, 1968).

[14] California State Education Code, Div. 9, Chap. 10 (California School Assessment Act of 1968).

[15] U. S. Office of Education, *Poor People's Demands on Education,* mimeographed (Washington, D. C.: U. S. Office of Education, 1968).

[16] "Symposium in Evaluating Educational Programs," *Urban Review,* Vol. 3 (February 1969).

forecasting?" Obviously, we routinely use numerical indicators as public policy tools without knowing all the intricacies underlying their computation. Indeed, specialists in most of these tools will admit to us that there are current imperfections in the methodologies used in constructing them, and that they still need refinement. However, the typical position generally is that we should be concurrently engaged in using and refining the indicators.

Apparently, a major key to the acceptance of any "synthetic number" by the public is a general agreement among qualified technicians that the numbers are reasonably accurate tools for policy determinations. In other words, if there is sharp disagreement among experts, the public will be reluctant to rely on the number of an important decision. I believe that most persons with competence in educational evaluation would agree that an adequate output evaluation system could be designed and put into operation today for a school district that honestly desired such a system.

Incidentally, please notice I did not say educators are the key persons to consult about evaluation indices: most educators may know something about budgets or school administration, but we do not ask politicians how to conduct political polls, manufacturers how to compute the GNP, or employers how to count the unemployment rate. Why then should we assume that educators know any more about school output evaluation than we do? Indeed, in statistics generally, the most suspect indices are generated when the computations are organized by persons and institutions with an operational responsibility for the item measured—for example, the crime rate statistics maintained by the FBI and many police agencies are notoriously controversial.[17]

Any system designed to produce output data will need improvement as it is operated. However, most corporate accounting systems also need improvement, and they are 500 years old. There are differences of opinion among evaluators today about methodological issues, but most of them spring from a concern as to whether or not certain data justify particular conclusions. These opinion differences persist even when all concerned recognize the data may have been gathered in limited or compromised form because schools refused to cooperate in the data collection process. With a cooperative school system, many of these disputes might disappear. Also, evaluators frequently seek to "tease" cause and effect information from their data. This is commendable. However, at the moment, the first public objective would be to see what is being done or not done, rather than seeking "whys." Then we

[17] Raymond A. Bauer, ed., *Social Indicators* (Cambridge: M.I.T. Press, 1966), pp. 112-29.

may move on to refinements. In fact, the best means of ensuring refinement of a data system is to base public policy decisions on it. When this is done, people can really question whether or not the system is right and how it should be revised. For instance, one of the main reasons the Coleman Report is the subject of critical attention is because some persons have attempted to base policy decisions upon its findings.

The output measure proposal is radical, in the sense that it aspires to provoke important changes in the way schools operate. Its radical nature possesses a potential for change; it excites the hostility of some noneducators who are often sympathetic to school change. This opposition must be frankly faced. The substance of the opposition is the charge that output measures may force schools to direct their energies into teaching for objective, quantifiable, cognitive goals, such as reading, grammar, and math. I believe such critics misunderstand the nature and the potential of testing. Many measurement specialists have repeatedly observed that if a goal can be specified, it can be described; if it can be described, it can be measured; and if it can be measured, it can be tested. In other words, any educational objective that can be described can be tested and measured. It is true that many test instruments today are not designed to measure the "softer," affective goals. However, these patterns are changing—the national assessment program is giving as much attention to citizenship, vocational education, literature, music, and art as it is to math and reading. For instance, consider the implications of this typical question that might be asked in the assessment: What procedures might the members of a group follow in selecting their first chairman, and why?

It may also be true that our skill in devising such tests is not as great as it is for testing in reading, and so on. However, this ignorance simply reflects the existing disinterest of the schools, *as currently run,* in seriously seeing whether or not noncognitive values are being transmitted. If schools wanted such tests, if they were seriously concerned with whether they were making any difference in the affective area, their demands would probably stimulate the production of such tests. In point of fact, *most* youths (with significant exceptions) today are performing reasonably well in learning cognitive skills. Thus, most schools are willing to administer such tests to students, even if they do not wish to be rated by the results. However, schools do not have great confidence in their ability in teaching softer, affective skills and attitudes. Moreover, schoolmen can see no public consensus regarding what the affective influence of school should be, and, hence, they fear disclosing what it is. In addition, lack of a machinery for defining and legitimating affective goals has probably further discouraged school interest. But the creation of such legitimating machinery would be accelerated by the development of better tests. In other words, we may have drifted into a self-reinforcing circle out of which we can escape by the use of goal-defining tests. Without such tests, we will persist in giving only lip service to affective goals.

This discussion leads to another important benefit of an output approach. What you test will determine what you teach. It is true this means teachers will teach for the test. However, good tests, designed by able professionals and administered by an honest structure, can militate against rote preparation and coaching. Good teaching for fair tests must emphasize student motivation, understanding, and flexibility. But "teaching for the test," in a broad sense, is a major objective of a *community-designed testing program,* to permit the community to determine, in general outlines, what they want their children to learn. If parents and the community do not decide, then who should? Indeed, who now is deciding what our children learn, and by what right do they do so?

What do I mean by *community-designed testing program?* A program in which the community, through its elected or legitimately appointed leaders, along with evaluators and schoolmen, has participated in the design of the goals to be tested. Also, community spokesmen should make the major policy decisions and use experts only where experts are most useful—in making technical decisions. This should result in a program where important community spokesmen are familiar with the rationale of the testing system because they have worked on its details and are prepared subsequently to translate the issues to their fellow laymen. The interaction produced by such discussions should immensely strengthen the ties between communities and schools and remove schools from the difficult-to-justify posture of determining subject priorities without community participation. Incidentally, as Dr. Tyler pointed out in Chapter Two, his experience in national assessment revealed that there are not great divergencies about school objectives within our society today. Consequently, if this is true, we need not fear a national convulsion over these issues. Perhaps the current goal-setting system, with its obvious lack of legitimating structure, encourages irresponsible attacks from spokesmen with narrow interests. Who can reply to them, "we voted to have this or that subject or goal taught"?

Assume that the output approach makes sense: How can we hope to put it into effect? How can we produce such a major change in our huge, amorphous national public education system composed of innumerable subsystems? There are problems of refining the basic concepts involved and getting a few districts to try them in order to demonstrate their value.

RESEARCH AND DEVELOPMENT

In the area of large social phenomena, we do not have a methodology that will permit us to establish test tubes or to conduct isolated, abstract experiments about proposed changes. Analysis and historical analogy will thus be important research elements. In this light, this chapter constitutes a portion of the research effort; it offers an analysis of the approach and makes it available to the criticism and assessment of others. When we talk of the fruits of analysis, this incidentally suggests that we will seek material to analyze. In addition to the material developed in the general studies in school change, there are instances in which parent and community groups have tended to engage in output evaluation. All such empirical experiences must be subjected to careful scrutiny.[18] The public and professional controversies surrounding publications such as the Coleman Report can also be enlightening. Anything that can be done, by actors such as parents and taxpayers, foundations, community action agencies, civil rights groups, and news media, to stimulate public application of this approach will also serve several purposes: it will supply data for research and analyses, serve to demonstrate the approach to other interested persons, and probably deliver direct benefits to the community and schools concerned.[19]

Such stimulation might involve preparing and distributing explanatory publications, financing the design of actual or model output systems, paying the costs of conferences or training sessions in which laymen and interested technicians discuss these issues, or subsidizing efforts of school districts to operate such systems.

There is also another research vein to be mined. A number of efforts are underway to promote public output evaluation of many government programs, such as the Office of Economic Opportunity, air pollution, and school desegregation.[20] The patterns of controversies that evolve about these incidents may supply us with enlightening analogies.

It is difficult to maintain hard lines between the category of research versus those of development and demonstration when evolving social action strategies. The forces and commitments that often are necessary to try a new idea on an experimental scale sometimes preclude a genuinely experimental, tentative approach. In the social-political arena, it

[18] Edward Wynne, "A Parent's Group Shows How to Evaluate and Change School Policies," *Phi Delta Kappan,* Vol. 50, No. 5 (January 1969), 294-95.

[19] Edward Wynne, "School Output Measures as Tools for Change," *Education and Urban Society,* Vol. 2, No. 1 (November 1969).

[20] B. M. Gross, ed., *The Annals of the American Academy of Political and Social Sciences,* Vols. 371 and 373 (May and September 1967).

is traditional to apply a hortatorical vocabulary for and against all efforts of experimental change. The fever which therefore arises about proposed school changes often discourages dispassionate analysis or explorations. Somehow, every change or barrier to change is seen as a life or death matter. This pattern takes on a special irony, when we recognize that research suggests there is very little evidence that most practices (or alleged changes) make much difference in the way children learn. In other words, there is no special reason for being so wedded to the status quo and little evidence that any conceivable changes will produce much harm. Indeed, most educational evidence suggests that, unfortunately, many changes make no important difference. However, despite the befogging fever of controversy that seems inevitable, we can hope that farsighted persons will maintain sufficient dispassion to consider these events in an objective light and reflect on questions such as: what can be learned from this event? How might things be tried differently "next time"? Can we do different things in different places?

Such a social-experimental approach can only evolve if there is a group of persons who identify themselves with the advancement of an output strategy, who regularly exchange communications, and who consciously seek to perfect and refine the strategy. Such a group apparently does not yet exist. Its evolution will be essential to the promotion of deliberate development and demonstration efforts. There may be effective research without such cohesion, but the conducting of several varieties of demonstration and the development of improved modes of operation will require an "organized base." This should be a group of persons who self-consciously exchange information, experiences, and insights. The group may be an informal, invisible college, or it may constitute itself into a formal organization or committee. It will eventually require money to proceed and, depending on the source of the dollars, may have to make some compromises to satisfy the donor. If the methods evolved from these efforts show continuing promise, the challenge of large-scale production and dissemination of the approach will arise.

PRODUCTION AND DISSEMINATION

The diffusion of a major innovation throughout our immense school system is an event of historical scope. Inevitably, such a step will involve important changes in existing institutions and probably the creation of major new institutions. The diffusion strategy for public output evaluation must assume that changes of such scope will occur concurrently with its nationwide diffusion. While the character of such changes cannot be anticipated with mechanical precision, one can attempt to forecast their nature. Such a forecast might enable disseminators to plan better and organize their efforts. It also could suggest some of the forces that might oppose and support the proposed change and indicate lines of argument and strategy that could be followed by the proponents of the change. Finally, the forecast, by giving us a picture of the "new educational world," can permit us better to determine whether or not the proposed change is desirable. Exactly how much do we like the new picture? The following forecast or scenario is based upon an analysis of major elements that may be affected by output evaluation.

1. The proposal radically changes the existing relationship between school systems and communities. Today, while all schoolmen give lip service to accountability, there exists practically no understanding of how such accounts are to be rendered. In general, most perceptive members of the community see education as a collection of obscure rituals, sometimes managed by persons they do not completely trust. However, despite this vague distrust, few community members feel comfortable about sharply criticizing the educational process—they feel they lack adequate perspective or competence to make effective criticism. The very restraint compelled by this inarticulateness creates additional strains between the public and educators. It is not so much that educators are seen as having won their spurs by accomplishment, in fair and open debate (as have businessmen or scientists), but rather that they have set up debate rules which have frozen out opposition. The proposal suggests a means by which laymen can use the competence of third party experts, evaluators, to supply them with data on which to judge school performance. The sociologist Weber observed that our control of the institutions about us depends on the "transparency" of the connection between such institutions and the events they effect. In other words, if the public can see how an institution causes or prevents certain events, the public is much better equipped to control the conduct of the institution. Conversely, it is in the interest of an institution to conceal the interrelationship between the institution and events that excite public concern, unless these events are universally seen as desirable. If output measures can cause the public to see schools in a new light, to know better where schools are teaching and not teaching well, the public will win new power over the management of schools.

But such radical transfers of power will not occur simply. Today, the national organ for citizen-school involvement is the National Congress of Parents and Teachers, the PTA. The word "teacher" in the name is a significant omen. The association's structure is premised upon the theory that there is a persisting and pervasive continuity of interest between parents, school administrators, and teachers. Therefore, in all of its deliberations, the association's policy is affected by the voice of schoolmen. This is especially true where issues of "professional competence" arise. The schoolmen's presence must inevitably cramp all efforts to discuss touchy questions frankly. There is an interesting analogy in the field of labor relations. Anti-union employers have long recognized that workers in any large plant will tend to associate together to exchange experiences and consider their self-interests. It is unrealistic to try and stifle such efforts completely; they will just continue underground. Under such conditions, what employers did was to organize (or encourage) "company unions," unions in which supervisors played an active role. Such associations distracted worker efforts from more effective forms of independent organizations. They appeared to fill a vacuum and permit employees to come together in an organization without experiencing the ill will of the employer (for forming an organization to which he was clearly opposed). When the Wagner Act was passed in 1936, to encourage union organization, one of its important provisions outlawed such company-dominated unions. The extinction of these groups encouraged the creation of genuinely representative unions. Interestingly enough, under the stimulus of the CIO's efforts in the 1930s, some company unions shook off their traditions of employer domination and became "legitimate operations."

As the output evaluation movement gains speed, and in order for it to be able to gain speed, the PTA, in whole or part, must be radically reshaped by activist parents. Otherwise, new and independent organizations must be formed. Probably, both reshaping and the creation of new organizations will occur concurrently (as was the case in the early stages of the civil rights movement). The ferment introduced by these changes, and the new responsibilities parent groups must assume (for example, for counseling parents about output evaluation), will generate an increase in parent group membership. It may also justify increases in dues as more services, and more valuable services, are rendered.

2. The changes may bring about the reaction of new professions. Persons with technical competence in evaluation will be in great demand if they have the skills to translate the language of their craft into concepts useful to policy makers and laymen. Such persons will have a golden opportunity to advance the technical state of their art, because the ensuing debates will inevitably raise questions about the correct interpretation of technical issues. Marx, Galbraith, Keynes, Robert Heilbroner, Arthur Schlesinger, Gunnar Myrdal, Kenneth Clark, and Walter Hansen stand out as social scientists who combined professional competence with a flair for public communication. While their prescriptions were not always finally correct, their eloquence focused public attention on important issues and helped establish priorities for their professional peers. Such debates stimulated their professions to greater heights of creation.

Probably the "new evaluators" will have their insights interpreted and applied by another new class of information brokers, semi-political figures who will use the data to advance their public status or office. (In the same fashion, different civil-rights activists now use varying sets of research data to support different ideologies or strategies. Of course, public acceptance of one strategy over another means the preference of one organization and class of leaders over another.) All of this is not a criticism of the information-brokerage process; on the contrary, this mechanism tends to increase the quality of public decision making. Major problems arise when research, theory, and professional articulateness lag behind evolving policy issues, as may be the case in education. Under such circumstances, information brokers can be driven to raise artificial and counterconstructive issues. Perhaps intellectuals have not yet supplied society with useful, change-oriented concepts for public education.

3. We may be able to correct a very unhealthy new development. An implicit alliance seems to be forming between teachers' unions and school administration in some school systems. Each group has a potent interest in combining against the public interest. Teachers can supply administrators with political muscle to resist important school change; administrators can supply the teachers with tacit support in their negotiations. At present, the public has only one weapon against this alliance: it can refuse to support teacher raises. However, this is a primitive tool; such raises sometimes are justified. The real question may be not whether to give any raises, but what kinds of increases will best increase productivity or reward current productivity. Unfortunately, salary raises based on productivity are not necessarily the kind promoted by teachers unions. This is the sort of thing that management must push on its own; but, if school administrators wish to act as pawns, it is next to impossible for the community to run the details of bargaining negotiations. Currently, the community's only tool is the meat axe. However, output pressures on the administration may correct this unhealthy imbalance. If administrators are under pressure to deliver real results, they may well act in the fashion of most other managers, that is, to use wage negotiations as tools to trade the advancement of their (and the public's) interest for concessions to their employees. Pay increases will be traded for new personnel practices that administrators believe will produce better learning. What will such changes be? We are not exactly sure, just because administrators have never needed to think about such matters in the past. They might relate to conducting school at different hours, requiring teachers to participate in new kinds of training, granting promotions and raises on new criteria, asking teachers to work in different types of classroom settings, and so on. These distinctions can never be effectively compelled by direct public pressures,

but they can be brought about if administrators are finally held accountable for results. In sum, output evaluation will discourage the tendency toward a broadcast alliance between teachers and administrators and bring about the return of the appropriate healthy tension.

4. We may see a revival and restructuring of that important American institution, the local school board. It is ironic that a discussion of school policy reshaping can progress this far without even mentioning the existing organ for community control of school policy. But this silence is simply a reflection of the judgment of many commentators upon the current role of the school board. In general, such commentators have concluded that most boards exist principally to serve as buffers which shield the policies adopted by the administrative staff from the judgment of the community. Somehow, school boards have not been able to translate much current public concern into constructive school change. It is not always that they are committed to the administration, but rather that they seem to become eternally involved in "fire fighting" and "bits-and-pieces criticism"; one just does not sense a pattern of firm, policy-oriented criticism of administrative dysfunctions.

Perhaps a major cause for the evolution of this pattern is the lack of conceptual tools for boards to use in evaluating existing policies. Administrators have evolved a lengthy list of accepted prerequisites to successful learning—certified, trained teachers, appropriate materials, certain class sizes, and types of buildings. It is inevitable that there will be shortages of these things. Boards now spend most of their policy making time attempting to obtain more of these "essentials," determining how to juggle the limited supply that exists, and being told that performance will not improve until some unattainable level of resources is achieved. Suppose boards spent their time (a) deciding what levels schools should be achieving in what subjects, (b) determining whether an adequate assessment system was being maintained, (c) devising rewards for superior performance by administrators, (d) attempting to detect the bugs that might arise as a result of such a new system, (e) concerning itself with the larger issues of budgeting, and (f) reporting to the community the results of the output measurement program.

It is likely that such a school board would have an important impact on school policy, and it likely would be seen as the focal point of all proposals for school change. Indeed, it is also possible that the type of person who would volunteer to serve on such a board might even differ somewhat from many present board members, who are often sincere and well-intentioned citizens, but who frequently appear unable to offer effective alternatives to administrators' proposals. Perhaps some more able persons now refuse to serve precisely because they feel they do not have the conceptual tools to devise alternatives, yet they intuitively believe that things are not right. I remember one very able person who rejected my effort to recruit her as a school board candidate, all the while saying that she did not want to touch that "can of worms." She had a public reputation for effectiveness to protect, and she just did not see how a school board member could demonstrate such effectiveness in the existing environment. Was she so wrong?

5. We may see new breeds of schoolmen and teachers evolve. Countless commentators have bemoaned the profusion of "inauthentic personalities" and "marginal men" [21] peopling the schools. At the same time, we have not been adequately conscious of the forces that have brought about these patterns. "Where there are few obvious criteria of performance, an institution must turn to indirect symbols of achievement, especially those which win public acclaim. An institution can become so preoccupied with marginal activities which enhance its prestige that it reflects the less visible work which makes up its true purpose." [22] This is a fair characterization of much current school administration. Since fair and honest structures for evaluating administrative performance do not exist, promotions at the top and intermediate levels must turn on criteria that involve superficialities and irrelevancies. Once such criteria are applied, they tend to corrupt the vision and conduct of teachers. Their superiors' advancement does not depend upon the skill of their teachers, but rather on whether the school is "smoothly run," whatever that has to do with learning.

At the same time, researchers have observed that achievement-oriented personalities, doers, self-starters, innovators, are "very much interested in knowing how well they are doing. They like to work at a task which gives them a *feedback*." [23] (Italics added.) It is hard for such persons to find satisfaction if the main feedback may be that they have taken the appropriate number of courses to achieve a promotion or raise. Concomitantly, an organization that evolves feedback can develop a less rigid and more open environment. The articulation of performance standards generates a "freedom from close supervision and from inflexible operating rules," "enhances work satisfaction," and encourages the evolution of a genuinely professional environment, in which relationships are based on shared concerns with improving results.[24] Today, the school "is a despotism in a state of perilous equilibrium," steeped in "irrelevant competition that discourages the strong." [25]

[21] Andrew W. Halpin, *Theory and Research in Administration* (New York: Macmillan, 1966), pp. 212, 236.

[22] Peter Marris and Martin Rein, *Dilemmas of Social Reform* (New York: Atherton Press, 1967), p. 46.

[23] David McClelland, "Why Men and Nations Seek Success," in P. C. Sexton, ed., *Readings on the School and Society* (Englewood Cliffs, N. J.: Prentice-Hall, 1967), pp. 157-58.

[24] Peter M. Blau and W. Richard Scott, *Formal Organizations* (San Francisco: Chandler, 1962), pp. 178, 179, 191.

[25] Willard Waller, *The Sociology of Teaching* (New York: Russell and Russell, 1932), pp. 10, 453.

Changes which permit important goals to be set and redefine performance in rational, recognizable criteria will (a) help revise the attitudes and conduct of current schoolmen; (b) change the types of recruits that are retained by schools today (plenty of the "right types" come in now, they just do not often stay); and (c) help recruit new types of persons into school work.

6. An output orientation may greatly increase the amount and productivity of educational research. Currently, such research is only a comparatively marginal activity. Throughout America, one-half of 1 percent of all annual education expenditures go into research; for industry, the equivalent figure is 3 percent; for health, 5 percent; and for defense it is 15 percent.[26] If we assume that there is some relationship between the size of the research effort and the results, we may feel that the productivity prospects for education research are encouraging—there may well be a lot of good things left to be discovered. But the paucity of education research expenditures leads us to another observation: This very paucity can be seen as the product of current efforts to escape output standards. In other words, education research expenditures are low principally because educators have not been desperately striving to increase the productivity of schools (or at least have not been striving to measure any such changes). Without such striving (there has not been any for large-scale or effective research), appropriations will not be lobbied for or passed. Moreover, when dollars are ostensibly appropriated for research, they will be siphoned off and used for what is not legitimately research, such as new operating funds.

Consider the unfortunate contrast with the military, where every general or admiral apparently believes that the safety of society (and the future of his career and the size of his unit) depends upon "his researchers" inventing a new threat or counterthreat annually. While it is not clear that all these inventions are desirable, it is evident that the generals' motivation has greatly increased the effectiveness of weaponry. How can we give our schoolmen the same desire to seek improvement? By making improvement definable and giving credit for it, just as officers are rated on the basis of the quality of the weapons they help to create.

The claim can still be made that the applied educational research that is done is too often unsatisfactory. But this is misreading of the research process. Effective research requires interaction between operators and researchers. The operator must feel an intense pressure to improve performance, to increase his profit, or simply to keep his company in business. (But "no public school has ever been put out of

[26] Communications (1968) with Hendrik Gideonese, Director, Office of Program Planning, Bureau of Research, U. S. Office of Education, and Leonard Lecht, Director, Center for Priority Analysis, National Planning Association.

business due to poor teaching.") [27] The researcher must have adequate resources, a prestigious status, the cooperation of the operator, and the feeling that the operators are seriously interested in improving output. These conditions do not appear to exist in education, and much current education research assumes the nature of a holding or justifying operation. Educators tend to admit that they need research, but nothing requires that the effort be taken seriously. Output measures should affect these attitudes and values.

The measure process will also produce invaluable research data. Output data (as defined in this chapter) is an essential ingredient for survey research. However, schools have often been unwilling to cooperate in developing such data pools, since they may be used for school assessment purposes. But when such data are routinely collected as part of the performance reporting process, researchers will be better able to (a) analyze the data, (b) identify more productive school programs, (c) find out why they are successful, and (d) design and assess new programs that capitalize on the successes of individual schoolmen.

7. We will see greater variety in school programs and operations. The shallowness of the current conventional wisdom has compelled its proponents to hold desperately to a narrow mythology which runs somethink like this: things must be done a particular way exactly because we cannot be sure that this is the right way. If we were sure it were right, we would feel more comfortable about permitting variation, since knowledge could only sustain the right. This tightness has reflected itself in diverse legislation, setting requirements for teacher certification, principals' promotions, and so on, and in similar civil service provisions. Output pressures may finally make the public conscious that there presently is no objective evidence in support of these restrictions. In other words, public focus upon results, rather than direct attack on prescribed rituals, may undermine the rituals and stimulate variations. What kinds of variations? New salary patterns; different measures of competence (not just teachers, clericals, and administrators, but many new types of skills at professional and subprofessional levels); better organized support services for the classroom teacher; more, or perhaps less, school days; shorter, or longer, school days; no requirement that children attend for so many years; much smaller, or larger, schools; and so on.

8. Schools will have to spend a larger proportion of their money upon data collecting and analysis (which is actually part of the research). This is consonant with the patterns followed in our more productive businesses. At one time, the idea in industry was to maintain and enlarge the investment in production workers, the men on the

[27] Halpin, *Theory and Research in Administration,* p. 200.

line. Money spent on paper work was a superfluous luxury. However, as our productive forces have increased, we have seen that the major challenge is for coordination and planning so as to obtain better organization of production forces: organization is the effect of intelligent paper work and data collection. Similarly, in schools, we often hear the plea that funds should be devoted to "classroom expenses," essentially higher salaries for teachers and more teachers. At the same time, we do not know what comprises an effective teacher; we do not know whether some types of teachers work better with some children and some with others; and neither do we know if children are learning any better as a result of these additional expenditures. Until we improve our diagnostic, analytic, planning, and incentive structures, we have only intuitive tools for increasing or upgrading manpower. We do not presently know what skills we need or what incentives to offer for what achievements. Essentially, our current low investment data collection and analysis is another aspect of the efforts to resist genuine planning, coordination, and community responsibility. All of these effects require more and better data.

EXACTLY HOW DOES ONE PROMOTE A NEW PRESCRIPTION?

After all these strategic considerations have been analyzed, one is still faced with the concrete problem of how to encourage any school district or districts to adopt this approach. This depends upon the judgment of the change proponents on the scene. Strategic discussions can enlighten activists to factors to consider, allies to seek, and arguments to use, but there is still the element of improvisations. Do you have the ear of a board member? Can he be interested in making a fight to get a system put in? Will he carry his fight into the media? Are existing output evaluations kept secret? Fight to make them public, and concurrently to improve their reliability. If evaluations are made public, propose they be used to affect school policies—what is working and why? If we cannot tell, then why can't we? Can experts be brought in to improve the quality of the measures? Has the public determined the goals being evaluated?

Explain to reporters the principle behind your efforts. Identify evaluators and educators who are sympathetic to your efforts, and obtain their counsel. Will businessmen naturally sympathize with your efforts? What about minority groups? Are there other districts with effective programs? Can their board members or parents be brought in to explain what they are doing, and how they got it done? Can outside funds be obtained to pay the installation costs of the system? (Not that the costs are so great, but lack of funds is often used as an excuse.) On a larger scale, can one promote state or federal legislation to pay the initial costs of such systems where the data will go to citizens, as well as administrators? Do you have pamphlets and explanatory literature available? Of course, all these questions only lead to others, but in the end, change depends on the determination, ingenuity, and persistence of the person on the spot. Essays such as this can be most useful if they provide such doers with the information that will permit them best to use their own good judgment.

A FINAL CAUTION

This generally optimistic proposal must close on a note of caution. Our public schools represent an enormous, decentralized, and somewhat irrational enterprise. Also, the research lag means there are many important things we do not know about the learning process. Increasing knowledge is the product of larger research investments *plus* time. These factors are not all drawbacks; for example, decentralization permits us to put new ideas into effect without having to change the whole system, and the very lag in research suggests there are great opportunities for improvement. But any persons who seek to improve school operations must recognize that there are no simple and expeditious steps. There are better and worse strategies, but effective efforts will require persistence as well as vision. It is upsetting to perceive that important defects in schools will not necessarily be quickly corrected. However, lasting changes in large institutions demand the continuing commitment of determined men and women. Perhaps a consolation may be found in the fact that the very toughness of these institutions argues that any beneficial effects we produce will endure for our children and their descendants. When Horace Mann abandoned law for educational reform, he said, "Let the next generation be my client." [28] He won his case. Can we equal such persistence and vision?

[28] L. H. Tharp, *Until Victory* (Boston: Little, Brown, 1953).

four

Strengthening the Present Model

Passage of the Elementary and Secondary Education Act in 1965 perhaps marked the single most significant event in education during the 1960s. With this legislation, Congress recognized the severe degree to which large numbers of economically depressed children were not being properly educated. Each year since its inception, Title I appropriations have approximated $1 billion. This infusion of federal funds has stimulated a gigantic effort at what is generally termed "compensatory education." The idea underlying compensatory programs is a simple one. The children of economically poor parents frequently do not perform in school as well as their peers from more fortunate economic circumstances. As a consequence, it is necessary to provide them with additional school services in order to compensate for their out-of-school environment and relatively slow academic progress.

Compensatory education has taken numerous forms, and it is difficult to describe a "typical" program. Both in concept and in practice, however, compensatory education has been controversial. Its critics claim that it has not elevated the achievement levels of poor children and, worse yet, has tended to undermine their self-image by suggesting to them that they somehow are possessed of a different "culture" and are inferior. Supporters of compensatory education defend the area by claiming that it is yet too early to assess its benefits, that it seldom has been provided with the resources necessary to do its task successfully, and, when properly operated, compensatory programs positively transform the self-image of the students involved.

The author of the following pages in this chapter, Wilson Riles, was the Director of the California Department of Education agency responsible for statewide administration of compensatory education programs. From this perspective, it is somewhat understandable for him to be a proponent of such programs. However, it is of interest to note here that, though statements are made regarding the effectiveness of compensatory education, Riles feels the primary significance of the movement is not so much the short-run positive results it may have for poor children, but the longer-range realization that "schools fail, not children." With compensatory education has come a new model for education, a model which says that if we are now attempting to school every child, then we must change our present educational system which was founded on the notion of educating only an elite. Under the new conditions, we must find a means to enable each child, even the "average" and "below average" student, to maximize his schooling experience. That indeed is what compensatory education is all about.

COMPENSATORY EDUCATION

Wilson C. Riles

Compensatory education is a program designed to meet the special educational needs of children from low income and poverty backgrounds. It is based on a commitment to a new definition of equal educational opportunity. Traditionally, educators and the public have spoken of equal educational opportunity in terms of sameness, for example, the same textbooks, the same curriculum, the same class size, and the same number of library volumes. We clung to the myth that we were doing an equally good job with all our children, that all the schools were equal, that they all provided a uniformly good education, and that, aside from disciplinary problems, nothing was wrong with ghetto schools. In other words, if the children failed, something was wrong with the children.

But "compensatory education" represents a new concept. We are being forced to recognize that equal educational opportunity means an educational program geared to the needs of each individual child, a program that will give each child an equal chance to succeed to the maximum extent of his potential, regardless of his economic, ethnic, social or cultural background. It means that more money, more individual attention, better teachers, and more curriculum experimentation must be poured into schools which serve economically disadvantaged children.

Where we have traditionally thought of a dropout in terms of the child's failure to succeed in school, a more realistic appraisal is that dropouts reflect the school's failure to succeed with the child. In effect, the child has not dropped out; he has been pushed out by a school that has ignored his educational needs and by a school program that has no relevance to his aspirations or learning problems. Our schools have been geared to the middle class child, his experiences and his values. Our teachers come from middle class backgrounds. Our curriculum, textbooks, and recognized teaching methods are all aimed at the middle class child. But the instructional program that is good for the middle class child is not necessarily good for the child whose background is one of poverty. Consequently, there has been a strong correlation between a student's educational achievement and his socioeconomic background. Traditionally, the child from a disadvantaged background has achieved at a lower rate than his more affluent classmate. He starts behind and falls further and further behind the longer he stays in school.

The problem is not new. What is new is the attention that is finally being given to its solution. Most of the students who are dropping out today would never have attended high school at all 50 years ago. They would have quit school before reaching the secondary level and would have taken unskilled jobs which were then readily available. They would not have been considered dropouts, they would have simply joined the working force.

What is new is that unskilled jobs are diminishing because of automation and the schools have been called upon to play a major role in breaking the vicious circle of illiteracy, poverty, crime, and dependency on welfare that is taking an increasing toll in human and economic waste. And, perhaps most significantly, what is new is that the poor and the alienated are no longer willing to accept the *status quo*. They are demanding what any middle class parent would have demanded long ago if his child did not seem to be getting anything out of the educational system. They are demanding an accounting and a change in the system to make it more relevant to their needs.

The top priority issue facing public education is improving the school achievement of the children of the poor, the disadvantaged, the groups that in the past have failed to receive the full benefits of American education. This then is the goal of compensatory education.

PROGRAMS AND THEIR SUCCESS

Some of the frequently implemented compensatory education activities are:

Intensified reading programs, using specialist reading teachers, language laboratories, and new curriculum materials.

Use of neighborhood teacher aides to free the teacher from routine duties so he can give more individual attention to each student.

Employment of extra teachers to reduce class size.

English as a second language classes for students whose primary language is not English.

Preschool classes for three-, four-, and five-year-olds to prepare them for a successful school experience.

Health and nutritional services, including medical and dental checkups and health education classes for both parents and students.

Intergroup relations activities to alleviate racial, social, and linguistic isolation.

Inservice training programs for teachers to improve their understanding of the effects of poverty on the child's learning progress and to enhance their skills in working with disadvantaged children.

These are not separate and unrelated activities. They must be parts of a multifaceted, comprehensive program. We have found in evaluating compensatory education programs that the best gains in achievement occurred where a comprehensive program was provided for the students. Piecemeal projects which attempt to overcome the learning handicaps caused by poverty usually fail to result in demonstrable improvement in student achievement. Evaluations of California's compensatory education programs reveal that where a concentrated effort was made, the students averaged one month of school achievement for every month of participation in the program, or one year of achievement during a year of instruction. Previous data indicated that children from impoverished backgrounds tended to average only .7 of a year growth for every year of instruction.

We have found that our best results have been school districts in medium-sized urban areas and in suburban areas. In the 1967–68 school year, the average growth in these areas exceeded one year per year of instruction, while less than a year's growth was shown for children in the largest cities and in rural areas. Also, the best results have been obtained in elementary grades. This is consistent with what educators have always believed to be true; we must reach disadvantaged children at an early age before frustration and failure become difficult, if not impossible, to overcome. We are talking about the difference between prevention and remediation. It is much easier to prevent the achievement gap from developing than it is to attempt to close the gap later.

Also essential is coordination and articulation between grades and grade levels to ensure that achievement gains are lasting and not merely dramatic, short-term improvements. The story of what happened in Headstart and other preschool programs has been well documented throughout the nation. Too many people were looking for a miracle and thought that if disadvantaged children were exposed to a few months of intensive classroom experience, all educational problems in the ghettos would be solved. What resulted was that preschool "graduates" lost their gains if they were placed in regular kindergarten and primary grade classrooms that were unprepared to build on the children's preschool experience. What we have learned then is that to be of maximum effectiveness, compensatory education programs must be comprehensive in nature, must start at an early age, and must continue until the student is able to maintain progress without extra help.

Compensatory education programs are not concerned only with students. High priority in California compensatory education programs is also placed upon improving school-community relations and on inservice education for teachers and other school staff members. In the area of parent involvement, state guidelines require that each school district operating a compensatory education program establish a district advisory committee, of which at least one-half of the members must be residents of the target area. In addition, parent advisory groups are to be established for each participating school. The purpose of these advisory bodies is to ensure that the community and parents are involved in the planning and implementation of compensatory education programs. School-community relations is not a one-way street; too often, school officials think in terms of the need to transmit information to parents—to improve the parents' understanding of school activities. There is an equal need for a structure whereby school officials can improve their understanding of the poverty area community they are serving and the perceptions of parents as to the educational needs of their children. The advisory committees and other parent involvement activities are based on the recognition that educators cannot hope to improve the classroom performance of children from low income backgrounds without involving their parents in the process.

Another required component of every compensatory education program is inservice education of the staff. Additional funds, new materials, smaller classes, and supportive services are all supplementary to the work of the classroom teacher. For, in the end, whether compensatory education is truly effective, or whether it becomes just another source of funds, depends on the quality of the teachers working with the children. The teacher, more than any other factor, will influence the performance of the child. Often, a student's achievement level will tend to be a mirror of the teacher's preconceived judgment of that student's capabilities. Where a high level of performance has been expected, disadvantaged youngsters have responded with remarkable achievement. One of our problems in the past has been that teachers really did not expect the children of the poor to succeed. And so they didn't. This attitude prevailed even among some of our so-called "understanding" teachers who would excuse the student's failure with a kind of "I know you're doing the best you can" tolerance. We do not need the type of tolerance and understanding that establishes lower standards and expectations for children from poverty areas.

The need for inservice education is not, however, limited to improving the attitudes of school personnel toward disadvantaged children. Emphasis should be placed on improvement of instruction by enhancing the skills of school personnel in diagnosing the learning needs of the children and by implementing programs to meet those needs. Inservice education should not be just a one time activity, but a continuous activity throughout the school year.

As more attention is placed on the problems of the disadvantaged, it becomes increasingly clear that we need more and better teachers in our poverty area schools. We are finally recognizing that teachers who work in poverty areas require more skills, more training, more sensitivity, and more devotion. We are recognizing that it takes a special talent to bring out the often hidden potential of the child from an economically disadvantaged background. We are, in effect, finally recognizing that teaching the disadvantaged is worthy of the best the profession has to offer, and not just the "leftovers" who do not have sufficient seniority to be "promoted" to the better neighborhoods.

Recruitment and training programs must be tied to the improvement of conditions in the schools. The talented and creative teachers and administrators will accept assignments in poverty neighborhoods only if working conditions are such that the assignment offers a challenge and a possibility of success rather than predetermined frustration and failure. Once a competent staff has been assembled, it must be provided sufficient resources and flexibility to exert leadership and creativity. The principal and teachers must be allowed to make decisions and experiment with new ideas without going through a tortuous bureaucratic maze.

COMPENSATORY EDUCATION AND INTEGRATION

In the last few years, there has been much discussion in educational circles as to whether integration or compensatory education is the best method of improving the education of minority group students from poverty backgrounds. There are some who say, "Let's forget about integration. It's too hard to accomplish. We'll pour extra resources into our ghetto schools and do the job through compensatory education." And then there are those who say, "Let's forget about compensatory education. Just desegregate the schools and the problem of low achievement among minority groups will vanish."

This schism exists among leaders of minority groups as well as among school administrators. Among civil rights groups, there are leaders who feel that compensatory education is just an excuse for maintaining segregation. And lately, there are minority group leaders, including those who a few years ago were in the forefront of the integration battle, who now are urging that we accept the fact of segregation and concentrate on building the "golden ghetto" school.

The answer is not *either* compensatory education *or* integration. The two are not mutually exclusive. It is not an either-or situation, and neither can substitute for the other. Both compensatory education and integration are needed to reach the goal of maximizing educational opportunities for minority group youth.

The U.S. Office of Education's study, *Equality of Educational Oppor-*

tunity, commonly known as the Coleman Report, reveals that a student's achievement is strongly related to the educational backgrounds and aspirations of the other students in the school. Segregation of students from the same racial and economic background operates to the disadvantage of those children whose family's educational resources are meager. Such segregation deprives these children of the learning environment that is engendered by more advantaged students with their higher motivation, better verbal skills and vocabulary, and higher achievement level.

For the minority child, the segregated school reinforces the attitudes and practices of the dominant society that have placed him in a subordinate position. Every day that the minority child enters his classroom and sees a sea of faces all of the same color, he is reminded that society considers him not equal enough to join it. The psychological effects of segregation on the student's learning cannot be erased by compensatory education alone.

But just as compensatory education is not a substitute for integration, neither can integration be a substitute for compensatory education. Just moving bodies around does not ensure that deprivations resulting from poverty will somehow disappear into thin air. Many persons have interpreted the Coleman Report to mean that integration alone will lead to increased student achievement. James Coleman himself has refuted this interpretation of the study.

In California, several city school districts have developed programs that involve both compensatory education and integration for disadvantaged minority group students. State guidelines for compensatory education programs provide that funds may be used to plan and implement integration, with compensatory education services following the children to their new schools. In this way, the enrichment and special services that children from poverty backgrounds need will be available in the integrated schools to facilitate their learning process.

A WORD ABOUT ADMINISTRATION—THE NITTY GRITTY

In California, the state department of education is responsible for reviewing compensatory programs funded under Title I of the Elementary and Secondary Education Act. While there are compensatory education programs not financed from these funds, a very large proportion of such programs are under Title I. For this reason, the federal-state-local school district pattern of relations that has evolved under Title I has unquestionably affected the administration and impact of all compensatory programs. It is useful to discuss some of the effects and implications of these patterns.

Title I provides that federal dollars are allocated to the state under a statutory formula keyed to the number of students from poverty families attending public schools. To qualify for its allotment, the state department of education must submit to the United States Office of Education a plan outlining the manner in which it proposes to administer and distribute funds throughout the state. Each school district in the state is entitled to certain proportions of the funds allocated to the state, depending upon the number of students (if any) from low income homes attending their schools. However, eligible districts do not automatically receive their money. To qualify for money, the legislation requires that they submit to the state a proposal or plan outlining how they will use the money in the coming school year to improve the learning of the target students. It is the responsibility of the state to review that plan to determine if it complies with federal and state statutes and guidelines and demonstrates reasonable promise of meeting the needs of students from low income families in that district.

It is not surprising that reasonable men sometimes differ about whether or not a particular plan or proposal is a sensible way of attacking a problem. As a result of its experience at the state level in considering such proposals, and in seeing plans in operation in many school districts, the California State Department of Education has developed some general principles to apply in these situations. The state urges that districts commit themselves in their plans to specific, quantifiable performance improvements. We realize large improvements in student performance do not come easily and we do not expect miracles, but it is the state's experience that a commitment to a definite, recognizable, worthwhile goal gives administrators and staff a point of focus and permits them to test the effects of their efforts as they proceed. They may not always succeed, but it is useful even to have a clear-cut definition of failure; it's a stimulus guide to midstream changes.

To help make this goal commitment more meaningful, the state expects all plans to include provisions for evaluation by competent professionals. The question of what kind of evaluation is an effective one is susceptible to differences of opinion, and different types of evaluation are appropriate for different program goals. State department guidelines for proposals provide that all evaluation plans must be reviewed by its own staff. This permits the state to engage in the same type of productive exchange with districts about evaluations as it does about the whole plan itself. With smaller districts we can often supply useful technical evaluation advice; in larger districts where trained staff are on hand, it is still useful for the local evaluator to have a chance to discuss a point with a fellow professional.

Evaluation findings have demonstrated the need for the concentration of resources upon the target population. In other words, since districts usually do not have all the resources they would like, they are often tempted to give some of the Title I benefits to all students that arguably may be disadvantaged; however, this temptation often results in the "funds" being spread too thin to help anybody at all. The most effective programs have been those that have offered a full pattern of resources to the students concerned, even if this has meant that other students who could have benefited may be excluded from the program. This is an uncomfortable choice, and there is understandably room for differences of opinion in individual situations, but we still strive to encourage districts to concentrate and be effective rather than disperse and lose impact.

Another factor that has influenced state level interaction with local districts is the matter of simple variations in individual human attitudes and abilities. All administrators, in making judgments about how to conduct their operations, must consider the characteristics of the persons with whom their organization must relate. While it sometimes may seem simpler to conduct operations on a formal basis and assume all persons with whom we work have equal abilities and perspectives, it is just not the way to get the job done. Inevitably effectiveness requires us to estimate how much attention must be given to the proposals and problems of one district as opposed to another. In one district indefiniteness in a proposal may simply reflect the fact that the district did not have time to put down all the preparations that were underway. In another district the same vagueness may mean the district staff had not completely considered the implications of some of the changes they proposed to make. If the state department staff is in tune with what is happening in the field, it will recognize that one application is essentially acceptable and that the other invites a phone inquiry or a personal visit.

Parent-school relations are another area where the state has played a helpful role. It is fair to say that, in some districts, there is a sense of distance between parents of low income families and school staff. Sometimes, in forming parent advisory committees, schoolmen, even with the best of intentions, have difficulty in reaching out effectively. At the state level we have tried to develop a special staff competence in such problems. We might suggest to the district the names of local community agencies, such as the local antipoverty program or an organization representing an ethnic minority, that may have better ties to the poverty community. Sometimes we even know community leaders who may be brought into the act. We also promote statewide and area conferences at which schoolmen have a chance to meet with other schoolmen, consultants, and poverty parents to form a better picture of how things are being done successfully elsewhere. Unfortunately, it is also sometimes true that some districts are not sincerely interested in reaching out to such parents. It seems that such districts fear parents may try to hold them responsible for remedying all suffering and discrimination; thus, in order to avoid such potential confrontations, the district prefers not to talk to parents at all.

Of course, the major effect of such a posture is to exacerbate all parent suspicions and to make every exchange a potential explosion. The only cure we know of is to help people to begin talking to each other. The first such talks are not always easy—they are sometimes traumatic for all concerned. But, in some instances, it appears that a degree of sickness has arisen in school-community relations, and it is not surprising that it may show itself in a trauma. Such traumas may even be the first signs of a step toward health: a break in the pattern of sickness. Because state staffs have sometimes played a part in promoting these first exchanges, the low income community may view them with more sympathy than it does local schoolmen. But no good purpose can be fulfilled by the continuing involvement of state personnel in a problem that must be settled in the local arena, and the constant aim of state staff must be to promote fruitful interchanges between persons on the scene. Since we do have a say as to whether or not Title I funds are granted, the state does have some leverage, but not much good is accomplished by depriving the schools, and the children, of the money. Our job is harder than simply saying no; it is to build.

School-poverty community ties in California are not always smooth, but important improvements have occurred. Perhaps one of the most interesting is the growing sophistication of poverty groups in "negotiating" with schoolmen. They appear at board meetings and present proposals. They visit their state and federal legislators. They raise questions about the Title I plans their districts file. Of course, they are not always satisfied with the answers they receive, but almost no human being is completely pleased with the institutions with which they must deal. The significant point is that they are speaking out, and when they are not satisfied, they talk with the next level. Eventually, these kinds of pressures produce results. Also, children are benefited by seeing their parents as vigorous, participating members of their communities. No longer are they the progeny of a voiceless, forgotten minority; their parents, like other members of the society, speak up, aspire, and sometimes get things changed. This has important carry-back to the classrooms.

This discussion of the state role in compensatory education has been somewhat extended, but it has attempted to explain an important feature of educational change in general, and a key part of compensatory education efforts. Our national and state education systems are decentralized. While there are great benefits from local involvement and direction, there is also a need to help individual districts benefit from the mistakes and experiences of other districts. An informal network for the communication of such information has naturally arisen among schoolmen, and word manages to spread. However, in compensatory education the efforts now being attempted by schools are comparatively new; they may have been thought of before, but often they have not been tried on a sufficient scale to evaluate their effectiveness. Therefore, the rate of change in this field must be faster than in many other fields of education. Thus, there is more information being developed and more need for this information by scattered individual districts. In these circumstances, the state is playing the part of an information disseminator and seeing that the right word gets to the right people. Because new information often causes people to see things differently, it is not always favorably received and sometimes is upsetting to the recipients. The information carrier must combine tact with persistence.

CONCLUSION

One of the major problems in our efforts to improve the quality of education for disadvantaged children is that the resources that have been allocated for this purpose fall far short of what is needed to do the job. Funds for compensatory education come primarily from Title I of the federal Elementary and Secondary Education Act.

The annual appropriation for Title I nationally is about $1.2 billion. This is the largest single federal aid to education program. However, the current appropriation is sufficient to provide compensatory education for less than one-half of the children who need special help in order to succeed in school. In the large cities, where poverty and educational deprivation is most acute, the percentage of children who can be served effectively with current resources is even lower. At the same time, evaluation results show that comprehensive programs must be provided in order to have sufficient impact to improve achievement. Therefore, any attempts to spread the inadequate funds to serve more of the children in need would be self-defeating.

The public must decide whether it wishes to solve the problem or whether it is content with the Band-aid approach of patching up the system hoping it will hold up a little longer. What is at stake is the entire public school system. There are many who have already given up and feel that public education is incapable of educating the poor. The future of public education will be determined by its ability to make the necessary changes without breaking down, or being torn apart.

five

New Models for School Incentives

In Chapter Two, Ralph Tyler discussed the value of measuring the output of schools and described the present national assessment effort in that vein. In Chapter Three, Edward Wynne extended the discussion of outputs to encompass the fashion in which they might be useful to motivate public pressures for educational reform. Here in Chapter Five, James S. Coleman pursues the usefulness of output measurements even further—their utility in providing performance incentives to students, teachers, and school administrators.

The great bulk of previous educational reform efforts have focused on different ways to teach children, train teachers, organize curriculum, structure classes, and so on. Although these reforms have typically been underfinanced, it is still true that it has been less productive for school change than one might hope. Schools seem to eat up and frustrate innovation like a steel mill uses scrap, but few important improvements seem to result.

One class of school critics has suggested that the issue is not so much the quality of the innovations, but the values of school administrators and teachers that frustrate efforts for improvement. Some of these critics, such as Jonathan Kozol or Paul Goodman, appear to imply that there are important flaws in the character, or perhaps "souls," of the professionals involved; somehow we must remedy this deficit of virtue, or recruit many more goodly men and women (though we do not know from where).

One senses that such critics have a point; schoolmen oftentimes project a rather devitalized, disheartening image. At the same time, there are important shortcomings in any "villain theory." Unless the system has deliberately and selectively recruited large numbers of "villains," it may be that the "villains" running schools have just as much virtue or vice as most other men or women. If this is the case, and we believe the sad state of schools is largely due to such villainy, we may have a hard time finding the necessary number of virtuous men to replace the villains. In other words, this theory may make us feel virtuous but leaves us powerless to effect change, unless we have access to a great pool of virtuous persons.

Other analysts have seen some merit in the approach of the modern day muckrakers, but have given it a different shift. James S. Coleman is generally known as the principal designer of the Coleman Report, formally known as *Equality of Educational Opportunity.* His basic discipline is sociology. Despite his competence in statistical analysis, he is equally concerned with another important sociological concept, the motivations that organizations set before their members. For example, an important piece of his earlier school research, *The Adolescent Society,* assessed the factors that affected student academic performance in high school. The study demonstrated that the academic values of the student body, whether they thought grades and learning were important, have as much to do with student rates of learning as anything done by school teachers and administrators.

In this essay Coleman begins with the insights inspired by this research and attempts to synthesize them with some of the themes arising from his output measurements survey. He suggests that the existing profound school resistance to change is not the product of villainy, but rather the rational response of educators to the incentive system that currently exists within schools. Such a nonvillain analysis may lack the color of a morality play, but it has other exciting virtues. Villains may persist until the second coming; incentives may be changed right now! The essay makes a number of concrete proposals that would result in important changes in existing incentive systems for students, teachers, and administrators, and discusses their implications. The changes do not necessarily cost more money than the present system. One should not expect the changes to happen easily, but they do offer hopeful possibilities.

NEW INCENTIVES FOR SCHOOLS

James S. Coleman

Every organization can be described as a system of incentives for its members. Sometimes these incentives promote conflict between different levels and parts of the organization; sometimes they lead to ends which are different than those announced formally by the organization; sometimes incentives are weak because so little energy is invested in the organization's activities. In an organization like a school, it is important to analyze the system of incentives because schools have numerous activities and several purported goals, and any system of incentives encourages certain of these activities and goals at the expense of others. From the point of view of educational policy, certain goals of education can be achieved only through modification of the existing structure of incentives; only by such modification will individuals be led to change their current distribution of time and energy.

In schooling there are three parties whose panorama of incentives is particularly important to the outcomes of education. One of these is the children themselves; a second is the teachers who are in direct contact with the children; and a third is the policy makers and administrators, including the school board, superintendent, principals, and other administrative staff. To be sure, there are finer classifications that are important for specific questions, such as the different incentives for school boards and superintendents, the differences among various levels and categories of administrators, and the differential incentives confronting children who are especially bright or especially dull in schoolwork. However, these three groups form a useful first way of looking at incentives in education.

I should note parenthetically that "incentives in education" does not automatically mean incentives in schools, for education need not be organized in schools, and indeed, most of a child's education is accomplished outside the schools within the incentive structures of the world of real actions and consequences. However, to examine the current system of incentives in formal education provided by government means to examine the incentives in schools. Thus, I will begin by considering the system of incentives that operates for each of these three groups in schools as currently organized.

EXISTING INCENTIVES IN SCHOOLS

INCENTIVES FOR CHILDREN IN SCHOOLS

The first point about the structure of incentives for children in schools is that it is very different from the incentive structure they confront in educational experiences outside formal school activities. In the education that occurs in everyday life, learning takes place essentially through action, feedback, and modified action. We learn to walk because the physical world provides us with contingent response: supporting us when we balance ourselves correctly, and letting us fall when we fail to do so. We learn to talk because the social world provides us with another set of contingent responses: satisfying our needs and admitting us into its affairs when we speak understandable language, and failing to do so when we do not. We learn because we have an incentive to relate socially to others.

Schools do not teach reading or arithmetic or the other "subjects" of school by this process. Instead, they attempt to bring about learning through a shortcut process in which incentives play almost an unnoticed role, creeping in at the back door because they cannot be kept out. The general model for teaching subjects in school is one of transmitting or imparting information or skills to the student. In this model, incentives to learn are either ignored or assumed to be present. The child is assumed to be a *student* or *pupil;* that is, he is assumed to have, from external sources, a desire or need to learn. There is little in the teaching process itself which introduces natural incentives of the sort that impel learning in everyday contexts. As a result, there are artificial incentives introduced in the classroom and the school, which partially and inefficiently repair the incentive-deficiency in the learning model of the school. These are ordinarily seen as "necessary evils" of school because they repair the incentive deficiency only at the cost of introducing extrinsic rewards and punishments into the classroom.

In the classroom, the primary incentive introduced by the teacher is that of setting one child versus another in disguised competition. Teachers call on certain children to provide "examples" for the other children of how well the work can be done; and, at least in the early years of school, children compete avidly to gain such attention and gratification from the teacher. Teachers sometimes use "bad examples" as well as "good examples," to keep the children toward the bottom of the ability or effort distribution from dropping to the bottom. In doing so, the children used as bad examples are implicitly seen by the teacher as expendable, following much the same principle that society does in incarcerating criminals to provide examples to potential transgressors. Both in society at large and in the school, the use of such punishment as examples is less than it has been in the past, though it is still widely used in schools, as it probably must be, given their present organization.

The implicit introduction of avid competition for the teacher's rewarding attention is probably the most widely used incentive in the classroom, but it is not the only one. There are others which come closer to the natural incentives for learning, and others which are even farther away. The latter are especially found in schools among poorly socialized lower class children who respond little to the teacher's attempt to introduce classroom competition for teacher's attention. Such children are often characterized as "discipline problems," because they are not responsive to this usual classroom system of incentives. It is here that incentive by bad example is most used, but this is not incentive to learn, but only to be orderly and not to distract others. Consequently, in such classrooms the principal incentives shift not only in the direction of escaping punishment and away from receiving rewards, but also shift to a different reward criterion: the criterion of maintaining order, not that of learning.

Some teachers who have both skill in teaching and insight into the process of learning are able to introduce incentives that are closer to the natural incentives for learning, though sometimes these are relatively weak. A social studies teacher may seek to get children involved in world events through field trips, newspaper clippings, and other means. Stronger and more effective devices are the staging of events that involve the skills or information to be learned. Such events as debates and simulation games, though they are themselves artificially staged, nevertheless introduce a natural and intrinsic structure of incentives for learning, through the role in which a child is cast. In the case of a simulation game, the incentive to a player is, as in real life, to function successfully in his role, gaining those ends that are important to the role. Such activities, however, are rare in the classroom.

The other major incentive system for children used by schools is grades. Grades parallel the classroom competition which the teacher uses, providing on a longer-range periodic basis the same kind of competitive structure, extrinsic to learning itself. At even longer range, entrance to the "college of their choice" is a similar incentive for some children.

Besides the incentives for children provided by the school, there are two other major sources of incentives for children in school: parents and other children. Many parents make both intangible and tangible rewards contingent upon signs of successful school performance, and thus the child has a high incentive to "succeed"—not necessarily by learning what he is intended to learn by the school, though sometimes this is the easiest method for receiving such rewards. (Other methods are pleasing the teacher in ways other than by learning, cramming before a test, so as to do well on the test without having really to learn the material, cheating, and other devices invented by generations of children to bypass learning.)

It is sometimes true that parents in their everyday activities provide incentives for children that are naturally and directly connected to learning. For example, in a household where there is much reading material and parents read a great deal, the child has a natural incentive to learn to read, and thus participate in the activities of the household. This incentive can only be satisfied by actually learning to read, and the much higher reading skill of children from such households suggests that this incentive is a very important one. Sometimes, but relatively rarely, topics of discussion in the home provide a strong incentive for the child to learn a great deal. Bertrand Russell says of himself that he was by no means the brightest boy in the neighborhood, but rather dull; but that his grandmother, through engaging him in incessant discussion, debate, and argument on intellectual topics, forced him to learn.

Other children constitute a final important source of incentives for a child, one which increases in importance for the child with increasing age. Other children provide incentives for a variety of activites, sometimes for learning the school subject, but more often not. Sometimes a good teacher will so structure teaching that incentives provided by other children are directly connected to learning, most often through the staging of "events" such as debates mentioned earlier—events in which the structure of activities causes children to provide incentives to one another for learning and achievement.

The incentives provided by other children are very strong, but are variable in direction. Activities that constitute success or achievement in the eyes of other children will differ from one subculture to another, and there will be different value hierarchies both between schools and even within the same classroom. Sometimes it is tied to marks in school; but seldom is it directly tied to the subject matter being learned. There are exceptions, particularly in mathematical problem solving. Sometimes a few of the best mathematics students in a class will compete for solving mathematical puzzles or problems, for mathematics is at its best simply a set of logical games. At the other extreme, however, achievement in the eyes of the subculture constitutes thwarting the aim of the teachers and the school. Incentives in this case are opposed to learning.

This is a brief review of the system of incentives that confronts a child in school. It is very complex, and not at all optimal for learning. Sometimes it induces learning almost by accident, sometimes it inhibits learning, similarly by accident.

INCENTIVES FOR TEACHERS IN SCHOOLS

No less than children, teachers are confronted with the task of surviving in school without extreme discomfort and distress. Several recent books by teachers in ghetto schools (Jonathan Kozol and James Herndon are two examples) are illustrations of teachers who were unable to survive without serious distress. The great number of teachers just out of college who survive only a year or less at teaching, especially in inner-city schools, also illustrate that survival in school is highly problematic for teachers.

In achieving such survival, a teacher has two primary groups with which to come to terms, the children in the classroom and supervisors and administrators, and two secondary groups, other teachers and parents. Probably the most important group is the classroom of children themselves, because most of a teacher's time is spent in this setting. The incentives offered by the children are incentives for accommodating to their levels of performance (which ordinarily means reducing demands), and spending classroom time on matters that interest them. Some teachers respond fully to these incentives and allow the classroom to be a playroom in which anything but the subject to be learned is discussed. Such teachers feel good because the children do not rebel; they frequently overlook the fact that nothing is being learned. A few highly skilled teachers appear to respond initially to these incentives, but then draw the children into learning without losing their attention.

But the matter is more complex than this. Because of the diverse motivations of the children, the teacher is often confronted with conflicting incentives from different students. From one small group of students, who are highly motivated to perform, and perhaps even to learn, the teacher has incentives to teach rapidly and at a high level. From other groups, the teacher has incentives to proceed at various slower paces; and still others present an incentive to avoid imposing any demands whatsoever. Different teachers respond to different elements of these incentives (i.e., are controlled by different portions of the class), and thus are good for one set of children in class and bad for all others.

Yet along with these various incentives that are directly offered by the children (in return for which they implicitly offer cooperation to the teacher), the teacher has an incentive to keep some social distance from the children to maintain control of the classroom. The incentive for maintaining control stems partly from the teacher's own interest in controlling the activities rather than being controlled by them, and partly from the incentives posed by the administrators of the school.

The incentives that derive from school administrative staff are primarily negative incentives, that is, primarily incentives *not* to cause organizational problems. These problems arise if the teacher cannot control the class, or if control is achieved at the cost of violating organizational rules or disturbing other classes. The cumulative impact of these incentives is strongly in the direction of maintaining classroom control, much less strongly in the direction of bringing about learning. There is also a negatve incentive against failing to bring about any learning whatsoever, but for two reasons this principally establishes a "floor," rather than a positive incentive to induce learning. First, the administrators are only very slightly able to measure how much learning the teacher has brought about, since learning is so highly influenced by factors outside the school. Secondly, administrators themselves have little incentive (as we shall see shortly) to provide positive incentives to teachers for extraordinary amounts of learning by children, except for a few of the highest-achieving students who may compete for external scholarships. Consequently, the major incentives they give the teacher to promote learning are negative ones.

Thus the configuration of incentives the teacher receives from the school administrators is primarily oriented toward discipline and student behavior, and only secondarily oriented toward learning. Learning incentives are largely negative ones that are applied when the teacher falls below a minimum level of classroom control and (secondarily) of student learning.

The incentives a teacher receives from colleagues depend very much on the relation of the teachers, as a body, to the administrative staff of the school. If this relation is a strong and positive one, the body encourages its members to support the positive aims of the administrators, which may be academic learning, or other matters such as strong extracurricular activities, most frequently athletics. If the relation is negative, the hostility spurs teachers to use their energies in other ways than promoting learning. Thus, primary incentives from teachers (to other colleagues) to teach especially well arise only under relatively rare sets of circumstances: when the teachers are strongly supportive of the administrators, and the administrators themselves have strong achievement goals for the school. Even in this case, the administrators' goals may be focused principally upon a relatively small group of students, such as the highest- or lowest-performing group.

Incentives to teachers from parents act principally as a constraint, for there are few ways in which parents can provide positive rewards for outstanding performance in either of their roles as taxpayers or parents.

Rather, they provide negative incentives for various aspects of teacher performance: constraints against giving their child too low a grade, against upsetting the child greatly in the classroom, and against any harsh actions taken by the teacher toward the child. A frequent constraint imposed by permissive middle-class parents is a constraint against any discipline measures imposed by the school.

Thus, teachers as well as children are confronted with complex incentives. Only a relatively small portion of these are oriented toward bringing about high amounts of learning, and most are focused on accommodating to the social and psychological needs of the children and the administrative needs of the organization.

INCENTIVES FOR SCHOOL POLICY MAKERS AND ADMINISTRATORS

There are various levels of administrative staff in school systems of the United States. The United States, in fact, is quite different from most other countries in this regard. In England, for example, the size of the administrative staff between the director of education for the London County Council and the teacher of a child is very small compared to the size of that staff in any large U.S. city. This fact signifies one important difference between the functioning of U.S. schools and schools in most other countries. In the United States the management of schools is far more centralized, with the school principal having far less autonomy and authority than in most countries. This centralization of management of U.S. schools exists simultaneously with evaluation procedures that are more decentralized than in other countries. In many systems outside the U.S., external examinations for determining the child's school performance are far more widely used. (In the United States, standardized achievement tests are given, but they merely enter a child's record and are sometimes used for diagnostic, assignment, or tracking purposes. They are not used as a measure of the child's performance in school.) Thus, in the United States, central school systems play a stronger role than in Europe in regulating the procedure of education and a weaker role in regulating the product of education.

This general pattern of centralized authority over the organization and functioning of schools means that a principal's source of incentives are his administrative superiors: assistant superintendents, associate superintendents, and the general superintendent. The direction of those incentives will differ, depending on the orientation of the central administrative staff; but there is one general bureaucratic tendency that shapes the direction of these incentives. This is the equilibrating and self-maintaining character of bureaucratic organizations—what may be called the conservative tendency of such systems. For the primary interest of occupants of roles in a bureaucracy is self-maintenance. This interest is manifested in striving for structural stability—administrators giving incentives to subordinates not to disturb the functioning of the organization. In applying this principle to schools, this implies that the pervasive and principal direction of incentives to a school principal is toward maintaining a school that does not disturb the school system or the community. In achieving this, he must maintain a reasonably happy staff, he must not introduce change so rapidly that it will disturb the organization of the school, he must give incentives to his teachers to keep order (or rather negative incentives for disturbing the general organizational functioning of the school), he must place the goals of achieving a product, that is, learning, second to the goals of maintaining equilibrium. Thus, whenever he considers an action (such as allowing the children the freedom of the halls and grounds outside of scheduled class time, or requiring children to wear a school uniform) which he believes might increase achievement, but which might upset the organizational equilibrium, he has a strong negative incentive against upsetting the equilibrium, an incentive to reject the action.

This does not mean that a superintendent may not also provide incentives for high performance of a school, nor that a principal may not also provide incentives to his teachers and to the students for high performance, but rather that there is a general bureaucratic drift of incentives toward organizational equilibrium. It requires an additional incentive, imported from the outside, so to speak, to generate incentives toward learning rather than solely maintenance.

The question of what leads to the importation of such an incentive toward productivity in organizations requires consideration of an organization's relation to its external environment. The matter is relatively simple: the organization's first incentives (that is, the first incentives of its managers) are toward organizational survival. In some organizations, survival depends on not disturbing the environment. But in other organizations, survival depends upon organizational achievement vis-à-vis the environment. Survival of a professional baseball team, for example, depends upon continual achievement, not merely upon nondisturbance of the environment. Survival of a business firm depends upon market success. In both these situations, rewards to the organization come from affecting choices of individual customers, whose patronage depends upon the character of the product it produces, and not merely upon its quietude.

In such a market structure where individual customers make individual choices, incentives to the manager (and thus incentives that a manager will provide to subordinates) directly link the organization's survival to its achievement. Thus, although his primary incentive remains toward survival, this incentive is linked to positive performance of the organzation, rather than to nondisturbance of the environment. It is seldom, however, that schools find themselves in such a market structure, or in any other structure where customers or clients selectively offer rewards to the organization based on its performance in producing learning.

However, although schools operate as a government monopoly rather than in a competitive market structure, they are subject to community pressures, as are monopolies in general. These pressures depend directly on the information available to the community about the performance of the school.

One facet of school performance on which information is freely available is order or discipline. Order means absence of fights in the halls, of student unrest, of disciplinary problems, of trouble caused by school children, either on or off school grounds. Information about this custodial function is ordinarily very visible to parents, and serious disturbances usually reach the mass media.

A second area of school performance which is highly visible is secondary school success in interscholastic endeavors, ordinarily athletic events, but sometimes other activities, such as band or debate. This visibility has many evident effects: higher levels of pay and status for athletic coaches, frequent career succession of athletic coaches to superintendencies in small systems, the firing of unsuccessful coaches, the disparity in many communities between elaborate athletic facilities and meagre academic facilities.

The academic success of the school or the system, however, is ordinarily much less visible. Except for a few indices, the measures of academic success are based on comparisons within each school; that is, grades of individual students relative to other students in the same school. This does nothing to make visible the school's academic performance.

There are exceptions to this lack of visibility of academic performance of the schools. These include numbers of college admissions, numbers of National Merit Scholarship semifinalists, finalists, and winners, and a few similar indices. But as a measure, college admissions has the serious defect that it is even more dependent on family background of the student body than is achievement per se; Merit Scholarships have the defect that they concern only the academically adept students; [1] and both have the defect that they are measures of the absolute level of student performance, rather than changes in performance due to school effects.

This review of the existing incentives for students, teachers, and school administrators leads directly to the question of policy: what policy

[1] Some schools which concentrate on their high performers do so at the expense of an abnormally high dropout rate, or a rigid tracking system that reduces academic mobility.

changes for education might modify incentives in a way that would greatly augment the social and intellectual development of children? The second section of this chapter deals with this question, and describes various modifications of American school systems that might successfully alter incentives.

CHANGES IN EDUCATIONAL INCENTIVES

INFORMATION TO CHANGE INCENTIVES

There have been several proposals to modify the structure of incentives for school board members, superintendents, and principals so that it is more oriented toward effective teaching and learning. One very simple policy is to publish nationally standardized achievement test scores for each school in the system, an action that has been carried out in a few cities. The potential effect of this change may be indirect: it provides various pressure groups in the environment with a criterion more related to learning than those they ordinarily use to appraise the system. The test scores may be used as a weapon by parents' groups, by teachers, by the superintendent, or others. (See Chapters Two and Three.)

One may expect that publication of such data will have two effects. The most immediate is to *change the direction* of pressures to which those who establish policy (school board, superintendent, principal) are subject. A second effect of such publication should be to increase the total resources for education, that is, the community's willingness to be taxed for education. The evidence for this is less clear, but there seems to be some indication, at least, that as the success of the schools in meeting their objectives is more precisely measured, community members are willing to expend greater effort toward those objectives.[2]

Thus, one important mechanism to change the incentives of policy makers in schools, both by changing the direction of educational pressure and increasing the pressure for additional resources, is the publication of performance information—output measures. Because it is effective, specific incentives created for principals and superintendents will depend on the specific information published. If that information is to bring about changes in school effectiveness, it must be information on those factors that the school can readily affect, such as increments, rather than absolute levels, of achievement. It should be recognized, however, that publication of academic performance data by itself changes only the information on which community members may take action; it does not provide different teaching procedures or other new action alternatives

[2] I have said "precisely" measured rather than "validly" measured, because I believe it is the precision of measurement rather than its validity that has this effect.

that might employ such information. In a subsequent section, I will indicate changes that can provide new action alternatives that can complement the information. First, however, I want to discuss briefly another change which modifies the reward structure confronting the community members themselves.

INTERSCHOLASTIC ACADEMIC COMPETITION

The example given of interscholastic athletics indicates the importance of such explicit competition between schools for directing resources into an activity. Yet schools do not structure academic effort in this way: competition is solely between students within the same school, thus providing no collective pressure in the community and the school toward greater academic learning. This was one of the principal conclusions in a study of ten high schools I carried out some years ago.[3] In particular, the study concluded that if academic efforts were governed by a reward structure based on competition between schools through academic games, rather than solely competition between students, efforts toward achievement would receive strong social support in the school, and would consequently be greatly increased. Since that time, at least one league of interscholastic competition has been initiated, based on several academic games pursued as an extracurricular activity. The program began at Nova High School at Ft. Lauderdale, Florida, and extended subsequently into a network of schools in several states and Puerto Rico. An annual "academic olympics" has been initiated using these games. There has not yet been an assessment of the effects of this activity in changing incentives of children, teachers, school administrators, and school board members, though indicators do exist: appointments have been made to provide game administrators or coaches for teams; travel expenses of teams to the olympics have been paid; and the success of teams has been published in local news media.

Obviously, the most direct change in incentives through interscholastic competition is in the incentives confronting the child himself. It becomes to his interest to encourage his teammates, because their success aids that of the school and thus his own. Interpersonal competition remains, but it is accompanied by mutual support as well.

Some of the same processes occur when academic activity is structured by games within the school. The mutual support to win for the school is not present, but the support for fellow team members does exist, and the incentive to succeed for the team does exist.

Academic games of this sort have been developed by a number of

[3] James S. Coleman, *The Adolescent Society* (New York: Free Press, 1961).

groups in the past few years, partly aiming at this effect, partly at other effects. These games have as one of their principal objectives an increase in students' motivation and interest. Their success in this appears due to the revised incentives a game creates for students, in some cases "collectivizing" the success and generating mutual support, and in all cases changing the goal from satisfying the teacher to winning in an encounter with another individual or team.[4]

There is one class of games, "simulation games," which is particularly important in changing the incentive structure for a child in the classroom. These games, by simulating a social, economic, or political structure, place the player in a situation where learning occurs through the natural process of action, feedback, and modified action. Such games reconstruct, through rules, role relations similar to real life. Therefore, the incentive to learn is intrinsic to the action-framework, as in real life. The child is no longer in a "student" role, but in a realistic role akin to the one he will later play in life, where he uses the action that has been learned.

Because the child's incentives in such games differ from those of the teacher-directed classroom by becoming incentives to function in the role itself, incentives that children provide to the teacher also change. The teacher's role changes from teaching to one of providing aid to children who genuinely want information and skills to perform appropriately in the game. The role changes from "teacher" to coach and aide. The teacher's incentives become the desire for vicarious gratification through the child's success. This change in activities and incentive structure is difficult for some teachers because the activities are so different from the usual ones. Nevertheless, the incentive structure does encourage the child's learning, for the teacher's incentives shift from those arising from his own performance to those arising from the child's performance, for which his activity is support.

INTRAMURAL COOPERATION AND COMPETITION

A related strategy for changing the reward structure of children and teachers is that of creating various cooperative and competitive structures in the school relating to traditional academic learning. This has been implemented extensively in the U.S.S.R. At the lowest level, a row in the class constitutes a unit, which competes against other rows. Various criteria of success are used, to ensure that mutual aid is provided by row members; for example, the score of the lowest scoring member is the criterion, or the average scores of all row members.

[4] A review and bibliography of such games in social studies may be found in *Simulation Games for the Social Studies Classroom* (New York: Foreign Policy Association, October 1968).

The class is also a unit, in competition against other classes. Sometimes this competition is competition against their own past performance, sometimes it is competition over the performance of another group for which the students are the aides. For example, two eighth grade classes will compete over the performance of two second grade classes under their respective supervision.

This use of intergroup competition and collective rewards in the U.S.S.R. is designed to create incentives for students to support, aid, and encourage the efforts of those around them. Observers (Urie Bronfenbrenner in most detail) have reported that it is very effective.

A second major set of proposals to change the incentive system is very different from those already described: to cut off completely the flow of resources from the government to the superintendent, and redirect those resources into the hands of the final consumers, individual families whose children attend school. These proposals take many forms and I will discuss each in turn.

DUAL COMPETING SYSTEMS

It was proposed to the Washington, D.C., school board several years ago that a second school system be established in the District of Columbia. Each child would be in two school districts, one school operated by one central school system, and one operated by a second central school system. The child and his family would choose which of the two schools to attend. Each school would be under a constraint to ensure that its racial composition was near to that in the school's attendance area, to prevent movement toward increased segregation.

For the individual child and his family, the situation would be similar to that he faces in other areas of consumer choice, except that he is limited to two choices. The budget for each of the two superintendents would depend on the income his system receives from the government, based on his record of attracting and holding students. Success of each school's principal and staff in attracting students would determine success of the system. This provides each superintendent with an automatic indicator of the success of each principal and staff in offering those things desired by children and parents. Insofar as the "clients" make their choices on criteria closely related to learning, the ability of the school to attract students is a measure of its quality. Further, the superintendent must react to such a measure by changing something about the school, to bring students into his system.

It is unclear how such a dual system would actually operate. It introduces a competitive market for the child and his family, but only increases his alternatives from one to two. It invites the two superintendents to collude and divide the market to minimize uncertainty (probably by agreeing to offer only token competition in particular districts). The market is a duopoly, and the possible unfavorable behavior practices of business firms in a duopoly are to be expected.

Some aspects of such a system are currently in force in those cities which allow free choice at the high school and junior high levels. Here, the pupil has a choice among all schools in the city, although schools are not located to make two schools easily accessible to a child. The incentives, to be sure, are fundamentally different at the superintendent's level, for although he is concerned about under- and overutilization of schools in the system, the size of his budget is independent of the child's and parent's choice. It is, in fact, only at the principal's level that such competition exists. The experience with such free choice plans indicates the importance of another free market element if such a system is to create the appropriate incentives for the principal: there is almost always a shortage of classroom space in every school; there is nearly full utilization of plant capacity. A successful principal cannot easily expand his plant capacity, partly because of physical plant constraints, but more because of administrative constraints. (For example, without administrative constraints, he could quickly add portable classrooms.) Consequently, the open choice merely leads to a greater burden (including sometimes double shifts) for attractive schools.

It is useful to point out the ways this proposed dual system changes each superintendent's motivation and ways it does not. They are still in the public sector. Hence, their personal gains from a successful system are not directly financial, but are limited to status and power. As part of the public sector, they would still be constrained, in much the same way that superintendents currently are, in their budget allocations. Thus, although their incentives to improve a low-performing school would appear to be vastly increased over those in present systems, the range of actions they may take (unless other constraints are loosened) for effecting change are not increased. This may or may not be important, for perhaps the actions superintendents can already take are sufficient to produce improvement if the incentive existed.

An important question concerning such a proposal is the superintendent's or principal's incentive to provide information (that is, in effect, to advertise) to consumers about the performance of schools in his system. Only if such an incentive (or incentive for others to expose such performance) exists will the child and parents have information to make their school choice a wise one. It is not clear, in the outlined proposal, whether an incentive to advertise would exist.

A TUITION GRANT OR VOUCHER SYSTEM FOR ATTENDANCE AT PRIVATE SCHOOLS

A proposal with some similarity to the proposal for competing public systems gives somewhat more authority to parents and child, the ultimate consumer (see Chapter Thirteen, "Recreating the Family's Role in Education"). Instead of two public systems, with budgets dependent upon numbers of students, this proposal allows a parent to buy education on the open market, using tuition grants or vouchers supplied by the government. The proposals differ in details that may be important. Should the public school system remain as a competitor to the private schools, or is it to be dismantled? Are private schools restricted to nonprofit enterprises, or are profit making ones allowed? What constraints are to be placed on these schools to ensure that the public interest, and not merely that of the specific parents or children, is being served? (For example, what mechanisms are there to prevent vouchers from being used for training in safecracking or in revolution?) Is there to be any restriction on use of the vouchers at religious schools? Must a potential entrepreneur have a franchise to operate a school, and if so, what limitations will there be on franchises? Is there to be any constraint against a school excluding persons on the basis of race or religion, or any requirement to maintain a racial balance? (If not, schools will obviously be used for ethnic and racial segregation.)

In this proposal, incentives for the school system superintendent (if the public system survives) and for the executive officer of his private competitors depend upon specific details. In general, the system is similar to the competitive dual system described earlier. Assuming perfect freedom of entry into the market for private schools, however, it differs in one important respect: it would not generate oligopolistic practices such as splitting up the market. There would be great incentive, as under the dual competitive system, to introduce greater efficiency, for one's competitive survival would depend on it. There would be incentive for high-performing systems to disseminate performance measures, and for low-performing systems to advertise on other grounds.

But there is already some indication of how such systems would operate. The private and parochial schools in existence are presumably little different from schools that would arise under the proposed systems, except possibly in the current schools' actions designed to attract sufficient funds from outside donors to supplement tuition, and the fact that the parents of their students (since they pay tuition from their own pockets) presumably have a special concern with their children's schooling. The headmasters at these schools appear to have far fewer incentives merely to maintain discipline, and far more incentives to increase achievement. In the United States, a large number of private schools have as their principal aim, in fact, the rescue of children who have been performing poorly in public school. Whether they are effective is unknown; but it is clear that there is a strong incentive for headmasters to raise each child's achievement to a level of college entrance.[5] There appears, on the basis of casual observation, to be more attention than in public schools directed to individual children who are not doing well, precisely the behavior one would expect if the parent has the option of withdrawing the child and financial support from the school. Note, however, that this is an incentive for the school's administrator, not the teacher, and there is no certainty that the incentive is transmitted to the classroom teacher.

It is clear that the provision of a tuition grant or voucher scheme has the potential for changing the administrator's incentives, and thus his behavior, but does not automatically do so. Its introduction must be carefully carried out to ensure that the desired competition does in fact arise. One of the most important of these additional elements, as indicated earlier, is the information provided to those who make the choice. Thus, the publication of output data as discussed in Chapter Three is complementary to the change that puts consumer choice directly into parents' and children's hands.

THE OPEN SCHOOL, WITH SUBJECT-SPECIFIC CHOICES

Similar to the voucher or tuition grant device is a proposal that the individual parent or child make choices for specific subjects.[6] Under this scheme, children would continue to attend their traditional neighborhood public school. They could, however, take any required courses they desire outside this school, instead of in school, from an entrepreneur paid from tax receipts. The entrepreneur would have to satisfy two sets of consumers, as is appropriate since the child's education has spillover effects on the community: the child and his family, and the community as defined by the taxation district (which may be local, state, or national). The child and his parents would use whatever criteria are available to them in their choice, including the ongoing satisfactions or dissatisfactions experienced daily, and at the end of each semester could make a new choice. The governments involved would impose

[5] There appears some indirect evidence that this effort is very successful. Several studies over a period of years have shown that when College Entrance Examination Board scores and background characteristics are controlled, public school students do better in college than do private school students. An explanation of this would be that private school students' CEEB scores are artificially high, due to more intensive training in school.

[6] See James S. Coleman, "Toward Open Schools," *The Public Interest,* No. 9 (Fall 1967).

either criteria governing school procedures or criteria governing performance increments, preferably the latter.

A modified form of this proposal that is made possible by the mixed funding of public education by state and national governments in the United States is for the federal (or state) contribution to go directly to the child's family as education stamps or vouchers. He could then use this voucher in or outside of his public school, depending upon the attractiveness of the alternative offerings.

The merits of such a scheme, compared to a voucher scheme for the school as a whole, lie at several points. One is that finer discrimination can be used by parents to make choices in specific subjects instead of the overall choice of one school rather than another. A school consists of many faces, and in shopping for a school, it is first of all difficult to assess specific subject offerings, and then not possible to make differential choices. Typically, a customer must buy "the whole package," and accept some undesired things along with those he likes. Particularly in the early grades, where learning of readings and facility with numbers is so important, the quality of these offerings may be obscured by other facets of the school.

Perhaps an even more important merit of this scheme is that it should generate a more numerous and diverse array of offerings. Beginning a school is a large venture, requiring capital expenditure, and a host of allied services (such as health, physical education, eating facilities), which must meet certain standards. Beginning a reading center requires only renting a storefront or other building, and a nucleus of teaching staff and materials. Thus, entry into the market is very easy, and one could expect many more entrepreneurs.

The existence of subject-specific vouchers would provide an incentive to local community leaders, such as those in a black community, who wish to establish their own educational enterprise in partial competition with the public school, but can mount such an enterprise only for portions of a school's activity. It provides, as an incidental benefit, a mode of decentralization that returns a large portion of control of the child's education to the child and the parent, and requires the local community group or the educational entrepreneur of the central public school system to compete for his customer. In effect, it allows the decentralization of specific functions, but does not dictate it. The option of who will deliver the child's education remains with the parent and the child.

PAY-BY-RESULTS

One other direct incentive scheme that has been proposed is payment of educational entrepreneurs on the basis of results they produce. This is not a wholly new scheme, for something like it was used in England from 1870 through the 1890s.[7] That period in England was one of uneasy establishment of a state school system. One step in that establishment was state subsidy to newly established elementary schools, on the basis of the number of students they got successfully through certain state-administered examinations. This method of state support was not regarded as successful, and in fact was generally discredited. Nevertheless, these schools in many localities quickly surpassed in quality the preexisting "voluntary schools."

It is instructive to note a major reason for the rejection of this system: the payments favored schools with students from good backgrounds because payment was based on absolute levels of performance, rather than increases in performance, and because family background was then, as now, more important than school for performance. The situation differed in other ways as well from that currently proposed. For example, there were not (at least at elementary levels) multiple competitors for the child's attendance; and the whole system was directed toward maintenance of a double standard for the working classes and middle classes.

A combination of payment by results and the subject-specific open market is possible. In this proposal, the child and his family would make the subject-specific choice, but payment to the entrepreneur would depend on increased achievement by the child. Thus, a program that provided a pleasurable alternative to school, but little increase in performance, could not survive.

A FINAL NOTE ON TWO SOURCES OF INCENTIVES

One point should be kept in mind with regard to the establishment of incentive systems. There appear to be two ways in which new incentives can be introduced: from a superior in an authority structure (for example, the principal establishing incentive pay for teachers, or the superintendent establishing incentive pay for principals); or through the power of choice on the part of clients or customers. In the latter case, rewards are not based on a superior's evaluation, but on success of the institution in a competitive structure (for example, changing principals' or teachers' incentives by giving the child and his parents free choice). The former type of incentive system, which is what is ordinarily meant by an "incentive system" in an organization, appears to engender more dissatisfaction, and more collusion to reduce output or destroy the incentive system, than does the latter. Thus teachers' unions oppose incentive systems where the reward comes from principal or superintendent, but find it more difficult to reject a change in the

[7] See E. J. R. Eaglesham, *The Foundations of 20th Century Education in England* (London: Routledge and Kegan Paul, 1967), Chap. 1.

market structure which gives the child and parent a choice, and thus indirectly changes the teacher's rewards "from below" rather than "from above." This principle holds quite widely with incentive systems: rewards that arise from differential success in a market are viewed as more legitimate than differential rewards that are "arbitrarily" distributed from a higher position in an organization.[8]

[8] The same principle applies to students, making their success or failure in an academic game more legitimate to them than the grades they receive based on evaluation by a teacher.

six

A New Model for Student Incentives

In the previous chapter, James Coleman describes a strategy whereby school incentive structure might be rearranged so that those who work with students would be encouraged to perform their various tasks more proficiently. Under such conditions, the hope is that their increased and increasingly effective efforts would ultimately result in increased performance on the part of students. The authors of the following article, Andrew Effrat, Roy E. Feldman, and Harvey M. Sapolsky, present a somewhat different strategy. Here emphasis is placed upon providing the student with incentives to perform.

Providing students with performance incentives is not in itself a radically different idea. Many readers will remember the "gold stars" for which they so slavishly labored in the vineyards of their primary classes. The distinction between the "gold stars" and teacher praise approach and that which is proposed here is, simply put, *money*. If the larger society is oriented toward material rewards, then why should schools be held out as a place which is somehow different? If it is important to the larger society that students acquire a set of minimal skills, then why not pay them for their acquisition? Moreover, if in the process, the child acquires a lasting desire for learning, a desire to continue inquiring throughout his lifetime, then the dollars paid for his basic learning may well be a bargain.

The authors of "Inducing Poor Children to Learn" have attempted to anticipate the many criticisms which will undoubtedly be offered of such a plan to pay for student performance. A question for the reader is, given a limited supply of dollars, where would you place them, on incentives for students to perform, or on incentives for educational personnel to perform?

INDUCING POOR CHILDREN TO LEARN

Andrew Effrat/Roy E. Feldman/Harvey M. Sapolsky

Despite years of concern for improving educational systems in this country, actual achievements have been disappointing. This has been especially true in low-income areas of American cities. We have a high literacy rate, yet a significant segment of our population fails to obtain the skills that are necessary for employment in a technologically advanced economy. States have periodically increased their investment in education, yet there is still a widespread belief that our urban school systems are inadequate and deteriorating. The proposal we describe here is suggested as a means for elevating the academic achievement of urban school students while preserving the integrity and diversity of the low income culture.

There is considerable consensus in the social sciences that important differences exist between lower income subcultures and upper or middle income ones. Although there is some variation within the working class, four important themes in lower income subculture seem particularly relevant. First, a number of studies suggest that the temporal horizons of the poor are shorter than those of the nonpoor. They tend to be more present-oriented, to have less ability to defer gratification, that is, to prefer more immediate rewards as opposed to longer run ones.[1] Second, the poor tend to value concrete, material rewards (such as monetary gain) more than abstract or intellectual ones.[2] A third major

---

A version of this article appeared initially in *The Public Interest,* Spring 1969, pp. 106-12.

1 Walter Mischel, "Father-Absence and Delay of Gratification: Cross-Cultural Comparisons," *Journal of Abnormal and Social Psychology,* Vol. 63, No. 1 (July 1961), 116-24; Louis Schneider and Sverre Lysgaard, "The Deferred Gratification Pattern: A Preliminary Study," *American Sociological Review,* Vol. 18, No. 2 (April 1953), 142-49; and Albert K. Cohen, *Delinquent Boys: The Culture of the Gang* (New York: Free Press, 1964).

2 Joseph A. Kahl, *The American Class Structure* (New York: Holt, Rinehart, and Winston, 1957).

theme that has been identified is that those with lower incomes tend to be more "peer-oriented." As Cohen has stated

> . . . the working-class child is more dependent emotionally and for the satisfaction of many practical needs upon his relationships to his peer groups. He engages in more activities and spends more time in their company. Satisfactory emotional relationships with his peers are likely to be more important, their claims to be more imperious, and the rewards they offer to compete more effectively with parental expectations.[3]

In his extensive study of adolescents in ten different communities, Coleman[4] also points out the general significance of recognition and respect from peers as a major reward in the adolescent subculture. Any educational system that could mobilize rather than compete with student peer groups would obviously be considerably more powerful. Finally, one segment of particularly lower income groups can be characterized by considerable apathy or pessimism—the feeling that one can do little to improve one's lot and that there is hardly any point to expanding effort on education. A system that provided attractive immediate rewards for such effort might do much to alter these attitudes.[5]

The American educational system, however, is built on white middle class values. Schools seek to orient students to work for what are obviously long-term goals, the vaguely defined and individually unspecifiable benefits that are said to come with continued academic achievement. The only relatively immediate incentives that the schools distribute during the educational process are grades and the social approval of the teachers, neither of which appear to be very meaningful to a large number of children from low income backgrounds.

Explicit recognition of the conflict between the rather middle class school subculture and the subculture of these students' backgrounds presents us with two alternative strategies of improvement. One would be to attempt to change the values of children from lower income backgrounds in order to make them conform to the values of the school system. Proposals for longer school hours, preschool training, and boarding school arrangements are designed to "capture" the child before he is "captured" by the subculture into which he is born. This type of effort is essentially what the schools have been employing with less than desired success. It is not clear, however, that this effort at subcultural change is either legitimate or feasible.

The second alternative is to recognize a subculture's right to its own nondescriptive system of values. Our proposal is to minimize interference

[3] Cohen, *Delinquent Boys,* p. 101.

[4] James S. Coleman, *The Adolescent Society: The Social Life of the Teenager and its Impact on Education* (New York: Free Press, 1961).

[5] August B. Hollingshead, *Elmtown's Youth: The Impact of Social Classes on Adolescents* (New York: John Wiley, 1949).

in the lower income subculture by modifying the external system to facilitate the acquisition of useful skills. Thus, the immediate interests and values of parents and children in low income areas would be explicitly recognized and employed as the basis of the school's reward system.

Let us briefly sketch an incentives system experiment consistent with these principles. Instead of being given a gold star, a pat on the head, or simply a letter or numeral grade for good academic performance, a student would receive a subculturally more desired reward: a cash payment. A payment schedule can be devised that will provide the student with incentives for improving his performance in the classroom so that he will be rewarded for working at his own capacity rather than in competition with other students. Thus the student is rewarded for improving his own performance or for maintaining an acceptable level of work in the classroom. Incentives would be distributed regularly for *incremental approximations* of correct classroom behavior. Long-range measurements of academic achievement could be based on periodic evaluation by the teachers and standardized independent measurements. We assume a student could earn about $100 to $300 in an academic year.

A change in the school reward system could also increase parental pressure for educational performance. Low income parents could note the increased performance of their children not only through the abstract grading system, but through tangible dollars. The payment for the very young could be such that a proportion of all dollar earnings would be sent to the child's guardian, who would then have even greater reason than at present to facilitate homework preparation and would be more inclined to become concerned over school work. Further, if the school's rewards were large enough, then the need for older students to supplement their family income through part-time after school activities might be somewhat redued.

Because having money is a positive value of low income students' subculture, a student with a good school record could expect to gain his peers' social approval for his efforts. This approval would provide further support and reward for his performance and aspirations. Thus, the material incentives program could not only reduce the conflict between the school and peer groups and remove a major social obstacle to an individual's educational advacement, but actually mobilize existing values to promote academic achievement.

The proposal has another important advantage. It could be implemented regardless of any changes in curriculum, the quality of the teaching staff, and the quality of the physical plant. If other changes are still desired they could also be implemented.

The social sciences provide some suggestive support for this proposal. Psychologists using different schedules of reward or reinforcement have demonstrated in a variety of contexts that children will learn specific instrumental responses when appropriate reinforcers and contingencies are present. Monetary and other concrete incentives have been employed with apparent success, for example, in helping juvenile delinquents to learn socially acceptable behavior, in helping the mentally ill, and in teaching remedial skills to children.[6]

Many anthropologists and sociologists working in and around the "Weberian" tradition have emphasized that an individual's or a group's basic values, "general conceptions of the desirable," are crucial determinants of their behavior. This orientation has apparently been influential in generating and guiding studies of the nature and effects of such phenomena as the "culture of poverty," the "lower class milieu," and "delinquent subcultures." Further, the "human relations" tradition in sociology and social psychology has amassed considerable data to support the idea that such phenomena as productivity and morale are, at least in part, functions of the organization's incentives system. Even educational theorists, such as John Dewey, have emphasized the importance of working from a child's interests and motives. These perspectives have much in common. They rest on a recognition of the fundamental importance of an individual's values, motives, or interests in determining his behavior.

A number of objections could be raised against the proposal. First, it could be argued that the use of material incentives in the schools is inappropriate and unwise since it is likely to increase the materialistic orientation of the children. From this viewpoint, the focus of education should be on more idealistic goals, and some believe that material incentives detract from the school's "real" purposes—the preparation of "better," not more selfish or more crass, citizens.

Second, it could be argued that the incentive program might involve major emotional costs for the children. Parental and peer pressure to improve academic performance and reap the payoffs could become so great that they would induce serious emotional problems in children who cannot meet these expectations. A payment system that is devised for the majority may be unsuitable or even dangerous for a minority.

Third, opposition might develop around the monetary costs of the program. Although the payoff matrix can probably vary considerably in order to be effective, the cost per child (excluding administrative expenses) would probably be between $100 and $300 per year. Are not school budgets already so overburdened with salary increases, construction expenses, and so on, that increased costs of this magnitude are likely to meet resistance?

6 Teodoro Ayllon and Jack Michael, "The Psychiatric Nurse as a Behavioral Engineer," *Journal of the Experimental Analysis of Behavior,* Vol. 2, No. 4 (October 1959), 323-34.

Fourth, it could be objected that there are many problems with the administration of material rewards in a school system. Teachers might play favorites or, having a substantial amount of money to distribute, they may feel themselves to be welfare workers and hence inflate the grades of an entire class or of the needier students. Further, teachers might find themselves subject to pressure from parents or students since they control the distribution of valued resources. Problems ranging from corruption to extortion are potentially present.

Fifth, the material incentives system does not provide inducements for increases in "general" education performance, but only for the criteria of the incentives program itself. That is, it may focus too much attention upon grades, discrete behavior, and performance on tests, as opposed to acquiring generalized skills and knowledge for its own sake. Presumably, students would focus on rote learning, "psyching out" their teachers, cheating, and every other means of attaining grades save the more complex one of becoming "educated." We would produce a generation that could obtain grades but that knew little of the subject matter for which the grades were assigned.

This proposal is not an attempt to reform our entire society or even to change the values of a particular segment of society. Rather, it seeks to take advantage of existing attitudes and values to facilitate the acquisition of skills acknowledged to be important by both upper middle and lower income subcultures. The gifted and motivated children are likely to pursue education for its own ends under almost any circumstances. For others, however, education is but a way to obtain material gains or at least freedom from material wants. An incentives program that facilitates improved academic performance enhances the children's opportunities to be qualified for the higher skilled, higher paying jobs which are increasing with the technological advancement of our society. Perhaps *their* children will then have the opportunity—some would call it luxury—of seeking education for its own ends. At least they will not have been denied access to society's rewards merely because their values and attitudes differ in some respects from those of the dominant upper middle class subculture.

We should also point out that many middle income families presently employ material incentives (such as vacations, cars, or allowances) to induce their children to perform in school. From this viewpoint, the incentive proposal does not corrupt society or the schools, but rather it takes a step toward equalizing the inducements available to people at different socioeconomic levels.

With regard to the second objection, it should be obvious that emotional stress is potentially involved in every educational innovation. In fact, the present educational system with the "culture conflict" that exists between the student and the school also has its psychological costs.

Whether or not the proposed incentives program will produce more severe conflicts is not clear. It is even conceivable that a material incentives program is more intelligible and "realistic" to the low income student than the status quo. Certainly, the proposal to correct the structural inequalities and motivational inadequacies inherent in the present system must be weighed against the costs.

Similarly, the dollar costs of the proposal would have to be measured against the gains. Although a program involving a per student expenditure of $100 to $300 is a large one, the costs are not out of proportion with some other educational reform programs. Moreover, if the proposal produces tangible gains, it would seem at least as worthy of adoption as the many proposals for a reduction of the teacher-student ratio or the construction of a new school in every neighborhood.

The problems of implementation are considerable but not insurmountable. Controls in the form of standardized tests would be used to discover welfare dispensing and other potential corruptions of the system. The fact that the idea of monetary incentives suggests possible corruption is an indication of the incentive's power and a justification to monitor the distribution better than existing school incentives are monitored. The teachers, however, do hold a great deal of power over a student's future, if not his present, and a greater awareness of this may actually be an improvement itself.

With regard to the fifth objection, it might be countered that increased student concern with classroom behavior and grades is actually desirable. What are really to be feared are tests that do not adequately measure generalized skills and grades which do not reward insight or creativity.

Of course, the final defense of the proposal must be its achievements. Although there are important reasons to believe the program will work, until it is experimentally tested, its appeal must rest on theory and analogy, a not uncommon fate of educational reform proposals.

seven

A New Model for Instruction

The tutorial community school described in this chapter is equally concerned with increasing students' formal knowledge, reading, writing, arithmetic, and aiding their emotional growth. The premise is that schools in which students teach students are schools in which students will become better informed and, at the same time, will feel more at home and fulfilled.

This concern for affective development has important implications for current school practices. While poor children may not be learning to read, it is perhaps just as true that almost all American students, from poor or well-off families, suffer from a lack of emotion connected with the school experience. They may be informed and literate, but still deprived of important satisfactions. The current college and high school unrest may in part be related to this form of noneconomic deprivation. While critics such as George Leonard may broadcast prescriptions in works such as *Education and Ecstasy,* the task of bringing human values into large institutions will not be solved by preaching; perhaps, however, new systems will enable us to be more free and human as we learn.

Ralph J. Melaragno and Gerald Newmark are psychologists working for System Development Corporation. The Tutorial Community Concept they are developing represents their effort to turn their skills to a new task. The description of their development operation is an instructive example of how systems analysis concepts may plan an important role in school change. At the same time, the innovation itself may have a direct effect on school operations.

THE TUTORIAL COMMUNITY CONCEPT

Ralph J. Melaragno / Gerald Newmark

This model is, in a way, the product of a progress from reflection to engagement. For a number of years, our research at System Development Corporation (SDC) had centered on learning psychology. The papers we published seemed to help advance knowledge in little ways, but when we looked at the education our children were receiving in school, we were dissatisfied. We determined to attempt a research and developmental effort that would try to influence what really happened to children in school. This chapter describes the model that is evolving from these efforts.

We decided to focus our efforts on trying to improve school instruction. While it is true that instruction appears to have undergone many changes in recent years, actual results have not matched expectations. Too many students leave elementary school without sufficient mastery of the basic skills of listening, speaking, reading, and writing. Too few have developed enthusiasm for learning or for school, or possess a capability for self-directed learning. Too many school practices seem more directed at confinement than learning. Numerous students are already on the road to becoming early dropouts. This is especially true of minority, or "disadvantaged students"; the average minority child today only completes the eighth grade.

To meet the wide range of needs among such students, it is generally accepted that individualized instructional methods are needed. However, education that treats people as individuals has become a cliché without ever becoming a reality. In a typical first grade class, there is a range of three years in reading achievement by the end of the academic year. This range extends through subsequent years so that by the sixth grade a six-year span of achievement can frequently be found. One teacher with a class of thirty or more students finds it impossible to serve such a wide range of individual differences in aptitude, abilities, interests, motivation, and achievement levels.

Students seldom have feelings that "this is my class, my school, a place where I come for important reasons, where I am important and respected." On the contrary, students tend to feel that "school is a place where I have to come, where people don't care about me, and where other children are competing to look better than me and to make me look bad." Older and younger students have little contact with one another; when they do, they tend to treat each other with disdain. Competition among students is fostered and one student's success may be bought at the expense of another's. Many of the rewards for success are based on the satisfaction of feeling better than someone else. All this is evident despite the fact that teachers care about children and are dedicated to the goals of education.

If learning to learn and self-directed learning are important educational objectives, as they should be in a world that changes so rapidly, then development of these capabilities should not be delayed until the student is in college. Rather, self-learning should be encouraged and planned for from the earliest possible moment, and should continue throughout the student's school career.

Improvements in materials, equipment, facilities, and teaching procedures will have little effect as long as students feel no responsibility for learning, do not care about school, teachers, each other, and (worst of all) themselves. What is needed is a radical change to a genuine learning community in which students, teachers, administrators, and parents share responsibility, concern, and participation to improve the learning of all. We believe such a community can be created at the elementary school level.

A promising resource for helping to individualize instruction and to change the climate of the school is the student himself—the use of elementary school students to assist each other in learning. A number of writers [1] have reported on attempts to have elementary school students tutor one another; these reports indicate that both "learner" and "tutor" profit from the interaction. Learners not only gain from the instruction, but also enjoy receiving help from schoolmates. Tutors take their roles seriously, have a sense of importance, and derive pleasure from their success. In some cases, teachers report that a tutor who was doing poorly in his own class, and who was considered a discipline problem, improved in his work and his attitude toward learning. Tutors' relationships to their teachers improve, and their motivation to learn increases.

[1] For evidence on this point, see: R. J. Melaragno and G. Newmark, *Final Report: A Study to Apply the Evaluation-Revision Strategy to Reading Instruction in First-Grade Mexican-American Classrooms* (Santa Monica, California: System Development Corporation, May 1968); P. Lippitt and J. E. Lohman, "A Neglected Resource: Cross-Age Relationships," *Children,* 12 (1965), 113-17; and J. Featherstone, "The Primary School Revolution in Britain," *The New Republic,* August 10, September 2, and September 9, 1967.

The tutorial process is not new; it has been applied in many ways and in many places. It has great potential for planned development as an educational force. However, its largest potential will not be realized as long as tutoring is limited to a piecemeal program, an appendage to the regular teaching procedures, used mainly for remedial work rather than to eliminate the conditions that initially made remediation necessary.

The Tutorial Community Project, the name of our effort to promote the use of tutoring on a large scale, is a systematic effort to design means to apply tutoring to broaden and extend the total climate of learning of an elementary school. The concepts underlying the project arose from our use of evaluation-revision procedures to design better methods of teaching Mexican-American first grade students in the Los Angeles area. From the beginning of this effort, we have progressed to the point today where it is possible to outline the primary components of an entire tutorial community.

PURPOSE AND CHARACTERISTICS OF THE TUTORIAL COMMUNITY PROJECT

The Tutorial Community Project is a developmental effort which is planned to take at least seven years to bring to fulfillment. The ultimate objective of the project is to develop a "tutorial community" involving an entire elementary school. The final tutorial school should operate at about the same cost level as the original traditional school. In this restructured school, students at every grade will interact with other students as learners and as tutors. In this way, hopefully, traditional barriers between teachers and learners will be broken down. Such an environment explicitly recognizes the extent to which students can learn by themselves and from each other. It also recognizes the need for continual refinement of school processes in order to help students achieve the cognitive and affective goals of the school.

CENTRAL ROLE OF STUDENTS AS TUTORS AND HELPERS

The process of students tutoring themselves and each other is not to be extracurricular, incidental, or remedial. Rather, it is to be an integral, essential part of the everyday school operation. The teacher's role should shift from teaching students to teaching and overseeing tutors. Not only are students to be involved in tutoring; they are also to be encouraged and assisted (by teachers, other staff members, and parents) to participate in establishing objectives, in planning methods and procedures, and in performing such support activities as testing, correcting papers, and keeping records of progress. Four aspects should characterize the tutoring: (1) careful diagnoses of each learner's individual needs by means of observations and test instruments; (2) provision of appropriate instructional materials for each diagnosed need; (3) training of tutors in their roles; and (4) evaluation of tutorial effectiveness in terms of cognitive and affective growth on the parts of both learners and tutors.

ENCOUNTER GROUPS

Literature on educational innovation is replete with instances where changes have been frustrated or warped due to lack of support or understanding from the school staff. The difficulties we faced in communicating to teachers our new methods for teaching Mexican-American first graders are typical. Researchers have observed that teachers often seek to exclude other adults from observing or participating in classroom activities or otherwise evaluating their classroom conduct. It has been theorized that a desire for such isolation is characteristic of the profession; that many persons enter teaching because the self-contained classroom offers them privacy. Yet the project requires school personnel to adopt new ways, and to work more closely with each other than is typical in schools. Teachers whose students are tutors, and those whose students are tutees, have to be in close touch with each other. We also hoped that the tutorial community would be concerned about the emotional climate of the school, as well as its intellectual elements. Finally, the developmental program has a great need to receive frank feedback about what is working, what is not, and why. In sum, we want the project to offer an atmosphere of openness.

To achieve these ends, we rely on what is called the basic encounter group. It is simply a technique for encouraging frank, wide-ranging discussions between participants who volunteer. (There are other psychologically oriented techniques that might also serve the need, such as T groups.) An encounter group usually consists of ten to fifteen persons and a trained leader. It is relatively unstructured, and offers a climate of maximum freedom for exploring interpersonal feelings and communication. On different occasions, teachers, administrators, researchers, parents, and students have participated in these groups. Sometimes the groups are restricted to one type of participant, such as teachers or students, plus a leader; sometimes they include mixes of participants, such as teachers, parents, and administrators.

Successful groups develop a climate of openness, risk-taking, and honesty among participants. This leads to better self-understanding, awareness of how one's behavior affects other people, and greater ability to listen, to understand, and to empathize and communicate with other people. Sometimes the process of attaining these goals generates tension or emotional discomfort. However, the project assumes that schools need major changes; it hopes to bring about important shifts in conduct and attitudes among the staff and students. It is unlikely that such change or growth can occur without some people becoming upset or uncomfortable. We believe that, without the encounter group or an equivalent experience, the change either would not occur at all or it would be far more painful.

COMMUNITY INVOLVEMENT

The concept of community in this project is viewed broadly to include all persons, particularly parents, who are interested in the education of students attending the tutorial community school. Active participation of such persons in the development and operation of the school is encouraged, and systematically pursued. Thus, mechanisms are established to enable interested community members to participate in planning, to suggest and react to new ideas, to keep informed of the latest developments, to observe in classrooms, to serve as volunteer teacher aides, to tutor children in the classroom or at home, and to participate in encounter groups designed to improve interpersonal relations and communications. Such a successful engagement helps to create a close harmony between the school and the community and embeds innovative elements of the school into the values of the community. This fusion permits the persistence of the tutorial system after researchers have withdrawn and the system is on its own.

RESEARCH APPROACH

In order to apply the principles we have described in the design of the tutorial community, we determined to follow a particular research or design approach. This approach contains two features which we turn to now.

GRADUAL DEVELOPMENT

The development (or, in a sense, invention) of a tutorial community for an entire elementary school is an extremely complex task and must be accomplished gradually. This gradualism takes two basic forms. First, changes to the total school program are introduced only after earlier changes have become stabilized. Thus, classroom encounter sessions for students are begun after tutoring procedures have reached an acceptable state. Second, teachers are also viewed as individuals and are encouraged to proceed at a rate that is comfortable for them. For example, a teacher may choose to have only four tutors come to her room for a period of time, then expand to have increasing numbers of tutors.

EVALUATION-REVISION STRATEGY

The entire approach in developing the tutorial community is an empirical one, involving successive evaluations and revisions of procedures until they are known to accomplish specified objectives. In this strategy, as we described earlier, objectives, the specific skills or information we want to teach, are described carefully. Tentative procedures are tested with students, staff, and community, and empirical evidence gathered on their effectiveness. Procedures are revised as a result of this evaluation, and the process of trial-and-revision continues until procedures are known to accomplish the objectives. This strategy is used for all facets of the Tutorial Community Project; it is applied to the development of procedures for tutoring, for community involvement, and for encounter groups.

CURRICULUM

The Tutorial Community Project is not limited to any particular type of subject content or objectives, nor is it a curriculum project for teaching some new and different type of subject matter. Rather, it represents a new approach for planning and conducting instruction that can be applied to any content. This is not to say that curriculum and curricular change are not considered important. The project has built-in procedures that make it easier to (1) introduce curricular change, and (2) give any approach a chance to prove itself. These are:

(a) Specifying instructional objectives in measurable, specific, behavioral terms makes it easier for school personnel to relate curriculum to goals and to communicate about goals and curriculum. For instance, by the end of the first grade, all the students (including those with Spanish surnames) should be able to comprehend twenty specified, important, concept-based English words.

(b) The evaluation-revision strategy, with its emphasis on continuous testing and measurement of performance, focuses attention on the need for curricular modification where the existing curriculum is not effective. It also provides an empirical basis for such modification by permitting us to see what is working, as well as what is not.

(c) The continuous dialogue provided by encounter group experiences reduces defensiveness and creates a climate of openness that facilitates change and experimentation.

EVALUATION

As we remarked in our discussion of research, evaluation plays an important role in our efforts. However, because the word "evaluation" has come to suggest many meanings, it is appropriate to discuss exactly how such evaluation is conducted. A distinction is made in the project between evaluating students and evaluating instruction. Traditional student evaluation is concerned mainly with ranking students and assigning grades, and generally has little to do with improving instruction. Evaluating instruction, on the other hand, requires a statement of teaching objectives in behavioral terms, development of criterion instruments, tests, and procedures that provide concise measures of performance on each important objective, and a detailed description of the instructional system to which test results can be related. In this context, evaluating instruction leads to teaching improvement by providing an empirical basis for modifying instruction.

To date, most educational evaluation is typified by standardized tests and teacher-constructed classroom tests. Essentially, it is directed at students and not instruction. Such tests sample from the content of a subject matter area and yield a relative rating of overall student performance. The results indicate that one student is more or less proficient than another, but provide little information about: (1) how much of the total content was achieved by any of the students; (2) which specific learning objectives each student mastered; (3) how realistic the course objectives were for the conditions under which learning took place; and (4) what conditions need changing.

Another form of evaluation that has contributed little to the improvement of instruction is the type of comparative study in which one course or method (usually some innovation) is compared with another (usually classified as "traditional"). The major weakness in this approach is that we know very little about the way in which the two alternatives are offered. In fact, two unknown quantities are being compared, and it is not clear as to whether or not the worst example of one is being compared with the best of the other. Further, these comparisons are difficult to conduct and to interpret because different objectives or conditions apply to the groups of students and teachers involved. Most such studies result in discovering no significant differences between the compared methods; in the small percentage of studies in which significant differences are obtained, it is usually unknown whether or not either method has achieved its own objectives.

Actually, the most important purpose of evaluation is feedback; the important questions to be answered are: "How well does an instructional system achieve its own objectives?" and "What procedures in the system are effective in getting it to the point where it does achieve its objectives?" In other words, what are we doing well, what are we doing poorly, and why are these effects occurring? Only after an instructional system is known to achieve its own objectives can that system be compared meaningfully with other systems, and then only if the objectives of the two systems are the same and learning conditions are comparable.

In the Tutorial Community Project, emphasis is placed upon evaluation as a feedback. This involves (1) ongoing, or *process,* evaluation, assessing day-to-day conduct, which takes place continuously during the development of the system and is an integral part of the development procedures, and (2) *product* evaluation, which is the end evaluation of the completed product.

PROCESS EVALUATION

Each year the overall outcomes of the Tutorial Community Project are assessed. This evaluation takes three forms: the administration of tests for specified objectives; collection of relevant anecdotal data; and the report of an independent evaluation team. In addition, other more informal measures are applied throughout the year, both by the teachers and the researchers: appropriately designed tests are used to measure interim progress, classes are observed, and so on.

Test procedures involve the assessment of both cognitive and affective growth on the part of students; pretests for different grade levels are administered to provide baseline data, and posttests are administered at the end of each year. Objectives are stated in behavioral terms and tests cover each major objective. Many of these tests were specially designed for the project. In the affective domain, in addition to attitude scales measured by pencil and paper tests, observable behavior indices are used (for example, change in attitude toward school may be measured by changes in the number and frequency of students volunteering for less desirable tasks). Results for each year are compared with original, baseline data, and the performance of students in the same grade for the previous year.

While every effort is made to use "hard" data to evaluate the tutorial community, it is nonetheless true that "soft" data in the form of anecdotal reports are necessary. In the main, this is true simply because the Tutorial Community Project *is* a developmental effort, and numerous unanticipated changes take place that need evaluation. Thus, teachers sometimes undertake to achieve objectives that were not planned for earlier, and it is important to evaluate even crudely their achievement in these efforts.

Finally, an annual independent evaluation is performed by a team of outside experts who visit the tutorial community school while it is in operation and prepare a written report on it. The team consists of six persons, an expert on curriculum and innovations, an expert on mental health, an elementary school administrator, an elementary school teacher, a high school student, and a member of the surrounding community. The team visits for five days.

PRODUCT EVALUATION

At the end of the seventh year, the "tutorial community" will be fully implemented, and all students in the school will have been a part of the community for their entire elementary school careers. At this point, it will be appropriate to conduct a product evaluation to determine whether it has achieved the operational goals implicit in a successful tutorial community. These goals might be characterized as student outcomes and project outcomes. The main student outcomes are:

1. Increased number of students mastering specified cognitive objectives.
2. Increased number of students achieving specified affective objectives.
3. Increased number of students achieving such "special" educational objectives as: capability for self-directed study; acquisition of positive attitudes toward learning, teaching, and school in general; and concern for the educational growth of other students.

In terms of the project as a whole, we aim to produce:

1. A model school that can be observed, or to which people can go to receive training and experience. It will also be a dynamic model; a school that continues to develop and change over time.
2. A detailed description of the final system.
3. A detailed description of the procedures used to develop the system, to serve as a model for other schools interested in establishing a similar type of "tutorial community."

SYSTEM GOALS

Two critical goals of our system development plan need to be highlighted. One is that the cost of operating the finally developed tutorial community school should be comparable to that normally experienced by an elementary school. The goal, then, is to find ways of operating the school within the resources available to that school. The second is that the development team must work itself out of involvement with the school. This goal implies the location of available personnel with adequate, but not unique, competence to take over responsibilities originally assumed by the development team.

With reference to these two system goals, a distinction must be made between the development and operational phases of the Tutorial Community Project. During the seven-year developmental period, many costs and responsibilities are assumed by the project staff (under a foundation grant). As evaluation-revision procedures indicate that some facet of the project is running sufficiently well to be widely implemented, the costs and responsibilities of that facet must be borne by the school's own resources and staff or by the immediate school community. Project staff members must constantly search for ways to eliminate themselves and the project's extra resources.

PROJECT ACTIVITIES TO DATE

The principles we have been discussing have been applied in our efforts to design and operate a tutorial community school in an actual school. One of the first activities undertaken by the Tutorial Community Project staff was the location of an elementary school in which to develop a tutorial school. Our Mexican-American project had been conducted in one of the elementary districts of the Los Angeles City Schools, and the area superintendent for that district was contacted during early 1968 and asked to recommend a school. Due to the developmental nature of the study, procedures were to be developed in the school rather than simply being presented as finished products. Two qualifications were specified: the school must be one with relatively harmonious staff relations, and the school must be one that was not embroiled in hostilities with the surrounding community. These two qualifications were felt to be highly critical for the success of a developmental effort; the school and community had to be in a position to tolerate mistakes. (It should be pointed out that such will not be the case for the expansion of the tutorial community concept to other elementary schools. When expansions take place, the model school will exist and operational procedures will have been completed.)

In response, the superintendent proposed Pacoima Elementary School and arranged a meeting with the principal. The principal reacted favorably to the proposal and expressed support of the need for change in elementary school operations. Next, the faculty of Pacoima Elementary School was seen on two occasions, and through a secret ballot unanimously agreed to participate in the study. Finally, active members of the Pacoima community were seen twice, and they, too, agreed to participate in the study. (Community reaction, while positive, was guarded. Parents agreed that the school needed to change to serve their children effectively, but their support of the project ideas was one "wait and see if it's worthwhile.")

Pacoima is a pocket barrio of Los Angeles. It is an economically depressed area, with a mixed racial makeup that is reflected in the school: of the 1700 students, about 45 percent are Negro, 40 percent are Mexican-American, and 15 percent are Caucasian.

INITIAL DEVELOPMENTAL TRIALS

The original design of the study called for gradual development of the tutorial community concept by treating one grade level at a time. Thus, the first year was to be devoted to the kindergarten, the second year to the kindergarten and the first grade, and so on. This plan was followed for the first year, then revised as project experience dictated (see the following section, Current Activities).

During 1968–69, project activities were divided into three phases: a preparation period during the summer vacation; a presystem period during the first semester; and a system trial period in the second semester.

In the summer preparation period, project staff and school faculty members planned specific objectives for the kindergarten year, and the faculty was introduced to the encounter group experience. Using the Los Angeles City Schools' *Course of Study for Elementary Schools,* a number of objectives were identified in language arts, mathematics, and social development; then preliminary behavioral definitions for objectives were prepared to serve as a point of departure for the first tutoring efforts. To help faculty members become familiar with encounter groups, intensive weekend experiences were made available; these were sponsored by the Western Behavioral Sciences Institute, the Human Development Training Institute, and a volunteer community organization (Encounters Unlimited).

About half of the teaching staff attended one or more of the encounter weekends. Most found the experience stimulating and profitable, as indicated by their reactions. Typical comments were:

> A most rewarding experience. I left knowing more about myself than I could have imagined. The growth that occurred over one short weekend was amazing.
>
> Personally the workshop was an "eye opener" for me and I feel that it was very worthwhile not only in learning more about how others see me (and working on changing the "not so good" qualities), but also in helping me realize more clearly the differences in others' feelings. . . . However I would not like to meet with a group of teachers with whom I work and come in contact with every day, it just might lead to very unhappy working conditions.
>
> The encounter group weekend helped me to be more honest in my reactions to others. It also magnified how complex people are underneath.
>
> I was impressed and depressed. I did not realize how ignorant and uninformed I was about social conditions existing in our society. I became aware of my own racial feelings.

Following the summer preparation period, the first semester was considered a presystem phase. The major effort was for teachers and project staff jointly to explore the classroom components of tutoring, such as tutor selection, tutor training, tutoring procedures, physical arrangements, materials development and utilization, testing, and record-keeping.

Twenty-eight sixth grade students underwent various types of training to become tutors. They subsequently tried out different tutoring approaches in four kindergarten classes. Some tutors supervised small groups of learners engaged in independent activities, such as painting, handwriting, listening to stories, and completing academic worksheets. Other tutors worked with individual learners to help each master mathematics concepts, listen to stories and answer content questions, write his own name, recognize letters and numerals, and so on.

These initial efforts resulted in the first system plan which was implemented during the second semester. The plan called for each kindergarten classroom to receive eight tutors from one fifth grade classroom, and for each tutor to alternate between supervising small groups in independent activities and tutoring individual learners. (We used fifth graders so as to have experienced tutors available in the next year.) In addition, teacher exchanges between kindergarten and upper grade classes were conducted. The kindergarten teacher described the kindergarten program and the nature of the young learner, demonstrated methods and materials, and discussed the role of the tutor with the upper graders; the upper grade teacher had an opportunity to observe his students tutoring and became more familiar with the kindergarten children and their activities.

Results of the first year's experiences were very encouraging. For the most part, upper grade students responded enthusiastically, seriously, and intelligently to the training and tutoring. They contributed excellent suggestions to improve the tutoring and demonstrated great pride in performing their assignments as tutors. Their teachers reported that the tutors benefited from the experience, and that it was evident in their attitudes and schoolwork. The kindergarteners demonstrated learning from being tutored; tests administered at the end of the year showed that kindergarteners improved the most in the area of language usage and other prereading activities. One particularly striking result was that more kindergarten students began reading in preprimers than had ever been the case previously. Moreover, almost all kindergarteners were ready to begin formal reading instruction in the first grade. Previously, the first grade teachers had spent from two to four months in reading-readiness activities; they now indicated that they could proceed directly to books and reading instruction.

The report from the outside evaluation team highlighted two points:

(1) the atmosphere in the school was extremely positive and supportive of the tutorial community concepts, with students, teachers, and project staff members exhibiting good working relations; and (2) involvement of the community with the school was very limited and needed stronger emphasis in the future.

CURRENT ACTIVITIES

As the first school year ended, a number of discussions were held between project staff and faculty members. One important conclusion stemming from these meetings was that the concept of changing the school by working with one grade level at a time was inappropriate. A majority of the teachers felt that the first year's activities within the kindergarten had convinced them of the validity of the tutorial community concept, and that they wished to become more involved immediately rather than waiting for their grade level's turn. Accordingly, the original design was abandoned, and a new one introduced that called for involvement of all grade levels. However, the importance of gradual development was maintained. The gradualism became more the degree of an individual teacher's involvement, with each teacher taking on increasing involvement as he felt prepared.

Tutoring goes on largely with classes paired together on a permanent basis. And, to accommodate the schoolwide interest in tutoring, pairings are between classes in immediately adjacent grades. Thus, sixth graders tutor in the fifth grade, fifth graders tutor in the fourth grade, and so on. There are special cases, particularly within primary grade classrooms where a few upper grade tutors are used to supplement the regularly scheduled tutors, since the latter do not possess sufficient reading skills.

In recognition of the community involvement deficiencies pointed out by the evaluation team, more project staff attention was focused on this area. The most important response has been to encourage and assist teachers to spend more of their after-school time in making home visits. These visits are different from those normally made; instead of the purpose being to inform the parent of a student's transgressions, teachers are making visits simply to get acquainted and to establish a relationship with the parent. The positive outcomes of such visits have been striking. Both parents and teachers express appreciation for the new mood that has been established. Moreover, students look upon their teachers in a new and more favorable light.

A number of adult encounter groups are in operation. Members of the groups include project staff, school administrators, teachers, and parents. While parents' participation was initially low, it is now growing, largely due to the personal invitations extended by teachers when making home visits. The most important result from these groups has been the improved relationships among teachers, many of whom feel they know each other better now than was ever the case in the past. Along with this improved relationship has come an increase in direct and open communication. This, in turn, has facilitated establishment and maintenance of tutoring relations and an increased tolerance for experimentation with the tutoring process.

FOR THE FUTURE

As indicated earlier, the two major products expected from this developmental effort are the establishment of a model tutorial community school and the preparation of an implementation plan for the extension of the tutorial community concepts to other elementary schools. However, two other points for the future of the tutorial community concept should be made, having to do with the maintenance of tutorial communities and teacher training.

MAINTENANCE OF TUTORIAL COMMUNITY SCHOOLS

Its has become increasingly clear that the tutorial community schools may be made up of personal interactions and roles that are significantly different from those normally found in elementary schools. One question that has emerged is, "How are tutorial communities maintained when key personnel leave?" That is, what can be done to keep a tutorial community from becoming overly dependent upon the commitment and enthusiasm of a small group of school personnel? If those persons leave the school, it could easily revert to a traditional elementary school. The most logical way to prevent this is to establish a base of support for the tutorial community with the stable elements in the school situation—parents and other community members. Thus, when there are key staff replacements, the replacements can be helped to maintain the principles of the tutorial community.

TEACHER TRAINING

Few teachers are prepared to accept the responsibilities inherent in a tutorial community school. During their undergraduate schooling, teachers learn little regarding individualization of instruction and even less about the use of elementary school students as cross-age tutors. Only in unusual instances would an undergraduate have extensive exposure to encounter group experiences. And, the need for increased teacher-parent interaction has only begun to affect teacher training. If there are to be more and more schools taking on tutorial community procedures, how are teachers to be prepared? Must each elementary school essentially reeducate its faculty through on-the-job training, or can something meaningful be done in the preparation of teachers to make them better participants in tutorial community schools?

While answers to these questions are not yet available, there are expressions of interest in the Tutorial Community Project on the part of teacher training institutions that could lead to meaningful interactions between the project and colleges. Another possible goal of the project is a plan for the close interaction of a college and an elementary school to provide realistic training for teachers. Such training must include extensive participation in the school's program—mastery of the concepts underlying the tutorial community does not appear amenable to a lecture-discussion method of learning.

CONCLUSION

We have only completed a fraction of our design effort. Undoubtedly, many revisions lie ahead. Still, these efforts encourage us to believe that the evaluation-revision technique is a powerful tool, that systematic cross-age tutoring holds great promise, and that staff cooperation and support can be obtained if one is prepared to listen as well as talk. If the progress rate of the past can be maintained, we are very optimistic about the long-run outcomes of the effort.

eight

A New Ecological Model for Schools

Like other authors in this volume, Frederick Erickson and Eliezer Krumbein believe that school improvement is more a matter of different structures than simply more dollars. Using an approach grounded on systems analysis, they have studied school operation as a mechanism for "processing" different inputs received from different sources and aimed at producing well-educated students. The basis of their work is the contention that a school's relationship with its external environment will determine its internal environment.

While many school studies have focused on the quantity of school inputs, the amounts of dollars, the kinds of services or programs bought with these dollars, or the amounts or kinds of things the students learn, Erickson and Krumbein have a different approach. To them, the issues are: where do the resources come from, and are they dollars, volunteers, or other nonmonetary contributions? The underlying idea is that resources that come from many sources, not simply local, state, and federal governments, but also parents, students, citizens' groups, and businessmen, have an especially beneficial impact on the operation of the school. Similarly, a variety of resources is held to generate a more productive school environment.

This theoretical analysis is illustrated by a discussion of a number of schools in the Chicago area that follow diverse patterns of operations. Some of these schools use varied resources, others do not. Some of the schools are private, others public. The discussion illustrates the different patterns of school operations that have evolved as a result of these diverse patterns of input, and demonstrates how the input patterns have shaped the character of the school. From the discussion, one can see some of the larger implications of the analysis and conceive of ways in which to apply the theoretical construct as a tool for partial school reconstruction. For example, in Chicago the authors (while serving as faculty members in the School of Education of the University of Illinois, Chicago Circle Campus) act as consultants to a network of small parochial schools that aggressively seeks diverse inputs from diverse sources, partly to cover the costs of school operations and partly to produce better student learning. Their ecological analysis of schools may provide a stimulus to similar experiments.

A SYSTEMS APPROACH TO REFORMING SCHOOLS

Frederick David Erickson/Eliezer Krumbein

Many people agree that urban schools are not good schools and should be changed. They disagree over how to do it. Although our conclusions are not definitive, we do have strong convictions which have directed our inquiry. It is only fair that we identify our position at the beginning. We do not believe that solutions to the problems of urban education *lie in spending more money on urban public school systems* in the absence of fundamental system change. We believe that urban schools are what they are because of the nature of their transactions with their surrounding community. In order to change the schools, these transactions must be changed before more money is spent. Indeed, to the extent that the availability of more money enables a school system to operate in the same old way, giving the school more money may prevent system change.

This chapter presents the rationale for our conviction. The school is considered as an institution and in relation to its environment. The basic system, the interfaces, and the systems with which it interacts can be termed an *ecosystem.* Within this ecological perspective, a variety of Chicago area schools are contrasted to see what makes them "effective" or "ineffective" according to our criteria. In the last section, a set of alternative strategies is proposed for improving urban schools by making use of new educational resources (including volunteers) which alter the school's ecosystem. The strategies are illustrated by new programs being started in the Chicago area. They are contrasted in terms of their political feasibility and ecological characteristics. We do not, at this time, take Peter Drucker's view that government is incapable of being an effective entrepreneur and provider of services in any areas except war and manipulation of currency.[1] We do, however, press the issue that, in education, alternatives to virtual monopoly of government control should be sought.

[1] Peter F. Drucker, *The Age of Discontinuity* (New York: Harper and Row, 1969).

Development of public school systems in the United States has been strongly influenced by five general characteristics.

1. Schools receive only one kind of input—consumable resources.
2. Only the board of education is a source of input.
3. Only one kind of resource is received: money.
4. No other systems in the environment compete with it (on approximately an equivalent basis) for the same resources.
5. Educational output is validated by the board of education, the same agency which controls and produces input.

Schools traditionally have had limited interaction with other systems. The vital link with these systems consists of the school board, a community governmental body empowered to conduct the intake of resources to the school. It is necessary that outputs of the school (graduates) be usable by the systems which absorb these outputs, industry and the university. These systems (theoretically) provide quality control information to the school board. Since the school board's search for revenue makes it sensitive to the political influence held by industry and the university, the board's accountability to the industrial-academic complex is high. Some revenue is also available from the state legislature which, in turn, is influenced by the industrial-academic complex. Together, the school, its board--legislature component—and the industrial-academic complex form an ecosystem. (See Figure 8–1)

FIGURE 8–1 *The Ecosystem of the Public School*

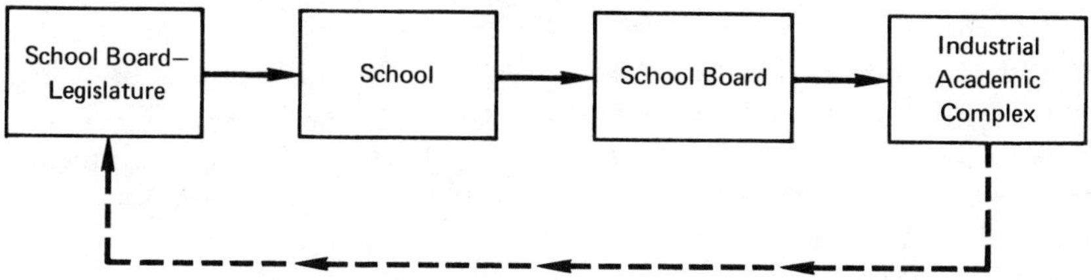

Absent from this model are two very important components, parents and students. Within the ecosystem, industry and the university are the consumers of the school's output. Parents and students, the school's primary clients, are structurally excluded from the picture. If one group of parents were members of the school board or had strong interactions with it, the school board might be accountable to them and serve their interests. The model would have to be revised. One factor in the strength of the interaction bond between parents and board in such a revised model is the degree to which local parents control school resources. In a community of affluent parents with political "savvy," the bond with the board is strong and accountability to parents is high. In a nonaffluent community, or in minority communities which live in a "colonial" relationship to the majority, the bulk of the resources come from the legislature, bypassing the parent group. The parent-board bond is weak, and accountability low.

Another factor in the ecosystem is the strength of the parent-local school interaction bond. This bond is a function of the resource link between the parent and the local school; what help do the parents offer the school? In large cities, resources derived directly or indirectly from the parent through taxation do not pass directly to the local school, but must be first collected "downtown." Thus, in an urban school system, accountability of a local school to its immediate parent community is really weak, even though the parents might be affluent.

By definition, in the school ecosystem, only those interactions within the model are vital to the school, even though many other transactions with the external environment take place. In our analysis, parent-teacher conferences, PTA, use of the school auditorium by community groups, membership by the principal in the Rotary Club, and the athletic banquet are all regarded as nonecosystem interactions and are superfluous. Many of them have political overtones and are indirectly related to resource intake, but the school could continue to function without them. The school need not be accountable to the groups with which it undertakes these superfluous transactions.

Not only is the number of intake interactions of the typical school extremely limited, but also the types of resources processed by the school are limited. School resources tend to consist of dollars generated through taxation. By comparison, consumption of nondollar resources is small.

The limitation of resources to dollars reenforces the nonadaptive, repetitive processes in the school structure. Dollars are processed relatively easily by the school. It is quite correctly feared that if other resources (for example, volunteers and contributions of supplies) are once introduced in the system they are liable to have a marked effect on internal system structure. Staff time must be used to convert the "raw material" nonmarket resources into more usable forms. System components must adjust to use the nonmaket resources that have been introduced. The renewed demands for nonmarket goods and services require the school to "hustle"; to become a free-ranging organism in searching for varied resources. Volunteers, "shared time" arrangements for professional services, information and new perspectives from many agencies, and symbiotic relationships with other systems—all these sources of resources must be sought, courted, and cultivated. And the nonsystem personnel that may be recruited cannot be dealt with universalistically, as ciphers, nor can such personnel be ordered about like ordinary employees.

On the other hand, market resources are easier for the system to assimilate. Lawrence Barnett, of the Center for Urban Education in

New York City, contends that what the schools have done is to use money to "buy pieces of the outside world and bring them inside the school." This contributes profoundly to the way in which the school is experienced by the child. When a piece of reality, a drillpress, laboratory apparatus, a policy, or a political event, is taken out of its context, it ceases to be real. The dynamics of the original social context—production pressures, quality control—are missing inside the conventional school.

It is unsound for the school insensitively to attempt substitutions for real world experiences. But involvement of the school and school children in the real world is avoided by the school because the use of non-market resources is cumbersome, and disturbing. The availability to most of today's schools of dollar resources creates a temptation to buy pieces of seeming reality and to deal with them inside the system. But this artificiality is really costly. To encounter the world, the school must enlarge its ecosystem. This would require the school to establish relationships with other systems which could enable it to offer learning materials in a real life context. Unquestionably, such adaptation might be painful, but, without it, we will continue to see the anomaly of the school offering partial pictures of life to students who, every day, stroll to an "artificial" school through a world teeming with real life events.

Thus, we contend that dependence on a single source of resources, and predominant use of dollar resources, leads to internal system rigidity and inflexible standard operating procedures. The school is not stimulated by its present limited interactions to maintain a libertarian ethos or to embark on alternative courses of action.

A final factor contributing to system inflexibility is lack of competition for resources and students between the public schools and other child-educating systems. State aid may be too low and the local tax base inadequate, but at least the superintendent does not have to worry about another school system taking what money he has away from him. He has a monopoly on tax support for education and his clients have no option; he has the only free school in a given attendance area. The legislature, the school board, and the industrial-academic complex have, through their formal and informal agreements, ensured that whatever the size of the pie, the superintendent does not have to share it.

On the other hand, systems under competitive pressure seek to maximize the ratio between (1) system input, (2) system maintenance, and (3) system output. Organisms unable to process intake effectively do not survive. The urban public school, with its virtual monopoly on resources and lack of accountability to parents and students for output can employ more and more of its input into system maintenance, instead of output, and still survive. It gets fat, lazy, and ineffective, but it continues to operate. Competition with another system would increase accountability for output, would generate forces for effective resource utilization, and would stimulate the school to look for new and various sources and kinds of resources.

THE SEARCH FOR NEW RESOURCES

The foregoing discussion has direct implications for urban school problems. As competition for limited dollars increases, one alternative for the urban school is to change its ecosystem, to search for new, non-market resources. Now components are added to the ecosystem and interrelationships between all components change, as shown in Figure 8–2.

FIGURE 8–2 *New Resource Components in the School Ecosystem*

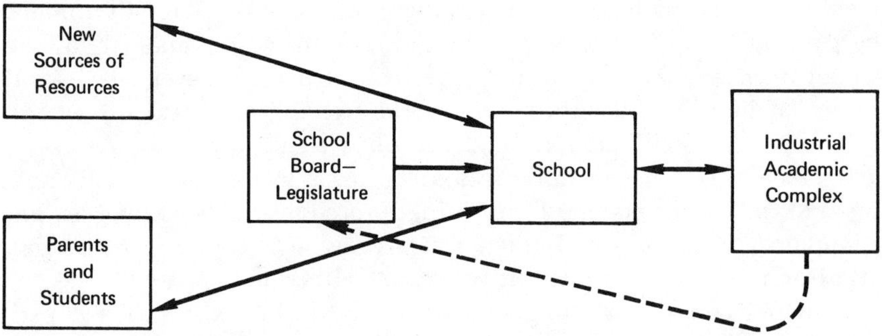

As we see, parents and students are a prime source of new resources—parents can perform a variety of roles in the school and students can teach each other. The industrial-academic complex can contribute research instead of just taking graduates; it can offer volunteers, consultant time, facilities, inservice training, and materials. Of course, as the school begins to depend upon parents for services, its responsibility to them for feedback and accountability increases. As industry relates directly to the school (rather than indirectly through the political process), its executives obtain a much clearer perception of what they have been paying for. Similarly, the university receives a closer look at what it has been monitoring; it no longer deals with the school through the single and frequently myopic interaction of the school of education.

The new interactions, shown by the two-headed arrows, are the two-way transfers of matter/information/energy involving mutual benefit to the school and the other subsystems with which it interacts. Such two-way interactions establish direct, symbiotic interrelationships between the interacting systems.[2]

In order for symbiotic relations between systems to remain stable, there must be a parity of benefit to each. It is extremely important that both systems have something significant to gain. Following are various sources of resources available to the urban school. Many are distinctly "urban"; available to the urban school because of its location in the heart of a large metropolitan area.

CULTURAL INSTITUTIONS

Libraries, museums, and zoos have long been identified by schools as a resource. However, they have usually been underused or misused. Typical use of such facilities consists of a whirlwind tour. In Chicago one sees these educational safaris at the Field Museum of Natural History. They arrive by bus and, led by the teacher and the museum guide, proceed in lockstep from exhibit to exhibit on a half-day expedition through a million years of human evolution. Libraries have children's collections, story hours, and a wide range of other materials, but they seldom are used effectively. History can come alive at the art museum, but it usually does not. The animals at the zoo are alive, but children rarely stay long enough to observe their life systematically.

Urban cultural institutions have much more to offer if used properly. Cultural institutions are service institutions. They need visitors to justify their fund-raising activities. Moreover, the quality of service they offer depends on the quality of services demanded by patrons. Symbiotic relationships with schools can be developed. The most notable example of this is Philadelphia's Parkway Project, the "School without walls," which makes intensive use of the museums and libraries clustered around a mall in downtown Philadelphia.[3]

SERVICE ORGANIZATIONS

Used in the colloquial sense, "service organization" is a rubric which includes youth-serving agencies, such as the YMCA, Boy Scouts, and settlement houses, and organizations such as the neighborhood Rotary and Kiwanis Clubs. Youth-serving agencies have valuable resources for schools. Often their staffs include professionals with group work skills.

[2] Peter M. Blau and W. Richard Scott, *Formal Organizations* (San Francisco: Chandler Publishing Company, 1962), p. 217.

[3] John Bremer, "The Parkway Program," mimeographed (Philadelphia: The School District of Philadelphia, May 1969).

These professionals could work directly with children and also conduct inservice training for teachers.

Jungman public school in Chicago uses group workers at Neighborhood Service Organization in Howell House, a southwest side settlement house founded by disciples of Jane Addams. Workers form groups of children diagnosed by the school as probably being emotionally disturbed. They meet at Howell House for education-related activities, but these relationships are often difficult for traditional school personnel. One school teacher complained, "How can I teach ordinary arithmetic to the class when the kids from the special group come in and tell everyone that they were learning fractions at Howell House by using measuring cups to make pizza?" Similarly, Cabrini parochial school on Chicago's west side has used the neighboring Sears, Roebuck–YMCA's gymnasium and pool under the direction of the YMCA youth program staff for the past five years without charge.

Youth-serving organizations, like cultural institutions, must justify their resource intake by having clients who need their services. Schools can help the agency demonstrate that need. The formation of symbiotic relationships is entirely possible.

VOLUNTARY TALENT POOLS

Volunteers are often considered unreliable. Perhaps the inadaptability of schools is a major cause for this allegation. When schools work with effective coordinating agencies, such as the Urban-Suburban Youth Project in Chicago, school needs and volunteer skills can be matched. Raymond public school in Chicago has, since 1962, operated a program of music lessons and attendance at musical performances for its students entirely through the Urban-Suburban Youth Project. This project identifies suburban housewives with musical training to serve as teachers and companions at professional concerts and rehearsals of operas, symphonies, musicals, and so on.

Large companies are becoming increasingly willing to releasc executives and lower echelon employees for part-time community service on a regular basis. The company receives favorable publicity, the employee obtains a breadth of community experience and prestige (service is becoming a must for the rising young executive), and the school benefits from the service.

High school and college students represent another resource which can be effectively coordinated. The Chicago Area Lay Movement made available hundreds of volunteers to the Roman Catholic parochial schools. Almost as large, the Northwestern University Student Tutoring Project worked indirectly with the public schools, using youth agencies as tutoring sites. Volunteers gained a rich education in the process of tutoring others.

COLLEGES AND UNIVERSITIES

The "tutoring movement" is now somewhat *passé* among college students, and community interest has decreased. Informal, self-help activities and projects to attain local community control are now more important in the ghetto.[4] Universities can still be a valuable resource to schools, however, especially through schools of education. Education schools need sites to provide experiences in formal pedagogy for their undergraduates, graduate students, and faculty. This makes available to the public schools many man-hours of labor in potentially large quantity. If public schools regarded the student teachers and aides as an asset, rather than as a nuisance, schools could be "saturated" with large numbers of university students, faculty members, and workers in educational innovation who would provide a variety of nonmarket services for the schools. The presence of so many wholesome personalities in the schools would make a material contribution to enrichment of the school environment.

This approach is being used by two programs at the University of Illinois at Chicago Circle. One, the Cooperative Program in Teacher Education (CPUTE), places education majors in teams of four or five in public schools in Pilsen, a Mexican-American neighborhood. Education students are placed in the schools two half-days a week from the beginning of their education course work, which is conducted in seminars. Supervising teachers in the schools participate in an inservice training program. Each group of university students and faculty members works in public schools for a period of two years. This provides an opportunity to experience the school in its natural environment.

Another teacher education program of the university involves west side parochial schools. Larger numbers of students are placed in the schools for field experience during their first education course. They begin by tutoring and working with small groups, moving to large group instruction by the time they enter student teaching. University

[4] Increasingly, lower social class, ethnic, and inner-city communities are becoming concerned about the control of educational resources. They view with suspicion volunteer tutoring projects, if they are conducted and operated by persons and groups from outside their community. Suspicion is based upon outsiders' lack of accountability. Similarly, students from colleges and high schools outside the target community are becoming sensitive to and respectful of the right of local groups to control who comes into their territory. Self-help activities of local communities in ethnic and lower class neighborhoods have always been the predominant approaches to survival in these areas. Middle class observers and students of the poor are becoming increasingly aware of such efforts.

facilities and staff are also made available to the school in this arrangement.

Schools of education need cooperative laboratory sites in "real" schools. Public and parochial schools, especially inner-city schools, badly need man-hours of effort. Mutual interest permits the formation of stable relationships between inner-city schools, especially those with some independence, and schools of education.

PARENTS AND STUDENTS

The clients of the school, parents and students, can provide instructional time and other services to the school. Parents are benefited by (1) providing education for their children, and (2) gaining the satisfaction of being a *patron* of the school. Students are gratified by being able to exercise leadership in teaching other students. As Bloom suggests, tutoring is a highly underutilized form of cooperation in learning.[5] Students teach each other very effectively, and teaching is an excellent way to learn.

BUSINESS, INDUSTRY, THE PROFESSIONS, AND GOVERNMENT

Finally, urban businesses, professions, and government agencies are a source of nonmarket resources. They can be used as educational sites. As with cultural institutions, it is important to use industry, the professionals, and government officials for more than field trips. Students and teachers spending a week or two at a major airline, television station, insurance company, steel plant, medical setting, engineer's offices and laboratories, architects' and stockbrokers' offices are able to learn a great deal about production and management, technology, industrial sociology, community relations, and interrelationships with other urban institutions.

The short-range interest of urban industry, the professions, and politicians may be publicity; however, their long-range interest is well-trained workers and a stable urban environment. The professions and industry pay taxes for urban public schools whose graduates presumably have mastered basic skills. Similarly, the professions and agencies of government can come to appreciate their broadly educational function. As Leon Lessinger notes, urban society is begining to hold the schools accountable for output quality. Schools are being expected "to develop a 'zero reject system' which would guarantee the quality of industrial production." [6]

[5] Benjamin S. Bloom, "Learning for Mastery," *Evaluation Comment,* Vol. 1, No. 2 (1968).

[6] Leon Lessinger, "Accountability for Results: A Basic Challenge for America's Schools," *American Education,* Vol. 5, No. 6 (1969), 2-4.

One of the most influential of the urban school's "publics" is urban industry. Corporate executives know about quality control and about *program planning and budgeting systems.* They are frustrated by the fact that it is so difficult to predict the skill level attained by the recipient of an urban public high school diploma. The only value of the diploma to a personnel interviewer is its function as a "docility certificate." A group of employment managers of major midwestern industries told us they often feel the high school diploma indicates little more than that the graduate was able to take orders, put up with frustration, and show up regularly. Such conditions create disillusionment among business leaders.

Members of professions are concerned about the preprofessional preparation of candidates. They complain about the absence of technical skill and humane motivation of their colleagues-to-be. Similarly, politicians and government agencies wonder whether representative government and administrative agencies, with their need for technical skills, will be properly served if a broad spectrum of the population does not continue to supply new interest and personnel for community enterprise.

SCHOOL COMPARISONS: A TEST OF EFFECTIVENESS

A number of public and private schools in the Chicago area will be compared (under pseudonyms) in terms of their ecosystem characteristics. To make this comparison clear, we have developed two-dimensional and three-dimensional models in which the schools can be located by their characteristics. Keeping in mind the "Joe" and "Harry" who developed the "Johari Window" to illustrate T-group processes, we have termed our two-dimensional scale the "Frelie Window," and our three-dimensional scale the "Elfred Cube."

THE FRELIE WINDOW

The Frelie Window is the first of our conceptual models and it has two axes (see Figure 8–3). The vertical axis indicates both the variety of (1) source of resources intake, and (2) kinds of intake. It constitutes a continuum from "Many Sources of Resources" to "Few Sources of Resources." The horizontal axis indicates the quantity of resources consumed per pupil. It constitutes a continuum from "High Quantity Consumption of Resources" per pupil to "Low Quantity Consumption of Resources." In the case of both axes, "Resources" refers to nonmonetary as well as monetary resources. Both variety and amount of resource consumption are presented here as rough estimates, subjectively derived and rather vaguely defined. The concepts are intended for il-

FIGURE 8–3 *The "Frelie Window"*

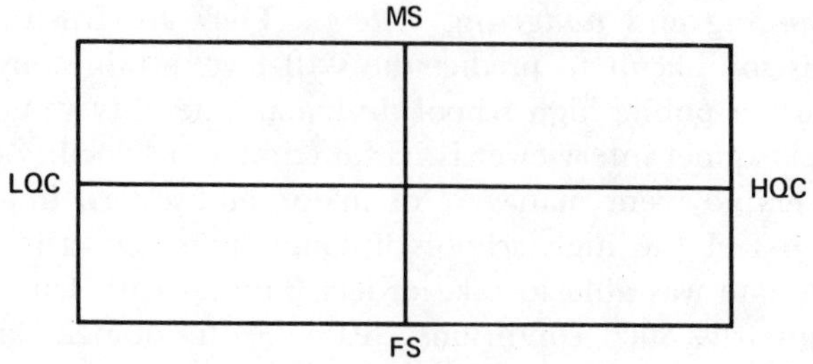

MS = Many Sources of Resources

FS = Few Sources of Resources

LQC = Low Quantity Consumption of Resources

HQC = High Quantity Consumption of Resources

lustration; although, with refinement, the model could be tested empirically.

THE SCHOOLS

Inner City High in Chicago is a typical ghetto public school. Overcrowded and dilapidated, it was designed for 2500 students and houses 4000. Staff and students are demoralized; 65 percent of its entering freshmen do not graduate and less than 5 percent of those who do graduate qualify for college entrance. Per pupil expenditure is roughly $700 (exclusive of federal funds). Almost no nonmonetary resources are used by the school.

If Inner City High is typical of the ghetto, *Suburban High* can be said to be archetypical of the suburban "Ivy League" public school. Located in an affluent Chicago suburb, Suburban High has 4000 students housed in two campuses, one of which is only five years old. Ninety-five percent of its graduates go to college; many are accepted at prestigious institutions. Per pupil expenditure exceeds $1400. The school is almost totally dependent upon a single source of resources, tax revenues from its community. Almost no nonmonetary resources are used by the school.

Hope Public Elementary is located near Inner City High on Chicago's West Side. Per pupil expenditure is $450. On the outside Hope appears as shabby as Inner City. Inside, morale is high. Children seem relatively relaxed. Doctors and dentists donate their time to treat the children. There is a dental chair installed in what used to be the anteroom of the principal's office. Clothing and books collected from community sources are available to the school children and their families. A voluntarily staffed social center operates at the school in the evenings. After long years of fighting to keep his unusual program going, the white principal was recognized by the U.S. Office of Education and placed on a national review committee for Title I programs. More recently, the Board of Education named him to direct a Title III program and then, at the request of black community leaders, he was selected as a local district superintendent.

Bleak Public Elementary, located down the street from Hope, looks similar on the outside. It makes use of little variety in kinds and sources of resource intake and has an oppressive atmosphere. Its annual per pupil expenditure is similar to that at Hope School.

Independent School is located near Suburban High. Many Suburban High students attended the lower school of Independent, a coeducational private K-12 school of 500 students. Tuition ranges from $1000 to $1200 for the lower and upper schools.[7] The school makes use of many community resources, including the neighboring Independent Music Center and field trips to urban industries and commercial enterprises in the Chicago Loop.

It was at Independent that a year-long seventh grade anthropology course was recently taught by a distinguished university anthropologist. The freshman year of high school includes electives called "Explorations," in which students can opt for special emphasis in anthropology, sociology, economics, history, or psychology. Morning exercises at Independent, a 45-minute period for all students, are nationally known. Presentations by students, teachers, and a wide variety of outside speakers are featured. Guests in recent years have included General Mark Clark, Gwendolyn Brooks, and Oscar Brown, Jr.

The school is described by former students as much less cliquish and "rah-rah" than Suburban. At Suburban, a marked division exists between Jewish and Gentile students, a division which was accentuated by the attendance boundaries established by the school board for the old and new high schools. At Independent School, anti-Semitism is far less pronounced, although the student body is equally heterogeneous religiously. That anti-Semitism is present at all, according to our informants, is due to the influence of parents rather than the school. The quality of teachers at Independent is judged to be extremely high. At Suburban, teacher quality is spotty, some are perhaps without peer nationally, while others are mediocre. Suburban is described as serving well "either the very bright or the very slow"; its outstanding strength is in science. Independent School is described as serving all students well, with teachers "really interested in teaching"; its outstanding strength is in the arts.

Chicago's *Classical Academy,* located on the posh near north side, is the most prestigious school in the city. A K-12 school with 400 stu-

[7] Urban Research Corporation, *Chicago Public High School for Metropolitan Studies,* Final Report to Chicago Board of Education (December 31, 1969).

dents, its tuition is comparable to Independent School. The Classical Academy is the within-city analogue of Suburban High. Although much smaller than Suburban, the Classical Academy has high per pupil expenditure and a traditional program. The school consumes few nonmonetary resources.

THE SCHOOLS COMPARED

When these schools are located in the Frelie Window, their similarities and differences stand out more clearly (see Figure 8–4).

FIGURE 8–4 *Location of Affluent and Non-Affluent Public and Non-Public Schools in the Frelie Window*

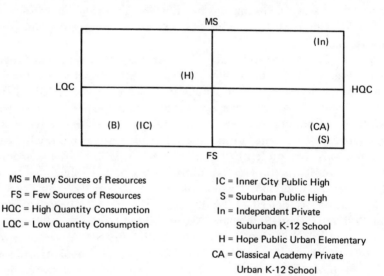

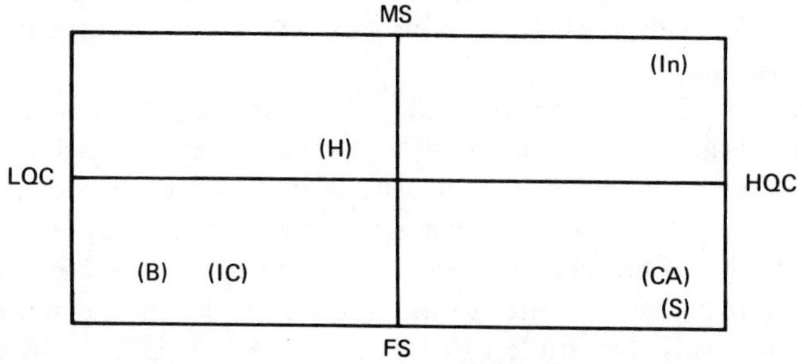

MS = Many Sources of Resources
FS = Few Sources of Resources
HQC = High Quantity Consumption
LQC = Low Quantity Consumption

IC = Inner City Public High
S = Suburban Public High
In = Independent Private Suburban K-12 School
H = Hope Public Urban Elementary
CA = Classical Academy Private Urban K-12 School
B = Bleak Public Urban Elementary

Inner City High and Bleak Elementary are financially impoverished schools, while Suburban and the Classical Academy are financially affluent. All of these use few nonmonetary resources. In contrast, Hope Elementary and Independent School use considerable nonmonetary resources. In terms of internal system characteristics, Hope and Independent are far more flexible. Both schools have vitality, even though one is an elite private school and the other a ghetto public school.

For all its affluence, Suburban High appears stultifying. Its administration and program are in many ways quite traditional, old things are done well there, or at least smoothly, by highly trained teachers. There is much of value in the program. But one aspect of the "old things" is the academic rat race, which seems to be increasingly frustrating for the students. Students at Suburban "drop out" emotionally by playing the game skillfully but without commitment. We feel, from reports of teachers and mental health officials, that there may be almost as much underachievement there as there is at Inner City High. If drug usage is any indication of alienation, it may not be a coincidence that Suburban was the first suburban school at which marijuana use became a major administrative problem.

"Playing the system" seems to be equally characteristic of students at the Classical Academy. College admissions batting averages figure prominently in the school's brochures. Suburban and Classical Academy students learn how to "drop out" invisibly. Many continue the pattern in later life, participating without commitment in college, career, marriage, parenthood, church and synagogue, and community affairs. They learn in school to be the lethally cool WASPs described by Philip Roth in *Portnoy's Complaint.*

Students at Inner City drop out very visibly. Walking through the halls one senses immediately that the school is a "total institution," which controls even minute aspects of his life—a prison. It takes longer to realize this at Suburban and the Classical Academy. There are similarities among the three schools, however, which transcend their differences in amount of resource intake. If Inner City had $1400 to spend per pupil, it might succeed in looking less like a prison, but it could never succeed in being an Independent School any more than could Suburban High. Hope, with even less money than Inner City, resembles Independent School in many system characteristics.

THE ELFRED CUBE

Here we discuss our second conceptual model. In a competitive situation, students become a school resource. Where they have an option as to which school to attend, students may bring resources directly through tuition and state aid, and indirectly through their power to legitimate the school by choosing it in preference to others. Competing schools must satisfy students' and parents' expectations to a considerable degree if they want to receive the latter's continued support. "Accountability," in this sense, means that parents and students assume important roles in setting school policy, such as the selection of faculty and staff, curriculum, and instructional media. "Accountability" also means evaluation of the output of the school in whatever terms are agreed upon by those governing the school. Under these accountability conditions, output quality becomes a matter of school *survival,* rather than *niceness* on the part of the school staff.

The concept of the "Elfred Cube" (Figure 8–5) attempts to add this element of interschool competition (for students and other resources)

FIGURE 8–5 *The "Elfred Cube"*

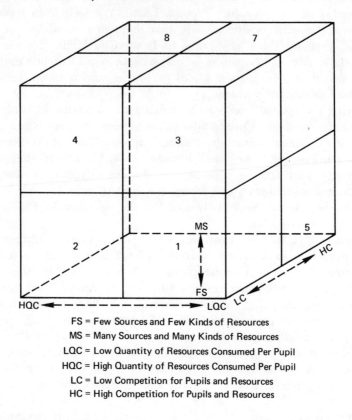

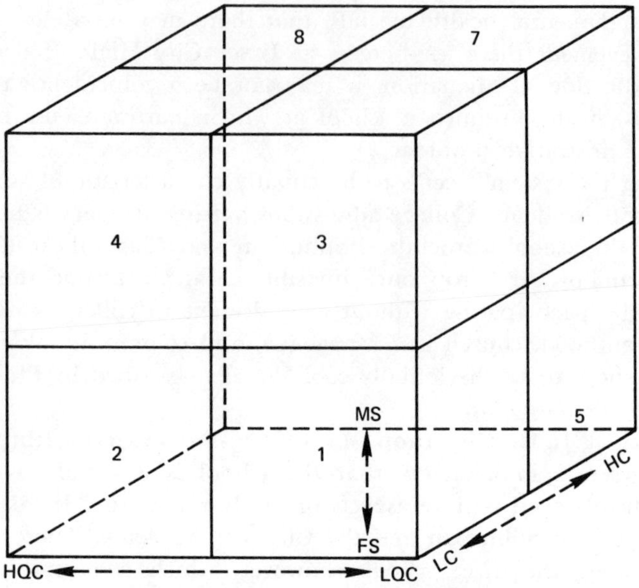

FS = Few Sources and Few Kinds of Resources
MS = Many Sources and Many Kinds of Resources
LQC = Low Quantity of Resources Consumed Per Pupil
HQC = High Quantity of Resources Consumed Per Pupil
LC = Low Competition for Pupils and Resources
HC = High Competition for Pupils and Resources

to the elements of resource consumption and sources treated in the Frelie Window.

When the schools we have discussed are located in the three-dimensional space of the Elfred Cube, the influence of competition for students on accountability for output quality becomes apparent. Eight regions within the cube are defined by the interaction of the variables: variety of resources, quantity of resources intake, and degree of competition. Each of the regions constitutes an ecosystem model.

EFFECTIVE SCHOOLS

Region 8, in our experience, represents an educationally flexible, accountable, efficient, and productive school ecosystem, and is optimal in terms of the Elfred Cube. Such a school would consume a large quantity of resources from many sources. It would be kept flexible by their variety, and would be kept accountable by the presence of competitors for the resources. Region 7 would provide the next most effective ecosystem model. Low quantity of resource consumption per pupil (indicating low availability of resources in the environment) might make life difficult for the school, but would stimulate diversification of resource interaction and keep the school flexible. Competition would keep it accountable.

INEFFECTIVE SCHOOLS

Schools situated in Regions 1 and 2 would both be disfavored. Schools in Region 1 would be inflexible because of little variety in sources of resources. They would be highly dependent on a single source of resources, small as they might be. Lacking competitors, accountability to clients would not be necessary. Region 2 schools would have little incentive to diversify their resources and become flexible because their quantity from a single source was high. They would be highly accountable to their single source of resources, but not to the clients, because of lack of competition. Such a school could be ineffective and get away with it. Like the schools in Region 1, schools in Region 2 could be ineffective and still continue to operate.

SUMMARY

In large urban school systems, local parents are not the direct source of dollars for the local school—state or federal aid, and citywide tax revenue are the source. The aid is channeled through "downtown." Increases in federal or state support of ghetto schools may only decrease accountability to local clients and bring about a reduction in local and state funds allocated to the school.

Financial grants to urban school systems from the federal government in recent years seem to have produced no increases in quality of output. The United States Commission on Civil Rights,[8] in its 1967 study, did not find even one of the major compensatory education programs undertaken by urban public school systems with outside funding to have produced significant change in students' achievement scores. Similarly, an assessment of the Higher Horizons Program in New York City indicates that monetary input may purchase more professional staff in the ghetto, but that this alone does not increase the quality of educational output. Similarly, our experience in Chicago has been that no significant change in public school ethos, standard operating procedures, or accountability to clients has resulted from such funds. Ghetto public

[8] United States Commission on Civil Rights, *Racial Isolation in the Public Schools*, Vol. 1 (Washington, D. C.: U. S. Government Printing Office, 1967).

schools now receive federal funds, but they have not ceased to be prisons. They continue to demean young people and ignore their parents with an impersonal and orderly brutality reminiscent of Auschwitz and the African colonies. Just as tragically, the flexibility and imagination found in humane public schools has also failed to produce educational output of quality.

If urban schools are to become effective, it seems that they must be forced into it. One way to do this is to reorder their ecosystems so that their transactions with the environment change. The way to do this is to begin by making the school competitive with other schools, while not increasing the resources from tax funds. This will force the school to become accountable and seek out new resources. Otherwise, it will atrophy and die. Financial intake can be increased after, *but only after,* competition and a variety of resources have produced changes in structure and process.

nine

A New Model for Governance

Decentralization of school district governance is an improvement strategy that has excited widespread interest. It is not difficult to conceive of important traditional management advantages that might accrue from such steps: more expeditious decisions, decision making by persons closer to the local facts, and a boost to the morale of teachers and other administrators. However, the decentralization movement has developed many features beyond simply administrative concerns. In fact, administrative concerns have become almost secondary to what might be termed psychological and political factors. However, this does not necessarily mean that the issue has shifted from improved schooling. Improvement may have as much to do with psychology and politics as it does with "better administration."

Henry Levin is a widely known economist interested in education. In 1969 he organized a national conference to consider efforts to promote greater community control of schools. As a result of this conference, and of his own studies, Levin has become deeply concerned with the governance of schools. His chapter considers decentralization as a means to improve the achievement level of black and other minority group students by enabling them to gain a heightened sense of self-worth from viewing their communities participate in the management of the schools they attend. The chapter, in a sense, rests on two legs: first, on a recognition of the frequent inadequacy of current arrangements for educating many big city students; and, second, on an explanation of how and why a greater delegation of school control to the local community would improve the tone and character of school operations for the better.

THE CASE FOR COMMUNITY CONTROL OF THE SCHOOLS

Henry M. Levin

Among all the major social movements of our time, demands for community control of the schools must certainly be one of the least understood. Perhaps this is the case for most complex issues, but it would seem that a major share of the confusion is due to the sensational, but relatively superficial, reporting of the news media. The press has tended to present this phenomenon in the context of a temporary racial crisis, giving greater emphasis to implications for "law and order" than to the education of minority group students. An analogy might be made to the journalists who, in reporting the causes for the outbreak of World War I, intensely explored events surrounding the assassination of Archduke Ferdinand, while ignoring the more complex set of economic and political relationships that led to the extensive international conflagration.

In an attempt to provide greater depth and balance to discussion of this issue, this chapter focuses on the rationale or justifiication for the community control movement.[1] Indeed, demands for community control cannot be fully understood without first recognizing the situation that presently confronts racial minorities in their quests for equality and dignity. Though two hundred years of slavery have been followed by one hundred years of "freedom," the black American still remains outside the mainstream of American life. By almost all standard measures, his welfare is substantially below that of the American majority; statistics on income, employment, life expectancy, housing, and infant mortality all reflect his unenviable position.

The substance of this chapter appeared in *Community Control of Schools*, Henry M. Levin, ed. (Washington, D. C.: The Brookings Institution, 1970).

[1] For a more detailed statement of the financial and administrative steps that might be involved in the establishment of such schools, see Henry M. Levin and H. Thomas James, "Financing Community Schools," and Marilyn Gittel, "The Balance of Power and the Community School," in Henry M. Levin, ed., *Community Control of Schools* (Washington, D. C.: The Brookings Institution, 1970).

He has migrated from rural to urban areas seeking opportunity, and he has worked hard at the jobs that were available. However, the rapid upward mobility that greeted immigrants from other lands has eluded the black American. In part this is due to his arriving in the cities at a time when opportunities for unskilled labor were fast diminishing and when the large-city political systems had already established themselves without his participation. Thus, he found himself caged by the walls of the urban ghetto with housing and job discrimination handicapping his chances of substantially improving his status. Massive discrimination and racism in both the government and private sectors have prevented any semblance of equal human rights for the black man, and while our society has recently begun to attempt to redress these inequalities, progress has been pitifully slow.

Of all the conditions facing the American black, the worst probably has been his feeling of powerlessness. Given the same high aspirations as his fellow citizens, the black is unable to fulfill them because of discriminatory barriers placed in his path. He is imprisoned in substandard, overpriced ghetto housing, and his choice of jobs is limited. He has neither the occupational nor residential mobility, nor the political power to counter these disabling conditions. Compounding this feeling of impotence is the fact that the very social institutions which were designed to improve his prospects have not been able to do so. It is this frustrating lack of control over his life's circumstances that may well be the most bitter pill to swallow. Without some measure of control over his destiny, his aspirations can never be more than pipedreams.

Thus, the basic problem of the black American is that of gaining control over his destiny, and in recent years a prospective solution to this problem has come into focus. Through racial cohesiveness and self-development, many black men intend to liberate themselves from racism and to gain equality and dignity. Foremost in this drive is the quest to redirect and reform those institutions that seem to have failed black Americans or, worse yet, have inflicted injury and further disadvantages on racial minorities. In the black neighborhoods of large cities, schools have become among the first of these institutions to be challenged.

One point that is not at issue is the fact acknowledged by urban educators and informed laymen alike that city schools have failed to help the black American to improve his status. The indictment of the schools is an especially serious one because formal education has represented the primary social device for more nearly equalizing opportunity among children of different races or social groupings. Yet, while about three-quarters of white males in their latter twenties have completed high school, only about half of nonwhite males in this age bracket have fulfilled a high school education. These data provide only a portion of the picture. Even among those students who do reach the twelfth grade, the average Negro is about three years in standardized achievement units behind the average twelfth grade white.

The black American, then, enters his adult life with severe educational deficiencies, and the nature of the schooling experience which is provided for him must share some of the blame for this condition. The average black in the large cities attends a school which is less well endowed than that attended by whites. For example, teachers in Negro schools have less experience and lower verbal ability than their counterparts in schools attended by whites. In addition, schools with black enrollments are more likely to be crowded and to experience shortages of supplies and other materials; and historically they have been characterized by lower expenditures.

But inferior resources are only one way in which schools handicap the ghetto child in preparing him for life. Even more destructive to his self-concept and growth is the cultural intolerance reflected by his schooling experience. The materials, curriculum, and teaching methods were developed for children of the white middle class, and they have been largely irrelevant to the experiences and special educational requirements of the black child. Thus the present schools situated in Negro neighborhoods tend to undermine the black student's identity by ignoring his cultural heritage. That is, in their effort to be "color blind," many schools have ignored color; they demand that the ghetto child reflect the language patterns, experience, and cultural traits of the white middle class. In this sense, city schools have been guilty of massive institutional racism by forcing black students to be captive audiences in a hostile environment, an environment that just did not have their needs in mind. In this respect, city schools tend not to reflect the pluralism that is claimed for our society.

Given the intention by blacks to take responsibility for those institutions which mold their lives and the lives of their children, it is no accident that the schools represent an initial focal point. As one spokesman noted:

> The schools are rather natural and logical vehicles for the first thrust because they represent the white underbelly of society. They are present. They are constant. They are not something that is hidden in a back room in city hall which you can't reach. The principal of the school is at hand. The teachers are there. So there is a very tangible instrument around which action could focus.

In addition to the visibility of schools, there is a widespread notion that in the long run education is a potent power in society, and that those who control schools, control something that is extremely meaningful.

An additional factor in favor of decentralizing control of the schools has been the fact that the black community frequently has the sympathy of a large segment of the white middle class who are also frustrated with the empty promises, administrative rigidities, unresponsiveness, and red tape that seem to characterize many city school bureaucracies. Yet another powerful element underlying the crusade for radical changes in school governance is the fact that the palliatives suggested by educational professionals for improving the ghetto schools have frequently been shown to be difficult to implement at best, and totally ineffective at worst.

Conventional wisdom of the late fifties and early sixties suggested that, through racially integrating the schools, educational problems of blacks and other minorities could be solved. In most cities, promises of integration were never fulfilled. Inaction on the issue or, worse yet, gerrymandering of local attendance districts to prevent meaningful integration, created great bitterness among many blacks whose top priority was racially integrated education. The fact that many city school boards could not deliver what they had promised led to much of the present minority distrust of centralized school boards. Where integration did take place, it tended to be token in nature, with black students placed in different "ability" groups or curricula than white students. Indeed, the U.S. Commission on Civil Rights found in 1966 that "many Negro students who attend majority-white schools in fact are in majority-Negro classrooms."

Today, white middle class outflow from cities in combination with black in-migration and political opposition to busing and other methods of alleviating de facto school segregation have made large-scale integration an improbable event. Of the twenty cities in the largest metropolitan areas in 1966, nine had Negro majorities among their elementary school enrollments, and fifteen had enrollments that were over 30 percent Negro. Thus, true school integration implies transgressing traditional political boundaries and incorporating metropolitan school districts that would encompass city and suburbs. Substantial opposition to this proposal by suburbanites will probably prevent such a development for the foreseeable future. In the meantime, inability of large city schools to adapt to the special needs of "minority" students will become increasingly a failure to adapt to the needs of a majority of students, most of these students obtaining their schooling in segregated environments. Among seventy-five cities surveyed by the Civil Rights Commission in 1966, three-quarters of the Negro students in elementary schools were already attending schools whose enrollments were 90 percent or more Negro.

Indeed many blacks reject integration as a solution not only because it is a phrase that is replete with false promises, but also because it has ideological overtones that are an affront to their dignity. As Floyd

McKissick has suggested, the view that quality education can only take place in an integrated school seems to be based upon the degrading proposition: "Mix Negroes with Negroes and you get stupidity."

A second approach to improving schools in the black ghetto has been that of *compensatory education* (see Chapter Four). During the early sixties, it became increasingly in vogue among educators to refer to the "educationally deprived" or "disadvantaged" child. In particular, most urban black children were considered to be disadvantaged, because it was said they lacked the home and community environment that stimulated educational motivation, achievement, and the derivation of middle class attributes. Therefore, additional school resources were to be provided to the disadvantaged child in order to compensate for his middle class deficiencies.

Unfortunately, the record to date for compensatory education is unimpressive. Most compensatory efforts have focused on smaller class sizes and additional personnel. The types of teachers, curricuulm, school organization, and educational methods that have consistently failed the ghetto child have been largely retained, and little educational progress has been demonstrated. Some school spokesmen have excused compensatory program failures by asserting that most of these attempts have been underfinanced. Perhaps this is true, but one can certainly question how spending more money on such traditional panaceas as the reduction of class size is going to change the qualitative nature of basic schooling processes that did not have the urban black youngsters in mind to begin with.

It is clear that schools as presently constituted have shown little evidence of being able to fulfill the educational needs of the disadvantaged child and particularly the black disadvantaged child. Both compensatory education and school integration have witnessed more failures than successes (with the possible exception of preschool programs), and most future plans for improving the education of black children revolve about these two approaches. In a sense, representatives of the black communities are saying to the educational professionals and the white community: "You've been given your chance, and our schools have not improved." Now blacks want a chance to solve their own educational problems, and the professionals have not been able to counter these demands with genuine alternatives. Instead, the rather tired response has been something to the effect: "Just give us a chance to provide really racially integrated, quality education." In the eyes of the black community, this reply has not only come too late, but it smacks of the same stale remedies that have failed to change the picture in the past. The surge for self-determination in combination with the failure of the professionals to prove themselves has made schools particularly vulnerable. This vulnerability has manifested itself in the increasingly voiced sentiment that the education of blacks can no longer be considered to be the "white man's burden." The black community has rejected this paternalistic approach and wishes to take responsibility for the schooling of its own.

MAKING SCHOOLS WORK FOR MINORITY CHILDREN

Before embarking on a description of how community-controlled schools might improve the schooling experiences of minority children, it is useful to offer a more precise analysis of why the present approach to compensatory education must inevitably fail the culturally different child. Inherent in compensatory education programs is the condescending view that the urban minority child is somehow inferior to the middle class child. Relative to the white, middle class child, he is "deprived" and "disadvantaged." Therefore, he needs remedial work and compensatory resources to improve his prospects. That is, *remediation* is considered to be the key to the minority child's emancipation.

That the minority child is different from the middle class white child is a mere tautology. Yet, in this case the schools assume that the child's cultural differences represent inferiorities that must be eliminated. Inherent in this approach is a total disrespect for the cultures and experiences of black and other minority children. Yet to a black youngster, his experience is certainly as valid as that of his white counterpart.

There is no reason that a minority child must deny or deprecate his background in order to "learn." Indeed, such forced self-denunciation can only guarantee the development of a serious and widening breech between the school and the child. "Quite the opposite, the schools must capitalize on the cultural strengths of minority children in order to build cultural bridges between the experiences of those children and the goals of the larger society." [2]

But this goal requires taking a specialized approach to educating minority students, one that violates the underpinnings of the present universalistic model. The present method tacitly assumes that the same approach is universally applicable to all children despite the pious rhetoric often espoused about "individualized" instruction. Unfortunately, large urban school systems have shown themselves to be incapable of building educational programs that capitalize on the cultural attributes of minority children. This fact becomes quite clear when one examines the way in which so-called compensatory education programs have been formulated. Most money has been spent on such traditional

[2] This approach is well documented and illustrated in Sylvia Ashton-Warner, *Teacher* (New York: Simon & Schuster, 1963). Also, see Frederick D. Flower, *Language and Education* (London: Longmans, Green, 1966).

methods as reducing class size, increasing the number of counselors and remedial specialists, and buying more library volumes. That is, more money has been spent on the same remedies that have not worked well in the past. The inevitable result is a larger version of the same dismal cake. There must be qualitative changes in the recipe in order to improve the quality of education for minority children.[3]

The fact that such qualitative changes have not generally taken place has meant that dollar resources have been misspent. The U.S. Office of Education in evaluating the effect of Title I monies on reading scores found that ". . . a child who participated in a Title I project had only a 19 percent chance of a significant achievement gain, a 13 percent chance of a significant achievement loss, and a 68 percent chance of no change at all relative to the national norms."[4] Further, projects that were investigated were ". . . most likely to be representative of projects in which there was a higher than average investment in resources. Therefore more significant achievement gains should be found here than in a more representative sample of Title I projects."[5]

In fact, comparing dollar inputs between schools attended by minority students and those attended by middle class whites is an erroneous way of measuring school resource endowments between races. To the degree that money is spent in both cases on teachers, curriculum, and other inputs that are more effective for white children than for black or Spanish-speaking students, dollar expenditures tend to overstate vastly the relative resources available to the latter group. Rather, nominal resources devoted to the two groups of schools must be weighted by their effectiveness to ascertain their true values.

The ludicrous nature of comparing schools attended by majority and minority students on the basis of checklists of physical characteristics or on dollar expenditures is reflected in the following illustration. If black schools and white schools have the same number of teachers with the same preparation and experience, the two sets of schools are considered to be equal according to conventional criteria. Now what if all the teachers have white racist views? Clearly, if black schools and white schools have equal numbers of white racist teachers, the two sets of schools are not equal even though the physicial quantities of teachers are. This example raises additional questions about the present definition

3 Certainly this idea is not new. It has been suggested by many persons concerned with minority education. An excellent example is Joan Baratz and Roger Shuy, *Teaching Black Children to Read* (Washington, D. C.: Center for Applied Linguistics, 1969). It has been rarely applied, however.

4 Harry Piccariello, "Evaluation of Title I," mimeographed (1969), p. 1. To be published in Joseph Froomkin and Dennis J. Dugan, eds., *Inequality: Studies in Elementary and Secondary Education,* U. S. Office of Education Planning Paper 69-2, Office of Program Planning and Evaluation.

5 Piccariello, "Evaluation of Title I."

of remediation and compensatory education. If we double the number of white racist teachers in black schools, class size will be reduced by 50 percent; yet it is difficult to argue that healthy increases in educational output will take place. Such a situation is perfectly consistent with the conventional arithmetic of spending on compensatory education. Attention is heavily focused on the amount of traditional resources available to minority children with almost no consideration of the appropriateness or the efficacy of those resources.

MAKING URBAN SCHOOLS MORE RESPONSIVE

For many blacks and members of other racial minorities, community control of the schools is seen as the only path that will succeed in making schools more responsive generally to the needs of the populations they serve. Under existing centrally administered systems, principals, teachers, and parents have found attempts to improve their schools frustrated by cumbersome procedures and regulations which protect the *status quo*. The school systems are so large that they cannot view themselves as being accountable to particular schools or parents, especially if those schools serve children whose parents lack political muscle. Since departures from tradition must usually be approved in the offices of the central school administration, bold and imaginative proposals for change are throttled by the lack of decision making power in individual schools and classrooms. In fact, the central school board's obsession for procedural order above other considerations has encrusted schools with a drab and uniform educational approach despite the large variety of educational situations and student needs that are actually present in large cities. To the degree that many of the methods, curricula, and personnel have not been appropriate and have failed to give minority children, in particular, the skills and healthy attitudes that the schools claim as objectives, the failure has become institutionalized and systematic.

The massive inefficiencies and rigidities evident in the existing approach have been documented by so many novelists and journalists that many members of the public simply take them for granted. In one city, schools have waited for two years for textbooks that could have been received within two weeks had they been ordered directly from publishers. Many city schools have reported storerooms full of unused scientific equipment and library books without having the programs, laboratories, and libraries to make use of these materials. Other schools have the programs and physical facilities but lack equipment. In schools of some cities, a simple request for stationery or paper clips must be approved by a dozen different signatories before the request can be filled.

Further, the choice of textbooks and curriculum can rarely be modified by a teacher, no matter how useless or deleterious they may be to his or her pupils. One of the better publicized incidents that illustrates the administrative callousness of large city schools took place recently in a black junior high school. A young white teacher was harassed by her principal, who received support from the office of the central school board, for daring to introduce the Negro play, *Raisin in the Sun,* into her English class and for encouraging and supporting her pupils' efforts to produce a student newspaper. Her creative attempts to introduce relevant activities were criticized as violations of the "required" curriculum. That she had succeeded in getting her students excited about their English classes was ignored in favor of administrative uniformity. There is evidence that many of our better teachers leave the schools in part because of these same frustrations. In fact, the general failure of compensatory education programs is a monumental tribute to the inability of large city school bureaucracies to adapt themselves to the needs of the sizable group of black children.

Thus, a major objective of school decentralization is that of making schools more responsive to the particular populations they serve, by making them accountable to the communities from which they draw their enrollments. The unwieldiness of the present highly centralized administrative structure prevents this type of accountability. It is expected that by being answerable to a local rather than city-wide governing board, schools will improve the learning environment for the children involved.

The direct impact of decentralization on schools would be derived from the ability of each community to select the curricula, materials, programs, and personnel that were most appropriate to the specific needs of its students. Experimentation and innovation, then, might lead to school environments that were more receptive to students and more successful in stimulating intellectual and emotional growth than are the present schools. In addition, decentralization would enable schools to handle logistical problems more efficiently by obtaining textbooks and other supplies in appropriate quantities at times when they are needed. Decentralization could also enable schools to obtain outside consulting on specific problems, utilize new types of personnel, such as artists and writers, and contract certain services that might be supplied more efficiently by private firms.

But, in addition to these direct effects, it is possible that the learning process will be enhanced indirectly by a healthy metamorphosis of community education attitudes. That is, the participation of parents and other members of the community in the operation of schools will lead to a more total involvement between the school and its constituency than is possible under the present bureaucratic structure. It appears that parental involvement in schools leads to more favorable attitudes toward education among their children; however, under the present system of highly centralized control, the school appears to be an impenetrable and alien fortress to the community and its parents. The inability of parents to have any meaningful influence in modifying rigid and anachronistic school policies has certainly led to parental frustrations and hostile attitudes that are easily transmitted to their children. It is believed that if the school were accountable to the community by being truly responsive to its educational needs, parents would show greater respect for schools and more favorable attitudes toward education. These attitudes would filter down to their children and would be reflected in the attitudes and performances of the students in those schools.

DECENTRALIZATION AND THE BLACK COMMUNITY

To the black community, the educational rationale for community governance is equally compelling, but the need for change is far more urgent than that suggested in the general case.[6] Not only is the present highly centralized system considered to be educationally inadequate, but also it is viewed as one which must inevitably have racist consequences. That is, the school system can afford to favor middle class white children at the expense of black children because black citizens simply lack the political power to do anything about it. In this respect, the schools reflect a type of racism which is ignored by the average white American. Kenneth Haskins, the principal who initially led the Morgan Community School in the District of Columbia, suggested that racism in this sense means ". . . that a public school system that fails black children can be tolerated, while a public school system that fails white middle-class children cannot." [7]

There is a strong belief that this dereliction might be reversed if the administration of those schools in black neighborhoods was responsive to the needs of large groups of black parents who were deeply concerned and involved in the process of education. In this regard, it is interesting to note that the Morgan Community School showed gains in the reading proficiencies of students in its very first year of community control. Only a handful of other public schools in the entire district exhibited such improvement over this period, while most schools showed declines.

Many black Americans also see a new and important educational focus emerging from community governance. They suggest that schools should

[6] While this discussion is generally limited to the black community, it is certainly applicable to such ethnic minorities as Mexican-Americans and Puerto Ricans.

[7] Kenneth W. Haskins, "The Case for Local Control," *Saturday Review*, January 11, 1969, p. 52.

be responsible for helping to fulfill the ideals and aspirations of the people served. The constituency of the school must necessarily include all the people of the community since the needs of the students cannot be divorced from the context in which they live. The school should be expected to promote the sense of self-worth and identity of the students served while imparting to those youngsters the ability to influence what happens to their lives. That is, the often noted observation that schools and the larger society tend to destroy the self-worth and identity of black children is considered to be as reprehensible as the academic failures of the schools.

In order to carry out these responsibilities, the community school must address itself not only to transmitting academic or cognitive skills, but also to affective skills, with particular attention given to the formation of positive attitudes. Indeed, community schools must be designed to compensate for the second-class treatment of black citizens in other sectors of society by building educational programs that will help black children to succeed.

But, even beyond that, many black Americans view community control of those schools in black neighborhoods as the beginning of a significant drive toward full equality. This approach springs from the widely held concept that as long as black Americans lack political and economic power, they will not be able substantially to improve their lot. Accordingly, community control of the schools represents the thin edge of a political wedge which would begin to redistribute decision-making power to those whose lives are affected by the decisions, in this case, the black community. Control of the schools is viewed as the first step in effecting a more just distribution of political power and a greater degree of self-determination for black citizens.

As one spokesman explained: "Improving the schools attended by black children is an urgent priority, but it seems to me that the bigger issue is one of how large numbers of people who have been effectively disenfranchised begin to find their way toward being a part of the society." It is interesting to ask, then, if large numbers of black communities did indeed obtain control of their school systems, how meaningful would that phenomenon be in securing complete liberation from the powerlessness that has hindered black advancement? His answer is that it could be very meaningful:

> While the answers are not in, it seems very clear that this could be an initial step toward more effective control of other institutions in the community, for it is the success patterns of communities which give those communities a sense of better future instead of futility. Given control of the schools, the community could sense a beginning of political potency. It is this factor which would enhance the community's ability to deal more effectively with other problems such as jobs and housing and which would construct the groundwork for full equality.

In this respect community schools represent a focus around which political and social structures would emerge for black Americans where such structures are presently lacking. The factors that link black men today are the largely negative ones of enduring racial discrimination at the hands of white society. While there is a recent emphasis on black culture, the school represents a tangible institution about which a sense of community involvement and black pride might develop. Responsibility for the schools represents a positive experience which can be shared by all blacks as opposed to the negative one of white racism.

The importance of the school in developing the communal ties that black Americans, and perhaps most Americans, desire so passionately cannot be overemphasized. As Robert Maynard has suggested: "An issue has been raised around which many residents can rally as never before and one in which their mutual, or community, interest is most clearly defined." In this sense it seems that the often cited term, *black community,* in fact, reflects the common attributes which blacks wish to develop and share with each other. Control of schools represents a setting within which these latent and somewhat mystical ties might emerge to form a true sense of community, a sense of a common purpose and destiny.

Thus, the black American views community control as a way of improving and broadening the educational performance of ghetto schools as well as more generally improving the status of black citizens. This would be done by breaking down many of the rigidities that characterize these schools, as well as by introducing programs, personnel, and materials that are specifically designed to transform black children into capable young adults. The historical evidence suggests that presently structured school bureaucracies are incapable of carrying out such changes. Therefore, community control becomes a logical alternative for educational reform.

In addition, many blacks feel that community support for operating schools will provide the nucleus for a community power base; and it is believed that strong and cohesive black communities represent the most effective strategy for obtaining a more equitable share of power in the larger society. While few critics might deny the importance of the immediate educational goals of the community schools, many have reacted strongly to these political implications.

POLITICAL IMPLICATIONS OF COMMUNITY SCHOOLS

The main criticism against community control of schools seems to be that the search for political "liberation" of black Americans has no place in the schools. One wonders whether it is not the ends of obtaining power rather than the means that are being questioned, for the schools have traditionally claimed the goal of preparing students for a participatory democracy. Courses given throughout the standard curriculum are designed to give students the requisite literacy, knowledge, and common set of values that enable them to understand and participate in the political life of our society. But blacks and other racial minorities have been excluded from the power structure. They have been unable to form a coalition or find any other group that will represent their needs, and the present objectives of the schools have not served them well. Indeed, present values reflected in the school curriculum are necessary for perpetuating the present distribution of political power; they do not encourage opening the game to players who have not been dealt a hand.

Since a significant portion of the black community feels that only self-development will invest it with the strength to reinforce its demands for a fairer representation in the larger society, it appears consistent that schools in the black community emphasize political goals of black cohesion rather than those of the beneficent democracy. Democratic trappings presently reflected by schools are clearly deceptive to black Americans who still lack political equality and meaningful representation. Thus, from the black point of view, there is necessarily an important educational precedent for relating its educational goals to its political ones.

SOCIALIZATION AND RACIAL SEPARATION

A second and related major social objection to decentralization is that it would institutionalize racial separation. Presumably neighborhoods would represent the initial basis of community, so that blacks would continue to attend schools that were predominantly black and whites would attend schools with white enrollments. Yet a major objective of the schools in a democratic society is that of exposing children to fellow students who are drawn from a variety of social, economic, and racial backgrounds. This goal is considered to be part of the socialization function of the schools, whereby individuals are being prepared to fulfill their interpersonal or social obligations in a multicultural setting. It is believed that exposure to a heterogeneity of cultures, races, and social classes improves understanding and interactions among the various groups and increases social mobility. These end products are considered to be prerequisites for an effectively functioning democratic society.

In this respect the community school appears to be both socially divisive and antidemocratic. But blacks are frequently among the first to point out that the concept of the "melting pot" has been a historical myth as far as black Americans are concerned. The fact is that blacks presently live in a separate society, and neither legal remedies nor the putative good will of the white community have been able to give them housing, education, and other social activities in an integrated setting. In the particular case of city schools, it was not blacks who rejected integration; it was the large-city school boards representing a sizable component of the white community. The vast majority of black Americans have always lived in a separate society, and past efforts to integrate them have not been successful.

But if we assume that a healthy America requires the full economic, political, and social integration of blacks and whites, the real question is how to achieve such a goal. Paradoxically, black cohesiveness appears to be a more effective strategy than any other existing alternative. The reason for its promise is a simple one. This society responds much more quickly to demands from powerful constituencies than it does to requests from weak ones, and black community is the basis for black political potency.

The effects of black separation in getting a larger piece of action are noticeable on the university campuses. The demands of newly formed black student unions for increases in black enrollments, black faculty members and administrators, and courses in Afro-American culture have been met with positive responses at many institutions. In addition, these demands have spurred substantial increases in the recruitment of blacks by professional and graduate schools as well as greater provisions of financial aid and counseling services for such students. These gains are particularly relevant because they represent the traditional paths of access to the middle class that have been heavily trodden by whites, but, until very recently at least, have been largely inaccessible to minorities. What the issue comes to in the final analysis is the view by community control advocates that integration and equality will never come until blacks have the power to pursue such objectives meaningfully, and the requisite power cannot develop without black unity.

COMMUNITY SCHOOLS AND WHITE AMERICANS

Is political decentralization of the schools an equally valid response to the educational problems of whites? One of the most serious flaws that characterizes city schools, as well as many other American institutions, is the fallacious assumption that identical treatment of different groups yields the same outcomes for all groups. The fact is that, given the different cultural attributes of racial and social groupings, application of the same educational approach yields highly unequal results. In particular, evidence suggests that the traditional schooling approach has been far less effective for black children and those of some other racial minorities than it has been for children of the white middle class.

If this is so, then the same logic must be applied to the choice of remedy. That is, organizational reforms that are drastically needed to improve the status of minority students are not necessarily the most appropriate remedies for curing the educational infirmities of those schools serving white populations.

In this respect, community control of the schools is far more urgently needed by minority Americans than it is by whites. Blacks (and other racial minorities) are a special educational case because their exigencies are not represented by the power structure or by traditional institutional arrangements. The result of their lack of representation is that blacks have been shortchanged in the allocation of school resources, and their needs have been ignored in determining the nature of the schooling experience that is provided for their children. As a consequence, there exists an enormous breach between the context in which the black child lives and the schooling that is imposed upon him. In addition, the central school authorities have shown themselves to be insensitive to other major concerns of the black population. Sites have been selected for new schools that are to be built in black neighborhoods without consulting inhabitants of the local areas. As a result, black residents and businesses have been uprooted despite the availability of suitable alternative sites that would leave housing and other neighborhood buildings intact.

On the other hand, no major contradiction is found between the values represented in the school and those embodied in the white community at large, and whites already have the political power to protect their major school interests. The central school authority is politically sensitive to both school resource demands and site selection preferences of residents in white neighborhoods. In fact, in these as well as other major respects, whites already send their children to community-controlled schools. The very failure of policies to reduce de facto school segregation is a tribute to the power of white neighborhoods to keep black students out of their schools.

To be sure, particular whites might not be altogether happy with their schools, but most white Americans can express their dissatisfactions through political channels or through moving to another neighborhood or school district, and many white Americans have the financial ability to send their children to private institutions. The minority American has neither the luxury of obtaining political responsiveness, the income necessary to seek private alternatives, nor the choice of a large number of neighborhoods or communities in which he can obtain housing and better schools for his children. Locked-in to his community, and locked-out of city hall, the minority American's only hope for improving his schools appears to be through their immediate and direct governance. Therein lies the case for community control of the schools.

ten

A New Model for the Suburbs

The schools populated by inner-city residents may not be the only ones for which reform is in order. Traditionally, suburban public schools have exemplified educational excellence in America. Their tax resources have enabled them to buy materials and skills that are unavailable to ghetto school systems. Concurrently, the parents of suburban students have the sophistication to supply their children with support and attitudes that assist school success. However, these resources and pressures can only be productive if parents and school systems have a sound vision of what constitutes educational excellence. Cognitive skills —literacy, mathematics, and physical science talents—are not the only knowledge that can be taught in school. Indeed, an insensitive focus on such values, especially when combined with lock-step teaching techniques, may generate tensions and produce alienation and hostility even among the most able students.

If we suspect that the vocational handicaps frequently faced by lower socioeconomic and minority ethnic groups are, in part, a consequence of the shortcomings in their educational system, is it not also likely that current college and high school unrest, often involving advantaged students, is a similar judgment on the educational system through which they have passed? In sum, is it not evident that something is seriously wrong with current practices, even (or particularly?) in the "best" public schools?

Dwight Allen is Dean of the School of Education at the University of Massachusetts. William Fanslow is a colleague of his. They both are concerned with ways to improve instructional techniques and with developing means to encourage more flexible school environments. In this chapter, Allen and Fanslow turn their attention to suburban schools, describe their shortcomings, and prescribe several steps by which they can be restructured into more effective and humane instructional institutions.

EDUCATION AND THE SUBURBAN "POOR"

Dwight W. Allen/William V. Fanslow

It appears to be rather fashionable these days in educational circles to worry loudly about the disadvantaged in our nation's schools. Like other phrases currently popular with the Establishment, "the welfare poor" and "law and order," to name only two, "the disadvantaged" is generally used as a euphemistic reference to nonwhites. In our ingrained liberal condescension it seems that we cannot imagine any other major group in our society which could properly be labeled "disadvantaged." Apart from the lingering racist attitudes inherent in this unquestioned association, there is another, typically middle class assumption, behind use of the phrase. It is simply our tendency to equate financial gain with social advantages, a fair enough equation on its face, and our rather uncritical willingness to make a converse judgment; namely, that financial poverty is equitable with social and educational disadvantage. While this statement also seems sufficiently indisputable, reflection will reveal it to be based on a restrictive conception of what creates and constitutes advantage and disadvantage in their broadest meanings.

If wealth alone were requisite to the "good life," we doubt that we would be witnessing the major cultural transformation which is now gaining momentum: the rejection of middle and upper middle class values by the offspring of those classes. If they are telling us nothing else, surely the children of affluence are making it quite clear that wealth and ease and luxury alone are not sufficient to their perception of a good life. "Money too has its price," they tell us who have bequeathed them so much of it, "and the price of your wealth and of our inheritance has been a loss of feeling, spontaneity, commitment, and joy." They would have us know that it is no bargain to barter feelings for objects. Thus, it is quite conceivable that the amount of disruption, dissent, and demonstration on our college campuses bears a direct relationship to the amount of frustration, boredom, and alienation which these same college students felt when they were students in grade school and high school.

Consider, after all, the nature of most "good" schools; rectilinear, smooth textured, clean to the point of being antiseptic, their physical style implies quite clearly what is expected of our students. They are to be neat, obedient, serious minded, and unemotional. There is little in either the architecture or the curricula of "good" schools which admits that students, or teachers for that matter, are human beings like the rest of us, and that like the rest of us, they are more than the sum of their homework or test scores. They are also emotional, idiosyncratic, physical, and sexual, and they are changing and, hopefully, growing in many dimensions. Do our schools, even our "best" schools, recognize the simple, irreducible fact that students are people? There is a considerable body of evidence being published which suggests the conclusion that our schools operate as though they were attended and monitored by robots rather than human beings. Frederick Wiseman's film, "High School," made at a "good" high school in a middle class Philadelphia neighborhood, depicts all too frighteningly the repressive, boot camp atmosphere to which seventeen-year-old human beings are daily subjected in the name of education. Education for what? College? Is it any wonder that many of these same students will later join a "radical left" when they reach their college campuses?

We would like to suggest that the largest group of disadvantaged students in our schools are precisely those whom we commonly assume to be the most privileged: the children of good America, the children of our subdivided, de-weeded, color televised, two-toned, college-bound suburbs. Although not economically disadvantaged, it is becoming increasingly apparent that the children of suburbia perceive themselves to be deprived in a variety of other ways, equally destructive if not as readily obvious to the middle class American mind: deprived of the capacity to express their deepest emotions without having either to "justify" themselves or to pay an exorbitant price of shame or guilt. (It is interesting to note in this regard that the economically disadvantaged, for example, the black and Puerto Rican, do not seem to be deprived of this latter capacity to anywhere near the same degree as middle class whites; the phrase "up tight" is generally used in reference to whites, not blacks.) It is no argument for poverty to state that our best schools seem to be graduating intellectual prodigies who are at the same time emotional retardates, people who know what is expected of them and can fulfill the expectations of others, but who honestly do not know what they want and seem unable to fulfill their own desires. Our students do not know what they want because no one has ever asked them. They have not been asked because, essentially, we do not consider them in their own right. You do not ask a puppy what it wants; you give it what you think it wants, or what you want it to have.

If the analysis we suggest is basically accurate, and the writings of others such as Friedenberg, Kenniston, Lindner, Fromm, and Goodman suggest that it is, then it is obvious that much of what we have been doing in American education is not only not good enough, but also it is producing positive damage in our students. Three hundred years after the hellfire sermons of Jonathan Edwards, we continue to view our children very much as the Puritans would have: as messy, silly, uncivilized, and untrustworthy little devils who must be made less emotional and more logical so that their rationality can ultimately triumph over their evil desires and vile emotions. Puritans never learned to live comfortably with their emotional responses, except constantly to guard against them, and neither, it seems, have we learned. Neither, as a consequence, have our children learned, and they certainly have not learned in school. Heaven forbid that our children waste their time in school expressing emotions when they could be "learning something," something that might help them get into a "good college." One wonders whether or not a good college is a suburban equivalent of the Puritan heaven.

It seems to us that the good which our schools have fallen short of and the harm which they have inflicted are intimately connected. It is simply not possible to divorce the rational capability of the mind and educate it in isolation, or as we seem to attempt it, in quarantine, from the rest of the emotions, the body, and the will of a human being. At this late date, is it too revolutionary to suggest that emotional expression, physical sensations, and volitional acts may actually be helpful, even necessary, in the growth of a fully rational person? The plain fact is that children are not humanoid-looking computers, nor are they miniature adults. Children are what they are, with the potential to be more if we will let them grow. Indeed, it is even conceivable that we might be able to devise an educational system which would actually encourage our children to discover what is possible in their physical, emotional, intuitional, as well as their intellectual, development.

There is also another major area wherein most suburban school children can be classed as "disadvantaged," that is, in their typical inability to function in a multicultural social environment. As Alice Miel and a group of researchers conclude in a study entitled *The Shortchanged Children of Suburbia,* ". . . there is little in their [suburban] education, formal or otherwise, to familiarize them with the rich diversity of American life." [1] In documenting its conclusion, the study describes the reactions of selected suburban children to people who are of different races, religions, ethnic, and economic backgrounds. Miel and her colleagues found that while most elementary school children from suburban backgrounds lacked direct experience with either Negroes or poverty cultures

[1] Alice Miel and Edwin Kiester, *The Shortchanged Children of Suburbia* (New York: Institute of Human Relations Press, 1967).

generally, they nevertheless tended to view Negroes as inferior and undesirable and poverty as both shameful and disgusting. Yes, Virginia, the Puritan work ethic is alive and well in Yonkers, Great Neck, Cicero, and Brookline. What is, of course, so frightening about these findings is that they indicate the perpetuation of an insular life style and an exclusive value system, hardly what our society will need if we are ever to bridge the yawning racial, cultural, and economic chasms between so many of our subcultural groups. For it remains a fact that, up tight or not, committed or not, the suburban American is the modern American prototype, the embodiment, like it or not, of most of our traditional values, myths, dreams, and nightmares. He is presently in the driver's seat, and if he is disadvantaged in ways that make the task of social remediation more difficult, then we are going to have to deal with him and with his children, and we had better start soon.

The challenge which we face in all of this, as human beings, as citizens, and as professionals, is not that of affixing the blame for our present plight on one or another group or mentality, but rather one of finding enough common cause in our crisis to begin to act in ways that will make a positive difference. We would like for the remainder of this chapter to outline a number of attitudes, strategies, and programs which we think might help us move down the road toward an educational system which does not cripple the spirit of our suburban, mainstream school children, and which may even develop in them enough personal confidence to permit them to open their experience and their values more than our present schooling encourages them to do. It was, after all, a suburban high school dropout who wrote the following poem about education in America:

> Everytime you go to school
> it's like a mine disaster.
> I think of all the people
> lost inside of you.[2]

Perhaps the biggest single mistake we educators have made in designing and administering our programs has been to assume that there is probably one best way to educate students. Having assumed that, we feel that we need only discover or concoct that *One Best Way* and our problems are more or less solved. From this approach, of course, follow the charming internecine educational wars which keep professional glands secreting at full throttle. The unavoidable pitfall underlying this approach can be sensed if we only alter the statement's direction somewhat and ask, "What is the one best type of student?" Was Einstein a good

[2] Richard Brautigan, *Trout Fishing in America, Inc.* (New York: Dell Publishing, 1967).

student, a model to be emulated? One would hesitate to answer no, yet Einstein failed in arithmetic in grade school. Was William Lear, the inventor, an exemplary student? William Lear dropped out of school before finishing. Was Picasso an ideal art student? Perhaps, but his teachers hated him.

We would like to suggest that we adopt a new approach toward education, which is to say, a new approach toward the people whom we presently and cavalierly categorize as "students." We suggest that we begin to think in terms of educational alternatives, human alternatives, surely not an heretical doctrine. Instead of spending endless hours at faculty meetings debating, say, whether to teach European or Asian history in the eleventh grade social studies slot, why not offer both, if the resources necessary to offer both are available. Can we at last wean ourselves from the medieval notion that all students must learn the same information at the same pace at the same time? We do not think there is any a priori basis for assuming, as we have for so long, that excellence means only that all must meet the same standards at the same time in the same way. That is excellence of a kind; it is excellent obedience. But is that what we are after?

On a broader scale, we suggest that we begin to think in terms of alternative, rather than competing, strategies for the maximum facilitation of learning in our school systems. Is it really necessary, for example, for all students to take the same series of courses; or even for all students in a given course to perform identical tasks? Is it necessary to expect all teachers of tenth grade American history to teach it in the same manner? No two teachers will treat the subject, or their students, identically, so why saddle them with the guilt of not having met a ridiculous expectation? Is there any reason why we cannot offer alternative curricula simultaneously, or why we cannot use a variety of evaluative tools within the same school system?

The argument that such procedures make the present system more difficult to operate is a hard one to justify, for there is a great deal of evidence to suggest that the present system simply is not producing the results we expect of it. The goal in education, after all, is not efficiency *per se,* and certainly it is not administrative efficiency. The goal of education, as we see it, is the enhancement of the human capacity to act. Education which remains in the classroom, like research which remains in the laboratory, is academic in the worst sense. It seems that if educators are to perform as professionals, they are going to have to begin to act, in spite of the many pressures to play it safe, in spite of trepidations, in spite of incomplete data about which directions are best to follow. The world is always in motion, and data will always be incomplete. If we can only accept the ambiguous nature of the world about us, perhaps we can move toward the goals we seek using a variety of educational methods which seem meritorious without hoping or claiming that any one alone will be a panacea.

We should like to detail several educational alternatives which we feel might serve constructively in reaching suburban school children in ways which our present system evidently does not. The first item is that of *performance criteria* and their possible use in schools, urban as well as suburban. Many suburban high schools point with pride to the high percentage of students who graduate, yet it is no secret that many of these graduates receive their diplomas for little more than constant attendance—putting in time, as it were. Equally evident is that many of the brighter students are bored beyond compare by their high school experience, a fact which has been legitimized as "senioritis" though it involves more than having reached the light at the end of the tunnel. One wonders how obvious many bright students would be about their dissatisfaction if they did not have to depend on teachers and principals for letters of recommendation to college admissions offices. Surely there must be a viable alternative to the present system of dealing with students on the crude basis of time spent and grades achieved.

The alternative of asking students to meet performance criteria does several things: it immediately individualizes the students' learning, since no penalty is attached to learning slowly, or rapidly for that matter. Grade levels, as such, become useless rubrics, since the goal is to master a specific body of information and skills, not merely to demonstrate one's ability to report for duty day after day.

By focusing on a clearly delineated area of competence, teachers are freed to deal with the particular learning situations and problems of individual students, rather than feeling, as many do now, that they have to ignore the "trouble makers" (who are usually students with severe learning problems, or are bright ones who are bored with the tedious goings-on), for the sake of keeping the class group together on its slow but steady course toward a group final examination. By setting performance criteria for students, we encourage brighter students to accomplish as much as they care to, while allowing slower students to learn at their own pace without making them feel like failures. The goal, after all, is to learn the material, not to get into third grade. In the present arrangement, if a student has not learned to spell "cat" in second grade, there is also a good chance that he will not learn to do so in the third, yet all the pressures conspire toward placing him in that class for fear of making him into an outcast and a failure so early in his school career. Why not simply forget about putting him in third grade, and teach him how to spell? The object of sending Johnny to school is to educate him, isn't it, and not merely to see him rise through the ranks as ignorant as the next student?

An additional virtue of using performance criteria rather than mere time and grade scales is the amount of freedom it offers both student and teacher in exploring aspects of their interest and curiosity which are not designed as part of the criteria to be met. If Johnny meets his spelling criteria in the fifth week of school, he is now free to learn what he wants to, and his teacher is free to encourage him to do so, rather than having to worry about how to keep his attention while other students are still trying to learn their spelling. In fact, with the advent of educational technology, machines can be used to teach the learning skills which require repetition and slow incremental learning, freeing teachers to deal with genuine student interest. Wouldn't it be a pleasant change to have the students competing for the teacher's attention? There is, of course, no guarantee that performance criteria would be in any way an improvement over our present time and grade system, but there is enough logic in such a method to suggest that we at least ought to offer it as one alternative to the present system whose limitations are already painfully clear.

Another educational alternative which we think bears attention is that of *differentiated staffing*. Rather than requiring all teachers, whatever their particular talents and limitations, to perform the same curricular tricks like so many trained dogs on a TV variety show, perhaps we can make better use of their strongest talents and minimize their weaknesses by requiring them to do primarily what they do best and probably enjoy doing most. If there is a first grade teacher who is excellent at large group presentations, but much less effective at the give and take of small group or individual instruction, can we not use her skill better by asking her to spend the bulk of her time preparing large group presentations which will be given to a number of student groups within a given school? We could then use other teachers whose strongest teaching occurs in small groups to act as small group facilitators. The only flaw which we can see in organizing school personnel in this manner is its marked difference from present practice. And that, sad to say, may prove to be a fatal flaw, and a peculiarly ironic one in a society where living styles are so diverse and where there is so little sense of tradition to begin with. Nevertheless, we submit that the task of education, and certainly the task of professional educators, is not solely to re-create the past but also to create the future. Surely, imagination and determination are valuable qualities in the educational process. Why can we not see more demonstration of them by educators?

In a suburban area, where there is generally little sense of social cohesion, there may be great opportunities for the development of *community schools* (see Chapter Nine). These schools, which might range from storefront operations in urban areas at which parents teach their children and each other to the hemispherical building in Berea, Kentucky, where elementary and high school students have classes side by side, would seem to hold considerable potential in a suburban context. Instead of continuing to assume that schools are for "The Education of the Young," which makes it all sound vaguely like torture, why not affirm the economic and legal facts that local citizens pay for their school systems and serve on the school boards which manage them. Surely, there is no reason in a situation like this why the schools cannot be designed to serve everyone in the community.

The benefits of developing community schools in suburban areas might be considerable. First of all, a community school would be open to all members of the community at all times. With that as a ground rule, one can imagine much more interest in education on the part of adults. Housewives might not only bring their toddlers to kindergarten, but might also stay in school for a while and thus become involved in the educational process. It is only a human process, after all, not some kind of mumbo jumbo. Housewives have a right to observe it at their leisure. Evenings might be used to hold various classes and seminars, not simply for adults—adults have no monopoly on the hours after 6 P.M.—but also for any persons in the community who were interested. In this way, adults and younger people might find in the school a common meeting ground where their issues and concerns could be discussed frankly and at length, a situation not often otherwise available.

In addition to bringing the community into the school, we might also think of sending the school out into the community, hopefully arriving at a state where neither place is sensed special or beyond the pale. Although we never allow our children to hear such heresy, it is widely recognized that they can often learn valuable lessons when they are not in school (see Chapter Fourteen). For brighter students who seem to be bored and confined, and for slower students who seem to have lost all interest and hope, the school could perform a positive service by acting as a broker in experiences. If several brighter students indicate a desire to study contemporary values, why not give them some audiovisual equipment and send them out into the community they live in? If slower students are intrigued by the work of doctors or policemen, the school should be able to place these students in squad cars or in certain areas of a hospital. A school in Cambridge, Massachusetts, has already had considerable success acting in just such a fashion. The school is a private, boot strap operation, and its clientele are high school dropouts from the Cambridge area, dropouts who number some 20 percent of the total high school population. It is interesting to observe as an aside that Cambridge in some ways is probably the most education-oriented community in the nation.

Part of the reason for the truly alarming dropout rates in Cambridge and elsewhere in suburban America is the essential irrelevance of most high school curricula. Our four-unit curricular model of English, social studies, science, and math is based on Greek and Latin models with few deletions and few additions. While we have attempted to bring the subjects themselves up to date, we have seldom seriously questioned their integrity as constructs of knowledge. However, at a time when so much communication occurs beyond the printed page, it seems more than a bit precocious to regard literacy in the media as a frill; at a time when pollution is a major threat to our health it seems a bit shortsighted to be still dissecting frogs and worms instead of relating them ecologically to their natural environments; at a time when people seem to be starving for personal contact with each other, it seems cruel and foolish not to regard students' emotional lives as a legitimate area of education and development; and at a time when so many of our sensory and psychological responses are programmed into us by the media, government, and industry, it would seem that a sensible investment in our national culture might be a systematic and serious program of education in aesthetics. Thus, instead of constantly tinkering with the curricular disciplines which we have inherited, we may find a viable educational alternative in the creation of entirely new curricular models.

One such new curriculum would embrace a four- or five-unit structure, and might be called a liberal or humane science curriculum. It would entail study in the following areas: communications, human relations, aesthetics, technology, and ecology. The major difference between these curricular categories and those of our classical models is that the skills taught in the earlier models—reading, arithmetic, a knowledge of history, and science—would not be put to use in an attempt to understand systematically the nature of the world into which we are bringing our children. Surely this is a legitimate function of education. Why then can we not legitimize it? Again, the objection will be raised, "But how will we evaluate students in these new classes if we have no bases of comparison?" Again, we can only reply that the point of education is not merely to evaluate students but to make certain that they learn as much as they care to. And there is every evidence that students today are more than a little interested in the world around them.

Another alternative strategy which might work particularly well in a suburban environment is the removal of the senior high school year as a requirement in its present form. Most seniors, particularly those who will be going on to college, spend the year frivolously anyway, while those who have no hopes of a college education are usually marking time until they receive their booby prize, the high school diploma. By not requiring attendance in standard classes in this last year, perhaps we can open the year up to a variety of educational experiences which would be of greater significance to the students at this stage of their development. There is also the considerable financial benefit of eliminating one year of classes: the pressure for new classrooms would be eased and, while teachers of former senior classes would not be dismissed, they would be used to augment programs at lower levels, in addition to working on independent study projects with seniors who were so inclined.

A number of useful things could be attempted in this last year. Students could be encouraged, and certainly allowed, to travel around the United States. Perhaps more than ever, in an encapsulated society, travel is the most liberal, most liberating type of education. Students could be encouraged to sample a variety of careers which had interested from afar; these experiences could be arranged for by the schools, as they are, for example, at Antioch College, and could be treated as the raw experience for later seminars and discussion groups, or they could be sought out individually by the students themselves. Students who were interested in a particular art or craft could spend the year profitably by working in their chosen discipline. Those students who were interested in education could be used to tutor students at earlier levels of development and could, in fact, be considered as part of the instructional staff of the school system.

Another major possibility which could be developed during a more flexibly organized senior year is that of creating intergenerational seminars in which students, teachers, and adults in the community would participate. Experimental seminars of this kind have been conducted in Dallas, Chicago, and at Exeter Academy in New Hampshire with considerable success. Parents who all but despaired of ever reaching their children, and children who despaired equally of communicating with their parents, found that, given a larger context than the family dinner table, long, frank, and fruitful dialogue was not only possible but also rewarding. Seminars such as these, on topics of mutual interest to participants, on topics in fact selected by participants, could be run for a semester or a full year, and could be instrumental in drawing parents and students together in their own home communities. The spill-over effects of such an endeavor might be considerable. Not only would such dialogue serve to educate the students, by requiring them to do their homework if their arguments were to hold up in open discussion, but also they might have the effect of liberating adults from many of their superficial, media-produced notions about young people and about education in general. One very likely result of successful intergenerational seminars might be a re-infusion of informed adult interest in the entire educational process. And, at a time when many taxpayers are voting down school bond issues with amazing consistency, such a renewal of interest would be a welcome by-product.

There are many ways in which we could improve the education of suburban communities. Rather than spending our professional meetings endlessly debating which one plan is best, we hope that we can begin to experiment with a number of alternative strategies. There is, of course, a calculated risk involved in such an approach to educational renovation, as there is no guarantee in advance that any given program will produce the expected results. But surely it is obvious by now that the functionally monolithic structure in which we are presently confined is simply not working for far too many students and teachers. We need to seek and gain the mandate to have the right to be wrong.

We think that the pressure of events has thrown down a clear challenge, and perhaps a rare opportunity, to those of us who are in any way involved in education. We are no longer going to be able to skirt the growing crises in our schools with annual conferences and limited research projects. The time has come for us to exercise all the leadership of which we are capable. Many may be concerned, and quite legitimately, with the matter of evaluating such experimental programs as have been suggested here and elsewhere. We suggest that there exists a great, untapped evaluative resource for our determinations about the relative success of large new programs: the students and faculty who will be directly involved in them. We see no reason why, in a democratic society, we cannot make legitimate use of democratic procedures in the education of our children.

eleven

Schools and a New Model for Racial Integration

Racial integration in schools has been and is likely to be a major educational controversy for a number of years. It is significant to recall that the original Supreme Court decision in *Brown* v. *Board of Education* cited research findings by Kenneth Clark as partial support for the ruling. Clark's research in social psychology dealt with the effect of segregation on the self-image of black students. Thus, the decision propounded a new educational model, grounded partially on research and partially on public policy needs. Predictably, efforts to implement that model have provoked further research, controversy, refinement of the original model, and the proffering of counter models by diverse interests and disciplines.

Since the court decision, new research methodologies have evolved and new data have become available. For example, we have seen the continuing refinement of the techniques of survey research and the collection of data from the Coleman Survey of *Equality of Educational Opportunity*. Concurrently, additional researchers have been attracted to this sensitive and significant policy issue. Thomas Pettigrew is such a researcher. He was a social psychologist residing in Arkansas at the time of the Little Rock school desegregation controversy in 1957. He studied the reactions of the black students participating in this episode and has since devoted considerable time to analyses of the effects of racial segregation and integration in schools.

In this chapter Pettigrew employs Coleman Report findings and similar research to support the proposition that properly structured school integration can be important in improving the school performance of black students. He then proceeds to suggest how such integration may be achieved in typical metropolitan areas.

The chapter serves a twofold purpose. First, it is an excellent summary and analysis of research in this critical area. Second, it is an example of the use of survey research data as a tool for policy development. Regardless of whether one accepts Pettigrew's conclusions, it is informative to see how systematic analysis of empirical data may permit researchers to induce the causes, or as they prefer to say, "the explanations," of differences in educational achievement among students. Undoubtedly, such techniques will grow in use and sophistication among educational researchers, particularly as more and more school output data become available. Therefore, Pettigrew offers us a model not only about education and racial desegregation, but also a model on how to approach school policy debates in general.

A RETURN TO THE COMMON SCHOOL: STUDENT COMPOSITION, ACHIEVEMENT, AND THE METROPOLITAN EDUCATIONAL PARK

Thomas F. Pettigrew

Contractual education services, "compensatory education," "community schools," "tutorial schools," "volunteer schools," metropolitan educational parks—all these models and more afford ample evidence to the effect that there is no dearth of ideas for the future education of America's children. This array of proposals has arisen because public schools in their present forms do not appear to be meeting national aspirations, not just in the central city but in the suburbs and rural areas as well.

Discussion of these various models often suffers from the suggestion that there is *only* one model for all of public education. Stated this way, of course, the assumption appears absurd; the problems and circumstances of public education in this large nation are too varied to be answered by a single approach. Indeed, even for a single, medium-sized school district, a judicious, well-planned mix of models would be needed in order to provide "the best fit" for its problems and situation. The correct mix of models undoubtedly will vary from area to area. However, little discussion has yet been directed to this critical planning issue to date. Proponents typically are too busy "selling" their particular model wares to initiate such overall thinking. The present interesting focus on "new models for American education" serves the valuable function of laying out contrasting approaches side by side. Hopefully, this task will prove to be a step toward the more systematic and less polemical approach of mixed models.

As part of such a systematic approach, this chapter will first discuss current research on the impact of diverse mixes of students on schools' educational effect. After that we will focus upon the operational implications of this research, emphasizing particularly the concept of *metropolitan educational parks.* Before beginning, however, I must realistically admit that there are many contemporary currents of opinion, ranging from black separatism to white indifference, which are hostile to the proposals I will raise. Nevertheless, if my position is supported by valid research, then these currents themselves will be running against the tide of facts and will be dissipated if we move toward achieving a whole and healthy America. So let us see what the record shows.

THE EMPIRICAL CASE FOR HETEROGENEOUS SCHOOLING

It is my opinion that competent research on race and desegregation is rare. Even authors of satisfactory studies frequently admit that they are not conclusive guides to policy makers and that continuous refinement is needed and (hopefully) foreseeable. However, while refinement is proceeding, children are still attending schools where they are not learning effectively. I believe that two recent federal studies, *Equality of Educational Opportunity* (the "Coleman Report"), and *Racial Isolation in the Public Schools,* issued by the U.S. Commission on Civil Rights, together with other related research, can provide us with an empirically based perspective for considering the critical policy issue of student mix. As we discuss these materials, readers without experience in considering statistical studies may find the first few pages a little heavy. However, I have attempted to keep the presentation aimed at the intelligent, concerned layman. The matter may be complicated, but if the policies I propose are controversial, the facts must be carefully scrutinized.

THE EFFECT OF SOCIAL CLASS

No short summary of James Coleman's volume, *Equality of Educational Opportunity,* can do justice to this massive and complex work.[1] However, the report, and other research, justify a few generalizations regarding Negro academic achievement in elementary and secondary schools. The generalizations will help us to identify the factors associated with better learning.

In the Coleman data, two items of information that were consistently correlated with student performance on achievement tests were: "home background of the child" and "student body quality of the school." Though each of these factors is measured in the report by a number of indicators, both basically involve social class differences between students' families. These differences are most effectively represented by two separate measures related to parents' education. "Home background" of each student can be measured by the average length of the parents' education; and "student body quality" can be rated by a number represent-

1 James S. Coleman, *et al., Equality of Educational Opportunity* (Washington, D. C.: U. S. Government Printing Office, 1966), pp. 3-7.

ing the average education of parents of all of the students in a particular school. Measured in this way, it is perhaps more accurate to speak of these factors as *individual social class* and *school social class.*

The individual social class factor is often said to be *the* principal correlate of achievement in the Coleman study; in other words, the most important piece of data for predicting a student's achievement score is his home background. However, the effectiveness of this predictor varies under different circumstances. For instance, individual social class proved a more important predictor of test scores for white than Negro children.[2] It proved of diminishing importance for all students as a predictor from the sixth to the twelfth grades.[3] (This decrease is consistent with considerable research on adolescents in American society that has shown the influence of family on student conduct recedes as the influence of student peers increases.) Consequently, the *school* social class factor, that is, the student mix, becomes particularly powerful in secondary education; and it is a far more important correlate of Negro than white achievement.

These trends can be elaborated upon by further analysis of Coleman Report data. For instance, the technique of regression analysis permits us to use the potential of the computer and classify each student in the data bank on the basis of two combined factors, his own individual social class plus the social class of his school. We then can attempt to determine what correlations, if any, exist between scores of students of the same age from equivalent home backgrounds in diverse sorts of school environments.

We find that the average verbal achievement levels for groups of Negro twelfth grade students range from slightly below an eighth grade level for low status students in lower status schools to almost an eleventh grade level for high status students in higher status schools. This is a decisive performance difference of three full grades.[4] School social class is thus an important predictor; moreover, it is a factor that may be changed by altering school policies, that is, revising boundary lines. Conversely, schools cannot affect individual social class. Therefore, *school social class* is the most important "school characteristic" we have found that is related to student achievement scores, white as well as Negro.

The Effect of Nonclass Factors on Achievement. The Coleman study also examined, by the use of regression analysis, a number of other identifiable school characteristics in order to see if differing patterns in these

[2] Coleman, *et al., Equality of Educational Opportunity,* p. 300. Replicated by Alan B. Wilson in his work in Richmond, California; see U. S. Commission on Civil Rights, *Racial Isolation in the Public Schools,* Vol. II (Washington, D. C.: U. S. Government Printing Office, 1967), pp. 172-74.

[3] Coleman, *et al., Equality of Educational Opportunity,* p. 300.

[4] *Ibid.,* p. 85.

variables produced variations in student achievement. These other variables covered differences in (1) teacher ability and (2) school facilities and programs. Teacher ability variables, ranging from the individual teacher's years of teaching experience to years of formal education and vocabulary test score of the teacher, proved to be the more important of the two in their connection with achievement. Similar to school social class, the teacher ability factor is a stronger correlate of Negro than white student verbal achievement scores. Also it is much more powerful in the secondary than elementary years.[5]

By contrast, the factor of school facilities and programs does not relate highly to pupil performance. Once individual social class is controlled, for example, per pupil instructional expenditure in grades six, nine, and twelve is not significantly associated with achievement test scores, except in one notable case of marked extremes—Negro children in the South.[6] Nor do such school facilities or program variables as pupil-teacher ratio, library volumes, laboratories, number of extracurricular activities, comprehensiveness of the curruculum, strictness of pupil promotion, ability grouping, and school size reveal any important relationships with achievement.[7] These essentially negative findings concerning the influence of school facilities and programs have received great attention. They have apparently threatened many educators who ponder what chances for success their next school bond referendum or salary increase proposal will have. Much of this concern, however, may be caused by a misinterpretation of these results. The chief finding is that school social class is such a critical achievement correlate that, in a gross survey approach such as applied by Coleman, it simply overwhelms the smaller effects of other school factors.

Moreover, Coleman's findings do *not* mean that school facilities and programs must remain unimportant. What they do signify is that the diversity of facilities and programs now in public schools is not sufficiently great to explain, that is, cause, wide differences in student performance. Consider the variable of pupil-teacher ratio. Most American classrooms range between twenty and forty students per teacher; and teachers are typically not trained to exploit the advantages to instruction of smaller classes. With such limited diversity, Coleman could not illustrate a consistent relationship between pupil-teacher ratio and pupil achievement scores. Yet one can still reasonably argue that it makes a major difference whether one is teaching 5 or 500 students, especially with teachers who adapt their styles to small groups of children. But Coleman could not test this proposition, since actual pupil-teacher ratios of 5 and 500 are virtually nonexistent. In short, Coleman could only

[5] *Ibid.,* pp. 316-17.
[6] *Ibid.,* pp. 312-13.
[7] *Ibid.,* pp. 312-16.

test the effects of facility or program variables in present-day schools. Just where, below twenty and above forty pupils-per-teacher, the instructional ratio variable becomes crucial for student performance, must await better trained teachers, and more studies of genuinely varied, experimental school programs.

One final set of variables analyzed by Coleman, however, did correlate highly with verbal achievement. A factor called "student attitudes" included questions measuring the student's interest in school and reading, academic self-concept, and a sense of control of the environment.[8] Each student's responses to such objective questions were fed into the computer. Regression analyses compared these responses with the student's achievement scores and his expected achievement performance as predicted by his social class and other factors. Student attitude variables were important correlates of performance for all groups of children at all three of the grade levels tested (sixth, ninth, and twelfth grades). Yet different attitude variables predicted white and Negro achievement. The academic self-concept variable, measured by responses to such items as "how bright do you think you are in comparison with the other students in your grade?" proves far more significant for white achievement. But the control of the environment variable, measured, for example, by responses to items such as "is good luck more important than hard work for success?" is much more significant for Negro achievement.

Clearly, these attitude-achievement findings are significant because they tap an attitudinal process involving a two-way causal pattern. Negro children with a sense of environmental control do better in their school achievement, and those who do well in school achievement begin to gain a sense of environmental control. Nevertheless, it is tempting to speculate, as did Coleman, that each child faces a two-stage problem. First, he must learn that one can, within reasonably broad limits, act effectively upon his surroundings. Second, he must then have a good opinion of his own relative capabilities for mastering the environment. The critical stage for white children seems to be the second stage concerning the self-concept, while the critical stage for Negro children seems realistically enough to involve the possibility of manipulating an often harsh and overpowering environment. In any event, more detailed experimental work seems justified in order to pursue Coleman's fascinating speculation:

> Having experienced an unresponsive environment, the virtues of hard work, or diligent and extended effort toward achievement appear to such a [minority] child unlikely to be rewarding. As a consequence, he is likely to merely "adjust" to his environment, finding satisfaction in passive pursuits. It may well be, then, that one of the keys toward success for minorities

[8] *Ibid.*, pp. 319-25.

which have experienced disadvantage and a particularly unresponsive environment—either in the home or the larger society—is a change in this conception.[9]

The Coleman Report's conclusions should, of course, be interpreted within the context of the data on which they are based. The Report is the target of considerable criticism, and it will be the subject of more in the future. In truth, the analysis and writing were necessarily performed in great haste; there exist major methodological problems, ranging from a relatively large rate of school system nonresponse to questionnaires, to special issues involved with a massive regression analysis of the data. Thus, a number of the Report's interpretations are open to strong challenge.

Yet all this careful scrutiny is, in its own way, a high tribute to this ambitious study. The Coleman group achieved a landmark accomplishment in an amazingly short span of time; and the Report and its data will influence American education for years to come. This is as it should be, for the Report's major conclusions will almost surely survive reanalysis and criticism.

Other Studies of Factors Affecting Achievement. Coleman's two chief conclusions, namely, the crucial importance of both individual social class and school social class as correlates of Negro and white achievement, are vital elements in any policy analysis. They suggest that varying the student mix may be an essential part of a performance improvement plan. The soundness of these key conclusions is attested to by two lines of supporting evidence. First, the U.S. Commission on Civil Rights' report, *Racial Isolation in the Public Schools,* includes an extensive reanalysis of Coleman Report data. Using more detailed contingency analyses on Coleman's metropolitan Northeast subsample, the Commission confirmed those findings of Coleman's which had originally been based on a regression analysis of the entire national sample.

Second, the central findings are substantiated by at least four detailed, though less extensive, educational studies that employed methods and samples different from those of Coleman's survey. Three of these studies antedated Coleman's emphasis upon school social class. In a study published in 1959, Alan B. Wilson demonstrates the special significance of the school social class factor in determining student college aspirations in eight high schools in the San Francisco Bay Area of California.[10] He found higher percentages of college aspirants in higher status schools, even after controlling for other determinants of college aspirations, father's occupation and education, mother's education, median academic grade,

[9] *Ibid.,* p. 321.

[10] Alan B. Wilson, "Residential Segregation of Social Classes and Aspirations of High School Boys," *American Sociological Review,* Vol. 24 (1959), 836-45.

and intelligence test score. For example, among those boys whose fathers and mothers were high school graduates and whose fathers held manual occupations, 60 percent in upper status schools wanted to go to college. This compares with 54 percent in the medium status schools and only 32 percent in the working status schools. Likewise, among those boys with a modest "C" academic grade record, 72 percent from upper status schools aspired to college. In contrast, only 55 percent from medium status schools and 41 percent in working status schools held such an aspiration. Finally, for those in the 100 to 119 IQ test range, for instance, 93 percent in the upper status schools, 72 per cent in the medium status schools, and 51 percent in the working status schools aimed for college.

A second early study on the problem was mounted by a research team at Harvard University. This study differed somewhat, however, in that it substituted social class level of the school's community for a direct measure of social class levels of the schools' students.[11] Controlling for father's occupation, boys from higher status communities were found to be more likely to go to college. In addition, community status, which determined the status level of the schools, had its crucial impact only at the high school level, the level Wilson studied. Consequently, community status predicted neither performance in primary school grades nor entrance into the college preparatory courses in high school from junior high school. This finding parallels the Coleman result that school social class gained in predictive value in the secondary school grades.

The most definitive early study was conducted by John Michael.[12] He analyzed the aptitude test scores and career and college plans of 35,436 seniors in a nationally representative sample of 518 American public high schools. Together with the student's scores on a scholastic aptitude test, not unlike that used by Coleman, Michael classified students on an index of family social class using such information as the father's occupation and education and whether or not older siblings had attended college. Further, he classified high schools into five status ranks according to percentage of seniors in each school who fell into his two top family status classifications, a method similar to the school social class measure of Coleman.

The first finding revealed that, with family status controlled, the higher the status of the school, the higher the average score on the scholastic aptitude test. Further analysis revealed that variation in percentages of students scoring above the national average on the test was evenly attributable to the individual and school social class indices.

[11] S. Cleveland, "A Tardy Look at Stouffer's Findings in the Harvard Mobility Project," *Public Opinion Quarterly,* Vol. 26 (1962), 453-54.

[12] J. A. Michael, "High School Climates and Plans for Entering College," *Public Opinion Quarterly,* Vol. 25 (1961), 585-95.

However, the variation in percentages scoring in the top quarter was considerably more related to individual social class than school social class. This is a result directly in keeping with Coleman's finding that school social class is most important for the more deprived students. It is also consistent with the Civil Rights Commission's finding that, among whites in the metropolitan Northeast, school social class was least important for the highest status students.[13]

Turning to student plans to attend college, Michael, as with Wilson and the Harvard investigations, demonstrated that school social class makes a difference. Michael's analysis revealed that these effects are strongest for students from lower individual class backgrounds. Consider first those seniors from lower class backgrounds who score in the top quarter of the aptitude test distribution. Among these talented youngsters, only 44 percent who attended the lowest status high schools planned to go to college compared with 57 percent who attended the highest status high schools. By contrast, among the talented seniors from the highest individual social class group, 80 percent who attended the lowest status high schools planned to go to college compared with 86 percent who attended the highest status high schools. In other words, a high status school exerts a far greater influence on college plans among talented lower status than talented higher status children.

Much the same phenomenon is true for Michael's entire sample. The percentage difference in college plans between individual social class groups is essentially the same at each type of school; but the percentage differences in college plans between scholastic aptitude test levels is far higher in the high status than the low status high schools. Put simply, attendance at a low status school does not deter seniors from upper status families in planning for college, but attendance at a high status school is an important aid to able seniors from lower status families.

All three of these earlier studies, then, demonstrate the significant consequences of attending high schools of varying social class compositions. Yet, as James Coleman himself states,[14] these initial studies did not differentiate between the effects of school social class per se on pupil performance, or the effects of some variable or combination of variables which are strongly related to school social class (for example, school facilities), which Michael demonstrated did co-vary with school social class. It remained, then, for Coleman himself to answer his own query; for the Coleman Report was able to provide the relevant controls and demonstrate that these effects were indeed associated with school social class per se even after other relevant types of factors are separated out.

In addition, these three earlier investigations suffer from the inter-

[13] U. S. Commission on Civil Rights, Vol. 1, 85.

[14] James S. Coleman, "Comment on Three 'Climate of Opinion' Studies," *Public Opinion Quarterly,* Vol. 25 (1961), 607-10.

related methodological weaknesses which limit the Coleman survey. The results are neither longitudinal nor corrected for initial pupil achievement and aspirations upon entering school in the primary grades. In other words, the studies (1) measured pupil improvement by comparing the test scores of lower grade students against the concurrent scores of other upper grade students in the same school (to see the amount or rate of pupil improvement) rather than testing the same pupil twice, several years apart, to see *his own* amount or rate of change. And (2) these studies did not permit testers to measure whether or not the pupils studied had different levels of skills and aspirations when they began school, which might have come from the efforts of upper status families to place their children in more effective schools. These weaknesses open the studies to the possibility that their findings result from special selection biases.

A number of Coleman Report critics have challenged the social class climate finding on precisely these grounds. They apparently choose to ignore the Civil Rights Commission's study replicating the Coleman result.[15] Wilson, in a follow-up to his earlier research, studied the school social class variable with a probability sample of junior and senior high school children in Richmond, California. He had the advantage of both longitudinal data and initial test scores upon entering school, thus overcoming the critics' objection. Wilson found that the social class context of the elementary school had a strong effect upon subsequent academic success at high grade levels, even after "allowing for individual differences in personal background, neighborhood context, and mental maturity at the time of school entry." [16] Thus, three earlier investigations and a later, well-controlled study by Wilson, closely agree with the major conclusions of the Coleman Report concerning the preeminent importance of a school's social class climate.

To sum up, the Coleman study is a broad-gauged survey of what exists now in American public schools. It could neither detail precisely how children learn nor test what American public schools could become in the future. The Coleman Report outlined the gross facts of American education today; the precision of the specific experiment is now needed to detail the processes that go unseen by the survey.

Some Research Policy Implications. Hopefully, the direction of future educational research will be strongly influenced by this study. The Coleman Report sets the context within which more limited data must be interpreted; and it provides a rich variety of exciting leads with obvious policy implications. In order to minimize the operation of indi-

[15] Alan B. Wilson, "Educational Consequences of Segregation in a California Community," in U. S. Commission on Civil Rights, *Racial Isolation in the Public Schools,* Vol. II, 165-206.

[16] *Ibid.,* p. 202.

vidual social class factors, for example, would boarding schools be an effective intervention for especially deprived youngsters in the early grades? Are there *any* truly effective public schools which are overwhelmingly attended by lower status children? If there are, by what means do such schools overcome the typically powerful effect of school social class? In other words, what works? If such schools do not exist, what methods not currently being tried might enable such schools to affect such pupils? What precisely is the process underlying the linkage between a Negro child's sense of environmental control and his achievement scores? How might this sense of control of the environment be imparted to the school? These and scores of other questions spring to mind from a careful consideration of the Coleman Report. Systematic funding, both public and private, of pertinent research is needed in order to make possible an attack upon these vital questions.

IS THERE A RACIAL COMPOSITION APART FROM SOCIAL CLASS EFFECTS?

Once we recognize the importance of the student social class mix on individual achievement performance, a question arises as to whether or not the effect on achievement of mixing races (desegregation) is attributable more to changing social class mix than to changing racial mix. In other words, what is the most appropriate explanation for the achievement benefits we often find associated with interracial schooling—the change in social class, when lower socioeconomic status Negro students mix with higher socioeconomic status whites, or simply the interracial mix itself, even where status of both groups of pupils is constant?

A discussion of this somewhat complex issue can deliver two important benefits: (1) to illustrate in depth the operation of many of the special problems that plague race and education research; (2) to help us better understand how desegregation affects both Negro and white children. Is its impact perhaps due entirely to the changing of the social class composition of schools via desegregation or to the concurrent change in the racial mix? This understanding of how desegregation achieves its effects is not critical for determining whether or not we want to improve Negro achievement via desegregated schools or merely through interclass schools. The relative "shortage" of middle class Negro families means that interclass schools can only be created by racial desegregation. However, such understanding will affect the kind of policies we explore and adopt to increase Negro achievement in desegregated schools. If the improvement from desegregation is actually a school social class effect, that limits our search for better policies to factors that should not be unique to interracial schools. If, however, improvement is also due to desegregation itself, regardless of social class, then our net must be cast more broadly in order to include racial considerations.

The Coleman Report provides only spotty and somewhat conflicting evidence on this focal issue; however, the Civil Rights Commission directed much of its Coleman data reanalysis to this relatively neglected question. Employing parents' education as the chief social class indicator, the Commission's study attempted to control for both individual and school social class while testing the relationship between racial composition of the classroom and Negro verbal achievement. This reanalysis uncovered relatively large and consistent achievement differences in favor of those twelfth grade Negro students in the metropolitan Northeast who came from "more than half" white classrooms.[17] For instance, among lower status Negro children in lower status high schools, those from "more than half" white classrooms scored at the eight-and-a half grade level compared to only a seventh grade level for those from "all-Negro" classrooms. At the other end of the scale, among higher status Negro pupils in high status schools, those from "more than half" white classrooms scored at the ten-and-a-half grade level in contrast to the ninth grade level of those from "all-Negro" classrooms.

In other words, these Commission findings, on the whole, maintain that the racial composition of the classroom is an important achievement factor. The Commission also recognized that other factors which typically co-vary with racial composition, such as school social class, are even more crucial for achievement than desegregation. However, for the moment, let us try to see how desegregation produces its beneficial effects. A number of explanations can be offered.

Do Predominantly White Schools Have Better Staffs, More Dollars? It could be maintained that, even in the metropolitan Northeast, predominantly Negro and predominantly white schools vary sharply in school quality, especially teacher quality, and that these distinctions are responsible for the improved scores in predominantly white institutions. This explanation could be challenged by the failure of the Coleman study to uncover sharp quality differences between "Negro" and "white" schools, for example, level of expenditures, amount of teacher training, in the metropolitan Northeast; but the Coleman finding can itself be seriously questioned.[18] In any event, controlling the analysis for school quality narrows slightly the performance differentials attributable to desegregation, but does not by any means exhaust them.[19]

Do More Able Negroes Get Into Predominantly White Schools? A second type of explanation involves sample selection biases, which are a typical difficulty besetting research in this area. One special form of

[17] U. S. Commission on Civil Rights, Vol. I, 90.
[18] *Ibid.*, p. 94.
[19] *Ibid.*, pp. 98-100.

biased selection explanation involves ability grouping, or "tracking." It can be argued that all the Commission found was that schools in the metropolitan Northeast do a reliable and accurate job of placing Negro students in "tracks." Given the social handicaps many Negro children bring to school, goes the explanation, only the very brightest do well; these gifted Negro children, who are apt students, eventually are assigned to high ability groups where most of their classmates are white. But less exceptional Negro students are assigned to low or medium ability groups where many or most of their classmates are other Negroes. Consequently, those Negroes with mostly white classmates score highest on academic achievement tests simply because only brighter Negroes are put into desegregated classes.

Another selection bias explanation concerns parental choice of community and school. One might maintain that, *within a given social class group,* more ambitious Negro parents will somehow manage to live in communities with interracial schools. Thus, what appears to be an advantage wrought by interracial schools is actually a result of the self-selection of highly motivated children of educationally minded Negro parents. A third possible selection bias explanation asserts that the likelihood is great that there are relatively more dropouts of poorly achieving Negro students from predominantly white schools. This is not viable here, because the Commission results can be replicated for the ninth grade which is before the vast majority of present-day dropouts take place.

These explanations suggest that the benefits of desegregation are really due to the types of Negroes that achieve desegregated environments, rather than to desegregation itself. The explanations based on selection bias receive some limited empirical support from the Wilson research conducted for the Commission and mentioned earlier.[20] He found that ". . . Negro students who attended integrated schools had higher mental maturity test scores in their primary grades, and came from homes better provided with educative materials." [21] Thus, when Wilson held constant the early elementary achievement of these students, he found that the school class effect remained, but that "the racial composition of schools, while tending to favor Negro students in integrated schools, does not have a substantial effect." [22]

Wilson's conclusion is limited, however, in a number of ways. For instance, among these 128 desegregated eighth graders, only eight of them (6 percent) were in lower status schools; but among the 777 segregated eighth graders, 378 of them (49 percent) were in lower status schools. In other words, there is not enough variance in school social

[20] *Ibid.,* pp. 100-101.
[21] *Ibid.,* p. 100.
[22] *Ibid.,* p. 101.

class among desegregated eighth graders for Wilson's statistical procedures to separate school social class and racial composition factors convincingly.

Since the Wilson study leaves open the question about the effects of desegregation upon the more disadvantaged Negro students, the Commission analyzed Coleman data to check the effects of interracial classrooms on the verbal scores of less gifted Negro ninth graders in the metropolitan Northeast.[23] These students had poorly educated parents and reported themselves to be in low or medium ability tracks. Both in high and low status high schools, these Negroes from predominantly white classrooms performed on the average from one-half to two-thirds of a grade better than comparable Negroes from predominantly Negro classrooms.

The selection bias that might arise from ability grouping implies that tracking may cause predominantly white *classrooms* to be associated with higher Negro scores; but it does not affect the finding that multiple tracked, predominantly white *schools* tend to relate to higher Negro performance, even in lower track classrooms. More importantly, the ability grouping does not typically begin in American public schools until the middle school grades and does not become nearly universal until the high school grades. Therefore, desegregation would appear to afford a better explanation for who gets into the high ability tracks than ability tracks do for desegregation effects. A Negro child of medium ability who begins his education in a desegregated school, for instance, has a far higher probability of being selected later for a high ability track than a Negro child of comparable ability going to a school of similar social status who began his education in an all-Negro school. Ability grouping, then, can serve as a magnifier of the differences already created by classroom differences in racial composition, a catalyst adding to the cumulative deficits of the segregated Negro.

The parental choice of community and school explanation is in some ways the reverse of the ability grouping explanation. It accounts for the fact that predominantly white *communities and schools* are associated with higher Negro achievement by suggesting that more effective Negro families move into such environments. However, it cannot account fully for the fact that the Commission found interracial *classrooms* also associated with higher Negro achievement, unless one is willing to assume that there is widespread selection by Negro parents of classrooms as well as communities and schools. There are other assumptions, too, that this particular line of reasoning must make, assumptions that are, at best, dubious. Since lower status, low ability Negro pupils also benefit from

[23] *Ibid.,* p. 101.

desegregation, these contentions require that poor Negro families possess a sophisticated knowledge of where to go to find the better interracial scools and the funds and freedom of mobility to move accordingly. All that is known about the extreme residential discrimination practiced against Negroes, especially poor Negroes, in American metropolitan areas today makes such assumptions most improbable.

Is the Improvement Really Due to School Social Effects? Two additional explanations argue that at least some of the apparent desegregation effects revealed by the Commission's reanalysis still reflect the operation of the powerful school social class effect. One chain of reasoning is based on the difficulty of controlling for social class across racial groups. This is so because the floor of Negro deprivation is below that of whites. For example, it can be maintained that "lower class" Negroes who attend a predominantly white school comprised largely of "lower class" whites are still benefiting from a higher social class student climate, than "lower class" Negroes who attend a predominantly Negro school comprised of "lower class" Negroes. While there is some merit in this reasoning, it should be remembered that the Commission's differences for twelfth graders by racial composition of classrooms (averaging about one and one-third grades, holding constant the social class variables of the Negroes and whites) were approximately 80 percent as large as those attributable to school social class directly (averaging about one and two-thirds grades holding the individual social class and racial composition variables constant).[24] Hence, it would seem that the small school class residual under discussion, that is, the difference between lower status Negroes and lower status whites, could account for only a small portion of the effects attributed to racial composition. Besides, the two factors, school social class and racial composition, prove most important as explanations at different grade levels. The racial composition of classrooms is most powerful for the achievement scores of children in the beginning grades, while school social class is most powerful in the high school grades.

The other social class explanation is limited but, perhaps, more subtle. It applies only to certain lower status Negro students who attend predominantly white, lower status schools. The majority of Negroes in such schools may well come from middle class Negro families. Even if the lower status Negro child is of fully equivalent status to his lower status white co-pupils, the main stimulant for his improved achievement may be his membership in a student minority comprised largely of middle class Negroes. This possibility is not as remote as it may sound; a larger percentage of middle class than lower class Negroes attend pre-

24 *Ibid.*, p. 90.

dominantly white schools, and the explanation only assumes that the middle class Negro minority in such schools will serve as a more positive reference group to lower class Negroes than the white majority. Though of limited scope, this explanation elegantly illustrates the subtleties and difficulties inherent in this type of research.

How Could Segregation Hurt Negroes? Still, none of those counter explanations, taken singly or together, eliminates the relatively large relationship found by the Commission between classroom racial composition and Negro achievement. If it is solely the effect of other co-varying factors, what could be the reasons for this association? How does segregation "hurt" Negro students? The process is undoubtedly complex, but a number of empirical clues are suggestive. For example, Coleman found that Negroes in interracial schools are somewhat more likely to feel they can control the environment, the attitude that proved such an important predictor of Negro scores. The Civil Rights Commission noted that (1) predominantly Negro schools often become stigmatized in the community as "bad schools" by Negroes and whites alike, even when at least the physical facilities are the equal of supposedly "good schools" for whites; and that (2) there are effective and ineffective interracial schools, and the differences between them point to the importance of interracial acceptance for high achievement and aspirations. A number of these considerations will be discussed in detail later in this chapter.

A practical educator might well wonder about the policy implications of this extended discussion about a racial composition effect on achievement separate from social class. For instance, does not the relatively small size of the Negro middle class make desegregation an educational imperative even if *all* of the benefits of interracial schooling for Negroes are a direct result of the school social class factor alone? For most practical purposes, the answer to this query is *yes.* There are, however, cases of predominantly Negro, high status schools with empty seats. Can one expect the same benefit for a lower status Negro child from attendance at such a school as he would receive from a predominantly white school of comparable status? The Commission report suggests that the child would receive much, *though not all,* of the benefits of racial desegregation.

While the foregoing discussion does not conclusively demonstrate the value of interracial (as opposed to intersocial class) schools, I believe that it does tentatively point to the operation of *both* social class and racial composition factors on Negro achievement. Since school operating decisions are being made every day which affect both these variables and will determine the quality of the education of the children concerned, it is incumbent on decision makers to take these factors into account. My tentative belief is further bolstered by the additional evidence presented in the following sections.

SIGNIFICANT DEFINITIONAL DISTINCTIONS CAN BE MADE BETWEEN "SEGREGATION," "DESEGREGATION," AND "INTEGRATION"

Coleman Report findings and Civil Rights Commission results suggest some empirically based definitional distinctions that might prove helpful in this semantically confused realm. To begin with, the legal distinctions between *de jure* and *de facto* segregation are of no practical importance for the consequences of racial isolation in the schools. The Commission's data speak to this issue directly; they suggest effects of de facto school segregation just as negative as those reported earlier for de jure school segregation. The legal distinction has little relevance for the Negro child in the all-Negro school.

Indeed, a realistic look at so-called de facto school segregation in cities today calls into question even the legal separation of the two forms of segregation. While de jure segregation has its roots in blatant state legislation, so-called "de facto" segregation generally has its roots in state action, too. Such state action may include anything from school board decisions to urban renewal plans and zoning ordinances. At some future time in American history, as Paul Freund has suggested, the judiciary will have to come to terms more clearly with the implications of the state action similarity of both de jure and de facto forms of school segregation.

Coleman Report and Commission data also have implications for the question of numbers and percentages which constitute "segregation" or "desegregation." This matter is of considerable importance, since the definition adopted will provide a conceptual framework for persons interested in advancing desegregation, the definition will describe the target towards which their policy should strive, and it will measure their success or failure. Two major alternative definitions have been proposed. One defines segregation and desegregation by pegging the definition to the nonwhite percentage of the area's overall school population. Thus, if 12 percent of a system's students are nonwhite, then ideally each desegregated school in the system would approach a nonwhite student composition of 12 percent. There are at least two possible criticisms of this approach. First, it is often impractical in all but reasonably small areas, and, second, it treats the individual school as a simple reflection of the community, rather than as an integral institution with its own dynamics and requirements.

A second definition attempted to meet these criticisms with a relatively fixed, rather than variable, gauge: on the basis of several social psychological considerations, the ideally desegregated school is one whose student body includes from roughly 20 to 40 percent nonwhites. The disadvantage here is that segregated schools could still result in systems with fewer than 20 or more than 40 percent nonwhite children.

The two federal studies suggest a more simple set of definitions. A segregated school is one whose student body is predominantly nonwhite; while a desegregated school is one whose student body is interracial, but predominantly white. Such definitions stem from the basic finding that the beneficial effects of interracial schools for the academic performance of Negro children are not linear; that is, Negro test scores do not rise evenly with increasing percentages of white children in the classroom. Rather, both analyses point to an achievement discontinuity which occurs past the midpoint, with the highest Negro verbal test scores reported from "more than half" white classrooms.[25] Indeed, enrollment in classes with "less than half" whites is associated with scores not significantly different from those of all-Negro classrooms.

This more simple definition receives further support from white test performance in interracial schools. As long as the class is predominantly white, white pupils' acihevement levels in interracial classrooms do not differ significantly from those of white pupils in all white classrooms.[26] But attendance in predominantly Negro classes is associated with lower white test scores. In other words, the same types of classes relate to higher scores for both Negro and white children; and these classrooms are predominantly white and may usefully be defined as "desegregated." Similarly, the same classes relate to lower scores for both Negro and white children; and these classrooms are predominantly Negro and may usefully be defined as "segregated."

IMPLICATIONS OF THE DEFINITIONS

The ideological difficulties of such definitions are apparent. As mentioned before, Negroes can rightfully argue that such definitions indicate that "white is right," that predominantly Negro schools cannot be "good schools." Commissioner Frankie Freeman of the Civil Rights Commission addressed herself specifically to this issue:

> The question is not whether in theory or in the abstract Negro schools can be as good as white schools. In a society free from prejudice in which Negroes were full and equal participants, the answer would clearly be "yes." But we are forced, rather, to ask the harder question, whether in our present society, where Negroes are a minority which has been discriminated against, Negro children can prepare themselves to participate effectively in society if they grow up and go to school in isolation from the majority group. We must also ask whether we can cure the disease of

25 *Ibid.*, p. 90; and Coleman, *et al.*, *Equality of Educational Opportunity*, p. 332.
26 U. S. Commission on Civil Rights, Vol. I, 160.

prejudice and prepare all children for life in a multiracial world if white children grow up and go to school in isolation from Negroes.[27]

The two federal reports also suggest that another useful distinction can and should be made between "desegregated," as opposed to "integrated," schools. Note that the definition of desegregation involved only a specification of the racial mix of students, namely, more than half whites. It does not include any description of the *quality* of the interracial contact. As we will see, merely desegregated schools can be either effective or ineffective; they can promote either genuine interracial acceptance or intense interracial hostility. In short, desegregation of a school can be but part of the process of improving pupil performance.

Recall that the Coleman Report revealed consistently larger standard deviations for the test scores of Negro children in desegregated (that is, "more than half" white) classrooms.[28] In other words, while the average scores of such Negro children were higher than those in segregated schools, an unusually large proportion of these children were achieving much higher than that average, and a similar proportion were far below (and perhaps might be better off in a "segregated" school). What accounts for these wide differences? The Commission's reanalysis of these Coleman data suggests that the explanatory intervening variable is *interracial acceptance* within the school. In desegregated schools where most teachers report no tension, Negro students evince higher verbal achievement, more definite college plans, and more positive attitudes than students in tense desegregated schools.[29] White students also evince benefits from the interracially harmonious school.

The term "integrated school," then, might usefully be reserved for the desegregated school where interracial acceptance is the norm. With these usages, "desegregation" becomes a prerequisite, but "integration" is an ultimate goal.

WHAT ARE OPTIMAL ENVIRONMENTS FOR RACIAL "INTEGRATION"?

The special efficacy of the desegregated school with interracial acceptance and low levels of tension is completely consistent with the growing body of experimental evidence on racially optimal performance environments. The basic work in this realm has been conducted by Irwin Katz.[30]

Katz first studied biracial task groups consisting of two Negro and

27 *Ibid.*, p. 214.

28 Coleman, *et al.*, *Equality of Educational Opportunity*, p. 333.

29 U. S. Commission on Civil Rights, Vol. I, 157-58.

30 I. Katz, "Review of Evidence Relating to Effects of Desegregation on the Performance of Negroes," *American Psychologist*, Vol. 19 (1964), 381-99.

two white students. In a variety of conditions, Negro subjects "displayed marked social inhibition and subordination to white partners." Negroes made fewer remarks than whites, tended to accept white contributions uncritically, ranked whites higher on intellectual performance even after equal racial ability has been displayed, and later expressed less satisfaction with the group experience than did whites. These complaint tendencies were modified only after a situation was presented which required Negro subjects openly to announce correct problem solutions to their white partners. That this procedure did work suggests the general technique for the interracial classroom of making sure that the Negro members have a public opportunity to display personal competence.

Katz also demonstrated performance effects of the biracial context on his white subjects. Accustomed to all-white situations, white subjects often failed to utilize the abilities of their Negro partners, even when they could expect a monetary bonus from the experimenter for good teamwork.

A second series of experiments by Katz reveals further effects of racial isolation by introducing threat into different racial environments. Thus, students at a predominantly Negro college in the South performed better on a digit-symbol substitution task under conditions of low stress when tested by a white stranger than under conditions of high stress when tested by a Negro stranger. Likewise, Negro students in another experiment scored higher on a digit-symbol code with a white tester, as long as they believed the code to be a research instrument for studying hand-eye coordination, a nonintellectual capacity. However, they did better with a Negro tester when they thought the code was an intelligence measure.

Katz has also isolated some effects on Negro Americans of anticipated comparisons with white Americans. Students at a Negro college in the South worked on easy and difficult versions of a digit-symbol task under three different instructions. One set of instructions described the task as not being a test at all, another set described it as a scholastic aptitude test with norms from the Negro college itself, and a third set described it as a scholastic aptitude test with national (that is, predominantly white) college norms. The Negro subjects performed best when they anticipated comparison with other Negroes, less well when they anticipated comparison with whites, and least well when no comparison at all was anticipated.

Another study again varied the anticipated comparison with whites or other Negroes, but at the same time varied conditions of white or Negro experimenter and different probabilities of success. The results of this experiment are consistent with those just cited. The Negro subjects performed best when tested by a white with a reasonable expectation (that is, 60 percent) of success and anticipation of comparison with Negro norms. They performed worst when tested by a white with a low expectation (that is, 10 percent) of success and anticipation of comparison with white norms.

Katz believes these findings are consistent with a four-factor model of Negro American performance in biracial situations. On the negative side of the ledger, he lists:

1. *Lowered probability of success.* Where there is marked discrepancy in the educational standards of Negro and white schools, or where Negro children have already acquired strong feelings of inferiority, they are likely to have a *low expectancy of academic success* when introduced into interracial classes. This expectancy is often realistic, considering the situation, but it has the effect of lowering achievement motivation. The practical implication of this factor is to avoid its operation by beginning interracial instruction in the earliest grades, an implication consistent with the Civil Rights Commission's finding that desegregation in the earliest grades generally has the most positive effect on the achievement of Negro children.

2. *Social threat* is involved in any biracial situation for Negro Americans; because of the prestige and dominance of whites in American society, rejection of Negro students by white classmates and teachers often elicits emotional responses that are detrimental to intellectual functioning. This Katz finding, too, is consistent with the Commission finding that Negro academic achievement is highest in integrated schools featuring cross-racial acceptance.

3. *Failure threat* arises when academic failure means extraordinary disapproval by significant people, parents, teachers, or peers at school. Low expectancy of success under failure threat may also elicit emotional responses detrimental to performance. But this need not always be the case. Sometimes, experiences in the interracial classroom act to dispel feelings of failure threat and group inferiority. When one of the nine Negro children, who, under the glare of world publicity, desegregated Central High School of Little Rock, Arkansas, in 1957, was asked what she had learned from her arduous experience, she exclaimed: "Now I know that there are some stupid white kids, too!" This insight into the white superiority myth could never have been acquired in an all-Negro high school.

Finally, on the positive side of the ledger, Katz notes that acceptance of Negroes by white classmates and teachers often has a *social facilitation* effect upon their ability to learn, apparently because it reassures Negro children that they are expected to be fully as talented in the classroom as anyone else. This anticipation, that skillful performance will win white approval rather than rejection for not "knowing your place," endows scholastic success with *high incentive* value. Katz believes this factor explains why his Negro subjects tend to perform better with white investigators on tasks which are free of severe threat.

A more recent Katz experiment adds another dimension.[31] Heretofore, he had employed primarily Negro college students for his subjects. But when he now uses as subjects truly isolated, grade school Negro boys from a New York City slum, the social facilitation factor previously evident with white testers disappears. In a verbal learning task, performance was superior with the Negro experimenter under all conditions of the study including the use of approval. This result suggests the original Katz model must be placed in a larger context of the past racial experience of the Negro subjects. It also emphasizes the need for early interracial experience.

Research such as Katz' offers educators both an opportunity and a challenge. His data suggest factors which might be found in an effectively integrated school and imply principles that should govern the planning and management of such schools. At the same time, they imply that effective integration is far more than the mixing of races, and that, in itself, is a difficult issue.

THE METROPOLITAN EDUCATIONAL PARK

Whether or not "common schools" of any variety will exist in the remote future, the first order of business is structural change of public education as it now exists. Is it possible to achieve effective racially and socioculturally balanced student bodies? Are there any "ultimate solutions" for our big city school systems? Is not integration really a nice but impossible notion? What about Washington, D.C., Harlem, South Side Chicago?

SMALL GHETTOS AND INTEGRATION

Initially, we must make a clear distinction between *small ghetto and big ghetto situations,* for what is possible and useful in the former may well be counter-productive in the latter. The small ghetto situation generally involves a city with less than one-seventh or so of its public school population Negro. Its high schools and often even its junior high schools are naturally desegregated, and with good faith it can correct its elementary school segregation *within* its borders. There are many such communities throughout the United States, and together they account

[31] I. Katz, T. Henchy, and H. Allen, "Effects of Race of Tester, Approval-Disapproval, and Need on Negro Children's Learning," *Journal of Personality and Social Psychology,* Vol. 8 (1968), 38-42.

for a surprisingly large minority of Negro children. They should not be confused with the Washingtons and Harlems, as apostles of segregationist doom are sometimes given to do.

The elementary schools in these small ghetto cities can usually be desegregated with a plan tailored to the system, utilizing an appropriate combination of the following within-district methods: (1) the districtwide redrawing of school lines to maximize racial balance (positive gerrymandering); (2) the pairing of predominantly white and Negro schools along the borders of the Negro ghetto (the Princeton plan); and (3) a priority for, and careful placement of, new and typically larger schools outside of the ghetto (the rebuilding plan). If there is a need to desegregate at only the junior or senior high levels, two other devices are often sufficient: (4) the alteration of "feeder" arrangements from elementary grades to junior highs and from junior highs to senior highs in order to maximize racial balance (the balanced feeder plan); and (5) the conversion of more schools into districtwide specialized institutions (the specialized school plan). Controversy is typically minimal because the small ghetto situation can usually be accommodated without widespread subsidized transportation of students (busing).

BIG GHETTOS AND INTEGRATION

The real problems of implementation occur for the big ghetto situation. The small ghetto devices discussed are generally mere Band-aid remedies in a city system with a substantial and growing percentage of Negro students. Thus, pairing schools along the ghetto's borders would have to be repeated every few years as the ghetto expanded. Or a new school built outside of the ghetto last year may become a nearly all-Negro school within the ghetto next year. Even in Boston, with only 26 percent nonwhites in its public school system, a sophisticated redistricting plan for elementary schools would have only minor effect. In a computer-simulated analysis, the ultimate limit of redistricting in Boston was tested with the rules that children in grades one through three would not be assigned more than one-half mile from their homes, and children in grades four through six not more than three-quarters of a mile. Under these conditions, the computer projection showed the proportion of Boston's nonwhite elementary students attending predominantly nonwhite schools could only be reduced from 78 to 66 percent, and for nonwhite junior high students from 65 percent to 50 percent.[32] Clearly, for Boston, not to mention the really enormous ghetto cities of

[32] Joint Center for Urban Studies of M.I.T. and Harvard, "Changes in School Attendance Districts as a Means of Alleviating Racial Imbalance in the Boston Public Schools," unpublished report, August 1966.

New York, Philadelphia, Washington, Chicago, and Los Angeles, more sweeping measures are required.

If the criteria for these sweeping measures are specified, the form and direction of future efforts begin to take shape. And these criteria were suggested earlier in the discussion of the causes of "de facto" school segregation. In planning for big ghetto desegregation, larger educational complexes drawing from wide attendance areas will be essential. These attendance areas will generally have to include both central city and suburban territory in order to ensure an optimal and stable racial mix. The sites for these facilities must not only be convenient to the mass transit network, but also must be on racially "neutral turf." Such locations would avoid immediate public labeling of the school as "white" or "Negro."

Racial specifications are by no means the only criteria for future remedies. At one time, big city public schools held national preeminence as innovative educational leaders; New York, Chicago, and the like, were the nation's scholastic pacesetters. Today, this role is filled by smaller communities such as Berkeley, California, and Newton and Brookline, Massachusetts. Thus, urban-suburban ties may accent and facilitate innovation. Indeed, future public schools should possess facilities which could rarely be duplicated by expensive private schools if they are to compete effectively for the children of advantaged parents. Such arrangements, of course, will cost considerable money; thus, a final criterion must be significant federal (or perhaps state) support of capital costs.

METROPOLITAN PARKS

Several designs would meet these criteria; but let us consider one as illustrative: *the metropolitan park plan.* Each park would be located on "neutral turf" in an inner-ring suburb or just inside the central city boundary.[33] It would be so placed that the same spoke of the mass transit system could bring both outer-ring suburban children into the park and inner-city children out of it. The attendance area of each park would ideally comprise a pie-shaped metropolitan wedge containing a minimum of 12,000 to 15,000 public school students. The thin end of the wedge would be in the more dense central city, and the thick end in the more sparsely settled suburbs.

But what incentive could generate the metropolitan cooperation necessary for such a plan? A number of systems have considered educational

[33] Other convenient and racially neutral sites would be appropriate to specialized metropolitan educational parks. Rather than near the central city and suburban boundary, sites near the art museum, the science center, the music center, and colleges and universities could possess enough appeal and status to attract suburban children into the central city despite the longer commuting.

parks, but they usually find the capital costs prohibitive. Moreover, many systems are currently hard pressed for expansion funds, especially as referenda for school construction bonds continue to be defeated throughout the nation. Federal funding, then, on a massive scale will obviously be needed, though it must be dispersed in a far more careful and strategic manner than the everybody-gets-his cut, "river and harbors bill" principle of the 1965 Elementary and Secondary Education Act.

If federal funding for capital costs is available without acceptance of metropolitanism, many school systems, particularly those exhibiting bad faith, will not choose to join a park plan. Therefore, federal construction grants must: (1) involve more than one urban district, and the consortium must always include the central city (note that any one park would not require the entire metropolitan area to join the proposal, though some coordination would be necessary, perhaps through review by each area's metropolitan planning commission); (2) require racial and social desegregation—and, hopefully, integration—in every school involved (metropolitan involvement makes this requirement feasible); and (3) exclude alternate routes for federal building funds (though if the first two criteria are met, the proposal need not adopt the metropolitan park plan as the model).

A 15,000 student, \$40 to \$50 million park, 90 percent of it paid by the federal government, would be a powerful inducement. Here lie both a great opportunity and an equally great danger. If the money is distributed in the easy fashion of the Elementary and Secondary Education Act to individual school districts, the antimetropolitan effects could be disastrous for both race relations and public education. Building money spent in such a manner would further insulate aloof suburbia and institutionalize de facto school segregation in the inner city for at least another half century. School construction money may be made available by the federal government; the vital question is: What will be its form and effects?

The educational park idea is not a panacea; there can be elegantly effective and incredibly ineffective parks. Yet ample federal funding combined with the nation's planning and architectural genius should be able to set a new standard and direction for public schools. This combination has successfully been applied to public facilities ranging from interstate highways to magnificent airports. Now the combination should be applied to the benefit of children.

From high rise structures to multiple unit campuses, educational parks themselves can be planned in a variety of ways. The most widely discussed design would involve a reasonably large tract of land (eighty to one hundred acres as a minimum) containing no fewer than fourteen or fifteen schools, serving grades from kindergarten through high school. One educator has visualized a campus design for 18,000 students consisting of two senior high, four junior high, and eight elementary schools.[34] If the park were to serve an especially densely populated section, it would be best if it did not include the entire grade spectrum so that it could still cover a reasonably expansive and heterogeneous attendance area. In general, however, an education park resembles a public university. Both include a variety of educational programs for a large group of students of varying abilities. And, like public universities in our major cities, some parks could consist of high rise structures and some could develop a more spacious campus atmosphere with numerous buildings. Hopefully, the metropolitan park could usually follow the campus model, since sufficient space would generally be obtainable at suburban-ring locations.[35]

Apart from offering racial remedies, the metropolitan park concept has a number of distinct advantages. First, there are considerable savings that accrue from consolidation; centralized facilities, such as a single kitchen, need not be duplicated in each of the park's units. Savings on capital costs, too, would accrue from simultaneous building of many units at one location. These savings, however, do not necessarily mean that the total construction and operating costs would be less than those for the same student capacity spread out in traditional units. The advantage is that for essentially the same cost metropolitan parks could boast significantly better facilities than traditional schools. Consequently, each child would be receiving far more per educational dollar in the metropolitan park.

Improved centralized facilities of a park should maximize innovations and individualized instruction. It is difficult to institute new approaches to learning in old settings. A prime finding of social change research is that new norms are easier to introduce in new institutions. The metropolitan park offers a fresh and exciting setting that should encourage new educational techniques and attract the more innovative members of the teaching profession. In addition, a park presents a rare design opportunity for building innovation into the physical and social structures of the schools. This, of course, includes the latest equipment for aiding the teacher and the student. Centralization enhances this process, for example, by providing efficient concentration of all electronic information storage, retrieval, and console facilities. Yet such centralization of equipment should not be viewed as leading inevitably to a wide assortment of frightening Orwellian devices cluttering the school. Poor

[34] G. Brain, "The Educational Park: Some Advantages and Disadvantages," in N. Jacobson, ed., *An Exploration of the Educational Park Concept* (New York: New York Board of Education, 1964), p. 16.

[35] In some of the thickly populated metropolitan areas, especially the older cities of the East, ideal sites are already scarce and rapidly disappearing. Hence, the recommendation below for park site land banks.

planning could lead to this result, but the accent should be on individualized instruction as the unifying and positive theme, a theme far more possible in the park design than in the present model of scattered "little red schoolhouses."

Many innovations made possible by a metropolitan park extend beyond the equipment realm. For instance, the teaching profession today suffers from being one of the most undifferentiated by rank of all professions, a characteristic which discourages a lifelong orientation to the field. While the medical profession has a graded rank order of roles from intern and resident to chief of a service, teachers must either enter administration and become principals or shift to more prestigious schools in order to move up the ladder. By concentrating a large number of teachers in a relatively small area, far more role differentiation becomes possible. Thus, a teacher might progress from an apprentice in a team teaching situation, to a master teacher in a team, to a supervisor of master teachers, and so on. Faculty concentration also allows more intensive, across-school, inservice training and the formation of departments across schools with rankings within departments as in universities (for example, a junior high history department consisting of all history teachers in the four or five junior highs on the campus).

Concentration of students also allows wider course offerings. Specialized classes, from playing the lute to seventeenth-century English literature, become economically possible when the students electing them are gathered from units throughout the park. Moreover, concentration makes possible some remarkable facilities that can be shared by all of the park's units, for example, an Olympic-size swimming pool and extensive auditorium and theatrical equipment. These special facilities could far surpass what is now available in all but the most affluent districts, become a source of student and community pride, and provide a competitive status advantage over private schools. They also would be used efficiently, rather than the minimal use expensive facilities receive in single site schools.

The metropolitan park offers unusual opportunities for an effective liaison with a local university or college. Nova, the extensive educational park near Fort Lauderdale, Florida, even plans to include college and graduate work right on its campus. But direct contiguity is not necessary to develop a mutually beneficial coordination.

Recall that an important cause of public school segregation in many central cities is the enrollment of large percentages of white children in parochial schools. This fact suggests closer cooperation between public and parochial schools; and the metropolitan educational park could facilitate such cooperation under optimal conditions. Most parochial systems are currently in serious financial condition, and tapping into the park's superior facilities should prove attractive. Roman Catholic educators point out that those items that cost the most—the physical science laboratories, gymnasium, and stadium—tend to be least related to the "moral training" that they believe to be the distinctive feature of their schools. Scattered site schools, public and parochial, make "shared time" and other cooperative arrangements awkward at best. And when parochial students come to take their public school class as a group, such segregation often reaps its usual harvest of intergroup tension and hostility.

A recent idea from Vermont introduces a more promising possibility. At the time of planning a large educational park, parochial school educators could be provided the opportunity of purchasing an adjoining plot of land and constructing a new facility of their own. As long as the land price is consistent with its true value, no constitutional infringements appear to be involved. The new parochial facility need only concentrate on courses directly needed for "moral training." Parochial school pupils would be free as individuals, not as separated groups, to cross the park's grass, not urban streets, and attend physical education, science, and other public school courses when they fit their particular schedules. The Vermont Plan offers construction and operating savings to hard-pressed parochial systems; and it offers a greater race and class student balance to hard-pressed public systems.[36]

Cost efficiency, educational innovations, more individualized instruction, wider course offerings, special facilities, and coordination with universities and parochial schools—all the advantages of the well-designed metropolitan park are features that parents, white and Negro, would welcome in the schools of tomorrow. This is politically critical, for desegregation efforts of the past have seldom had the advantage of being intrinsic parts of a larger package promising across-the-board improvements for *all* children.

BUT WHAT ABOUT THE OPPOSITION?

In addition to the natural resistance to change, four major objections have been raised to the park concept: (1) executive capital costs; (2) the phasing out of existing schools; (3) the problem of impersonalization in large complexes; and (4) loss of neighborhood interest and involvement in the school. Each is a serious objection and deserves comment.

The park *is* expensive, and major outside funding is necessary. Further-

[36] The old stereotype of parochial school students as children of working class immigrants is outdated. Roman Catholic children who comprise the students for the Church-operated educational systems tend as a group to be distinctly higher in socioeconomic background than Roman Catholic children who attend the public systems. Thus, inclusion of parochial pupils in public school courses and programs is likely to facilitate social class as well as racial balance.

more, mistakes in design and location could be disastrous. A park is an enormous commitment of resources, and, if poorly conceived, it could stand for years as a major mistake in planning. This is precisely what would happen if parks were operated totally within central city systems, for demographic projections prove the folly of building parks for a single central city system as a desegregation device.[37] It is for this reason that the parks of the future must be *metropolitan* in character.

Present schools were expensive, too, and raise the problem of phasing out existing facilities. For many urban districts this is not a problem; they already have overutilized schools with double shifts and rising enrollments or old schools long past their usefulness. But some urban districts have many new schools and would be hesitant to join a park consortium. The program, however, is a long-term one. Hopefully, in the 1970s, most of the nation's leading metropolitan areas would boast one or more parks; these in turn could serve as models for completing the park rings in the decade. Moreover, elementary and secondary student enrollments will rise rapidly: from 48.4 million in 1964 to a projected 54.9 million in 1974, and to 66 million in the fateful year of 1984.[38] Metropolitan parks, then, could be phased in as older facilities are phased out and as enrollments rise.

Such a process would be ideal nationally, but there will be special problems in localities with "planned de facto school segregation." These are cities, such as Chicago, which in recent years have purposely built new schools in the heart of their Negro ghettos. If racial progress is to be made in these cities, recent structures will have to be converted to new uses, perhaps, to much needed community centers.

The third objection to parks centers upon the impersonalization of organizational bigness, "the Kafka problem." Indeed, much of the park's description, 15,000 students, a staff approaching 1000, the latest electronic equipment, has a frightening Kafka ring; and one can easily imagine how an ill-designed park could justify these fears. However, such a prospect is not inherent in the park plan. Nor is bigness a park problem alone; many of today's huge urban high schools accommodate many thousands of students in a single unit and arouse the same uneasiness. In fact, imaginatively designed parks could act to counter the urban trend toward ever larger public school units. *Smaller* schools at each level can be economically built as units within the park; and careful planning can afford a reasonable degree of privacy for each unit while still providing access to the shared facilities of the park.

37 The Philadelphia Urban League, in proposing nonmetropolitan parks for a central city system whose student body is already majority nonwhite, has advanced just such a plan.

38 F. Keppel, *The Necessary Revolution in American Education* (New York: Harper & Row, 1966), p. 19.

Some critics are particularly concerned about the park's loss of neighborhood interest and involvement. The criticism assumes that most urban public schools today are neighborhood based, and that they generate considerable neighborhood involvement. Serious doubts can be raised about both assumptions: we may well be worrying about the possible loss of something already extinct. In any event, there is no evidence to indicate that only a neighborhood-based school can generate parental concern, or that a metropolitan park could not duplicate this feat, or that there is a close and negative association between the size of the attendance area and involvement.

The criticism does raise an important planning issue: How can the park be initiated and planned to heighten parental and community interest? Certainly, special facilities, university liaison, and cooperation with parochial schools could help generate community pride and interest. So could smaller schools and a park school board of parents with wide authority. Furthermore, widespread use of the park for adult education, community affairs, and so on, might also contribute to public involvement. Indeed, special facilities of the park lend themselves to such adult use more readily than the typical school today.

Finally, one might ask how such a metropolitan educational park plan fits with other such widely discussed possibilities as "decentralization" and "community-controlled schools." First, it should be noted that decentralization and community control are typically advanced either apart from integration considerations or as outright alternatives to integration. "The Bundy Report" for New York City, for instance, could well lead to racially homogeneous districts that would institutionalize racial segregation for generations to come. Yet there is an obvious need in such large and unwieldy systems as New York and Chicago to decentralize authority, as well as a general need to increase parental and community involvement in public education.

Similar to compensatory education, however, these possibilities acquire force and meaning when they *accompany* the drive for integration rather than substitute for it. Thus, effective decentralization need not take the form of isolated social class or racial islands, but should assume the metropolitan wedge shapes described earlier as ideal attendance areas for educational parks. New York City's schools *could* be organized along the lines suggested by "The Bundy Report" in such a way as to help rather than hinder integration.[39]

In summary, then, those who say there is nothing we can do about the

[39] Private communication from Professor Dan Dodson of New York University. Of course, *no* decentralization and redistricting plan in New York City can solve the problem of desegregation alone. The point is that it can be made to seal in racial and class segregation or to improve slightly the situation depending on how it is accomplished.

educational segregation of our major cities are fortunately wrong. This is not to say that desegregation progress will be easy, or even that we will do what is necessary to achieve such progress. But it is to say that it potentially *can* be done for a significant number of urban Americans, white and Negro.

A FINAL WORD

Stripped to its essentials, the argument of this chapter is as follows:

1. It is widely acknowledged that public education needs a major restructuring. While numerous proposals and models for the future exist now, little discussion has begun on a systems approach of optimal mixes of these models.

2. Despite difficulties in evaluating present and proposed programs in public education, there is growing empirical evidence, especially from recent federal studies, to indicate the critical importance of the social class climate of a school's student body. And, this evidence strongly suggests a model of learning which stresses that children teach children, and the need for public education that is heterogeneous in both social class and racial terms.

3. It is demographically possible to provide such heterogeneous education everywhere in the United States. The chief challenge to this statement are our largest metropolitan areas; and it is here that the metropolitan educational park, with its advantages and disadvantages, becomes *one* important structural component for any future design for American public education.

In short, then, we *can* provide "common schools" again; a question remains as to *will* we?

twelve

A New Model for School Finance

One of the goals for which schools have traditionally been held responsible is to assist in the societal effort to provide each individual with "equality of opportunity." But how can schools do this when some children begin their formal education with clear-cut advantages over others? Even if schools were able to treat each child equally—spend the same amount of money on the education of each student—the child who initially entered school from a comfortable home and stimulating environment would almost assuredly graduate having maintained or even increased this advantage. What makes reality worse is that not only do all children not now receive equal services, but also the discrepancy tends to favor the already advantaged student. Simply put, children from wealthy homes have a better chance of attending good schools than do their less fortunate peers. Moreover, school finance formulas in the fifty states typically do not alleviate this condition and, in some cases, they even reinforce it. The sum consequence is that schools under present circumstances frequently exacerbate, rather than eliminate, disparities in opportunity.

Attempts to reduce educational opportunity gaps have been unsuccessful for many reasons, one being that it is difficult to measure precisely what needs to be spent upon the schooling of each child in order to enable him to enter the post-school race for society's rewards on an equal footing. The authors of the following article, Henry M. Levin, James W. Guthrie, George B. Kleindorfer, and Robert T. Stout, suggest a means whereby this measurement difficulty might be overcome. Their "remedy" is to utilize the concept of "capital embodiment" as a device to measure a child's educational "bank account" upon his entry into school. If the child is experiencing a "deficit," then a computation can be made as to the additional resources he will need over the course of his schooling in order to enable him to graduate with a learning ledger which is balanced relative to his peers. This procedure would place school financing on a substantially more rational basis than is presently the case and would represent a large stride toward achieving true equality of opportunity through the schools.

CAPITAL EMBODIMENT: A NEW APPROACH TO PAYING FOR SCHOOLS

Henry M. Levin/James W. Guthrie/ George B. Kleindorfer/Robert T. Stout

In this chapter we wish to discuss the problems of school finance by employing a new concept, "capital embodiment." We feel this conceptualization provides a powerful rationale for distributing educational resources in a manner which is very different from the present pattern. We proceed in three stages: (1) to define equality of educational opportunity, (2) to describe the discrepancy between that definition and present reality, and (3) to suggest an alternative means for financing schools which should decrease the discrepancy and lead to equal educational opportunity.

DEFINING EQUALITY OF EDUCATIONAL OPPORTUNITY [1]

In our society's present race for "spoils," not all runners begin at the same starting line. Children from higher socioeconomic strata (SES) presently begin life with many advantages. Their home environment, health care, nutrition, material possessions, and geographic mobility provide them with a substantial headstart when they begin schooling at age five or six. Lower SES children begin their education with more physical disabilities and less psychological preparation for adjusting to the procedures of schooling. This condition of disadvantage is then compounded by their having to attend schools characterized by fewer and lower quality services.[2]

What must we do if schooling is to compensate for these disparities

[1] Almost the entire issue of the Winter 1968 *Harvard Educational Review* (Vol. 38, No. 1) is devoted to the topic of "Equal Educational Opportunity." The article entitled "The Concept of Equality of Educational Opportunity," by James S. Coleman, provides historical perspective on the development of the concept.

[2] The relationship between a child's social status and the quality of schooling available to him is described in James W. Guthrie, *et al., Schools and Inequality* (Cambridge: M.I.T. Press, 1971).

and to provide equality of opportunity? What actions are implied in such a goal? In responding to these questions it is important from the outset to make clear that we are *referring to equality of opportunity among groups of individuals,* that is, by race, socioeconomic status, residence in city or suburb, and so on. We recognize fully that genetic differences and variations in other characteristics among individuals within such groups will continue to promote *within* group differences in attainment. However, we reject explicitly the necessity of having differences *among* groups with regard to the equality of their opportunity. Equality of opportunity implies strongly that a representative individual of any racial or social grouping has the same probability of succeeding as does a representative individual of any other racial or social grouping. Stated in another way, if there is equality of opportunity, then there should be a random relationship between the social position of parents and the lifetime attainments of their offspring.

We believe strongly that the task of the school is to equalize opportunities among different social groupings by the end of the compulsory schooling period. This belief is reinforced by the fact that most states require all minors to attend schools until at least age sixteen. Inferred from this mandate is the view that formal schooling will enable representative youngsters from all social and racial groups to begin their post-school careers with equal chances of success. In a true sense, while the race for spoils may still be won by the swiftest, if schools are functioning properly, then typical individals from all social groups should be on the same starting line at age sixteen. Our society would wish that representative children of each social grouping begin their adult lives with equal chances of success in matters such as pursuing further schooling, obtaining a job, and participating in the political system. It would seem that equality of educational opportunity could be interpreted in no other way.

THE OPPORTUNITY GAP

Table 12–1 is a hypothetical illustration of the proportion of children at three socioeconomic levels who, under present conditions, are likely to achieve "lifetime success." Success can be thought of as a hypothetical set of generally desired outcomes. Examples of such outcomes on which a favorable consensus might be derived include lifetime income and occupational attainment. In this illustration only about 15 percent of the low income children are likely to achieve "lifetime success," while 50 percent and 85 percent of the medium and high SES children, respectively, should attain that goal. Yet, equality of educational opportunity requires that, at the end of that period of social investment in schooling, all social and racial groups should have an equal probability of achieving success.

Table 12–1 PROPORTION OF CHILDREN AT THREE SES LEVELS WHO ARE LIKELY TO ACHIEVE "LIFETIME SUCCESS" (A HYPOTHETICAL REPRESENTATION)

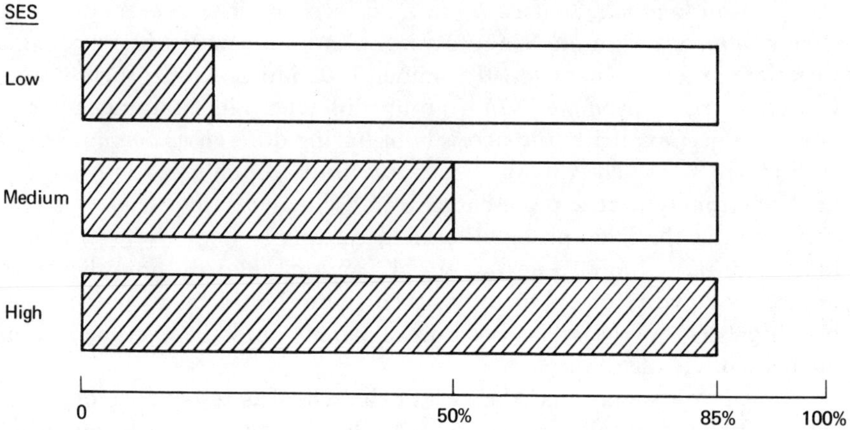

The gap between equal opportunity and actual opportunity is represented by the white portion of the bar graph for the low and medium SES groups. That is, the opportunity gap is greatest for the low SES group, smaller for the medium SES group, and almost nonexistent for the highest group.

CAPITAL EMBODIMENT AND OPPORTUNITY

An appropriate means of illustrating the cause and magnitude of the opportunity gap is to conduct an analysis in the context of *human capital development.* Beginning in the 1950s, economists have employed the human capital approach to understand the process of increasing social and private well-being through investing in the health, education, and training of people.[3] Briefly, economists have found that financial investments in raising the health and proficiencies of human beings yield substantial social and economic dividends to society. Indeed, when translated into monetary terms, productivity and earnings attributable to human capital investment generally exceed the rate of return associated with investments in physical capital.[4]

The concept of human capital investment is readily applicable to our concern with the opportunity gap. To a large extent, differences in op-

[3] For more information on the human capital concept, see Gary S. Becker, *Human Capital* (New York: Columbia University Press, 1964).

[4] For a review of several studies in this area, see Theodore W. Schultz, "The Rate of Return in Allocating Investment Resources to Education," *The Journal of Human Resources,* Vol. II, No. 3 (Summer 1967), 293-309.

portunity among individuals from different socioeconomic levels represent differences in the amount of capital investment embodied in them. Investment in human capital, then, is defined as resources that are devoted to an individual's growth, investments which increase his proficiencies. And, at present, both the family and our larger society invest more resources in the growth and development of higher SES children than they do for lower SES ones.

Even before birth, the lower social class child is more likely to face prenatal malnutrition, and in his early years he is a prominent candidate for protein starvation.[5] He is less likely to receive adequate medical and dental care as well, so he is more prone to suffer from a large variety of undetected, undiagnosed, and untreated health problems. The meager income levels associated with lower SES children typically translate into less adequate shelter and a more modest overall physical environment. These factors are less likely to stimulate cognitive development than are the richer and more varied material surroundings of his higher SES peers. Limited family income, also, inhibits or precludes travel and exposure to the large variety of worldly experiences that increase the knowledge and sophistication of the more advantaged child. Finally, and perhaps most important, both the quality and quantity of parental services tend to be less for the lower SES child. Lower SES children are more likely to receive limited parental attention because they are frequently situated in families with many children and where one or both parents are missing.[6] Further, the low educational attainment levels of lower SES adults limit the amount of knowledge they can transmit to their children. This is a particular drawback in the area of verbal skill development,[7] an area upon which school success depends so heavily.

Perhaps the most important component of parental investment related to SES is that of educational services provided by parents. It appears that parents with greater educational attainment themselves inculcate in their children much higher skill levels than do parents with less education. Indeed, the greater investment of human capital embodied in children from families with higher educational attainment can be estimated in terms of dollar values. That is, a parent, and particularly a mother, has the option of working or providing services to her children. The higher

[5] See Nevin S. Scrimshaw, "Infant Malnutrition and Adult Learning," *Saturday Review,* March 16, 1968, pp. 64-66.

[6] For a discussion of the effect of family structure, see Lee Rainwater and William L. Yancey, eds., *The Moynihan Report and the Politics of Controversy* (Cambridge: M.I.T. Press, 1967).

[7] See, for example, Ellis G. Olim, Robert D. Hess, and Virginia Shipman, "Role of Mothers' Language Styles in Mediating their Preschool Children's Cognitive Development," *School Review,* Vol. 75, No. 4 (Winter 1967), 414-24; and Robert D. Hess, "Maternal Behavior and the Development of Reading Readiness in Urban Negro Children" (Paper prepared for the Claremont Reading Conference, Claremont, California, February 10, 1968).

the educational level of the parent, the greater the value of that parent's services in the labor market, and, therefore, the greater the imputed value of parental services in the home. A parent with higher educational attainment must forego a larger amount of income in order to stay home with children than a parent with lower attainment. Indeed, the educational level of parents, multiplied by the time that they invest in their children, can be converted to aproximate dollar amounts of capital embodiment in each child. This can be accomplished by valuing parental educational efforts according to the market value of such services (of course, market value of services is in turn determined strongly by parents' education).[8]

Dennis Dugan, an economist, has constructed such estimates for a national sample of children. He presents calculations of the total value of parental educational services embodied in children at various age levels according to the educational level of the parents.[9] These calculations are based upon " . . . (1) the proportion of a mother's time devoted to educational related activities (as opposed to household chores), and (2) the number of children among whom the mother's time is divided." [10] The estimated amount of father's time devoted to educational activities of his children is derived similarly.

For purposes of illustration, we will display only the value of mother's educational investment in children at different grade levels by educational attainment of mother. Table 12.2 contains these results for 1965. The figures shown are dollar values of accumulated educational services invested in the child by one source, the mother.

According to the estimates displayed in Table 12–2, the six-year-old whose mother is a high school graduate has had twice as large a maternal investment as the child whose mother terminated her education at elementary school. The child of a college graduate has 2.7 times the investment from this source as the offspring of an elementary school graduate. These figures illustrate the substantial inequalities in human capital formation among children of different socioeconomic levels as they begin their formal schooling. Over the period of schooling, while all the values increase for all groups, the ratio of inequality remains constant.

Moreover, values of mother's and father's contributed educational

[8] It is important to make clear that the dollar amounts derived in this fashion are only indicators of the differences in parental investment between lower and higher SES children. They are meant to be illustrative rather than conclusive. Most important, they are meant to measure the differences in capital embodiment between children at different SES levels attributable to only one component of human investment, parents' services. Differences in human capital due to differential investment in health, nutrition, physical environment, and other factors are not measured directly in our estimates.

[9] See Dennis J. Dugan, "The Impact of Parental and Educational Investments upon Student Achievement," mimeographed (Paper presented at the Annual Meeting of the American Statistical Association, New York City, August 21, 1969).

[10] *Ibid.*, p. 5.

Table 12–2 VALUE IN 1965 OF MOTHER'S EDUCATIONAL SERVICES FOR MOTHER'S EDUCATIONAL ATTAINMENT BY GRADE OF CHILD *
(All Amounts in 1966 Dollars)

Mother's Education	GRADE 1	6	9	12
Elem. School				
0-7 years	$2,724	$ 3,412	$ 4,126	$ 4,989
8 years	3,397	4,231	5,135	6,235
High School				
1-3 years	3,972	5,012	6,094	7,409
4 years	6,964	8,898	10,797	13,080
College				
1-3 years	7,091	9,051	10,995	13,365
4 years	9,044	11,560	14,076	17,148
5+ years	9,322	11,919	14,644	17,978

* *Source:* Dennis Dugan, "The Impact of Parental and Educational Investment upon Student Achievement," mimeographed (Paper presented at the Annual Meeting of the American Statistical Association, New York City, August 21, 1969), p. 8.

services represent excellent predictors of academic success at grade one. That is, differences in human capital formation at grade one are related to differences in academic performance. For example, Dugan found that measures of human capital embodiment explain approximately 95 percent of the variance in pupil verbal skills for white first graders and 85 percent of the variance for nonwhite first graders.[11] Stated in another way, there is a close correspondence between the value of embodied parental services and a child's academic achievement or between the investment in a child and the academic returns to him.

Dugan also addresses himself to the relative efficacy in raising academic performance of dollars invested in school services. That is, he estimated the combined effect of parental investment and school investment on student achievement. In this way he attempted to approximate the amount of additional school investment in lower SES children which might be needed to place them on an academic par with the larger parental investment in their higher SES peers. His results are interesting, but they are limited by the use of an inadequate expenditure measure.[12] Nevertheless, he presents a provocative finding with regard to equalizing academic performances of whites and nonwhites. Dugan found " . . . that an additional $6,662 per nonwhite student is required to raise the nonwhite mean achievement to the level of the white achievement mean for sixth

11 *Ibid.,* Table 3.

12 He used state averages for expenditure rather than districtwide or school averages. The latter are the most appropriate for this type of analysis, but they are not always available.

graders."[13] Distributed over the first five years of school, this translates to a mean annual expenditure of approximately $1,300 a year per nonwhite pupil above the amount which was being spent, about $400. The point is that if we are addressing ourselves to equal educational outcomes, then substantially higher dollar amounts must be spent on school services for lower SES children.

AN ALTERNATIVE PEDAGOGICAL STRATEGY

Differences in dollar investment must be translated into differences in educational effectiveness if the fortunes of both lower and higher SES students are to be equalized at the end of the mandatory schooling process. In order to satisfy this goal, a new educational approach must be implemented, one that addresses itself to the specific needs of each child. In this respect, just as more money is presently spent on special educational arrangements for some children because of their physical incapacities, so will we have to differentiate among children of different SES origins. For example, more money is already spent on children with learning problems stemming from brain damage, emotional handicaps, and severe physical disabilities. Following the individualization of instruction for these groups, we suggest specially tailored courses of study for other children as well.

By implication, the greater initial needs of lower SES students will necessitate greater expenditures. But, how should these dollars be spent? We begin with the general belief that additional resources received by school districts should be employed in a manner which will maximize their effectiveness. This concern does not focus exclusively upon the schooling for lower socioeconomic status children. Rather, we believe this alternative strategy to be applicable to the schooling of all children, and as much in need of being implemented in Scarsdale and Grosse Pointe as in Detroit and New York City. Before progressing to this rather simple proposal, however, let us make clear that we are not about to prescribe a specific school program in all its operational detail. Rather, our purpose is to propose a simplified description of a schooling strategy which would have as its central objective the preparation of children capable of succeeding in the out-of-school world regardless of their social standing or racial and ethnic identity.

WHO SHOULD ADJUST TO WHOM?

Almost regardless of the social or physical characteristics of the child, he presently is subjected to a similar mode of schooling. From the time

[13] Dugan, "The Impact of Parental and Educational Investments upon Student Achievement," p. 24.

of his first contact with school, whether it be in kindergarten or the first grade, whether it be in the lowest expenditure or in the highest expenditure school district, the child is placed in a four-walled room, with an adult teacher at the front and chalk boards around the sides. He is surrounded by other students who are much like himself, at least in terms of matters such as size, skin color, and social standing. Upon his entry into this system, the assumption is made that he is like his classmates on almost every other dimension as well. Unless he is somehow dramatically different from his peers, that is, he is blind or otherwise organically incapacitated, he will receive the same kind of treatment as all his classmates. If the treatment does not fit exactly, then generally the child is asked to adjust to it. The closer he is able to shape his attitudes and actions to conform to that of the norm of his group, the greater the benefit he is likely to derive from the instructional system. The greater he deviates from the norm, the less likely he is to benefit. He is expected to mold himself to fit the procedures of the school. The educational procedures are not likely to be molded to fit his needs. If he cannot adjust himself suitably, either one or two alternatives typically transpires. One, he is provided with some sort of remedial or specialized attention, which is aimed at reshaping him to fit the system. If this does not succeed within some specified period of time, usually not a very long period, then option number two is invoked. He is, in one fashion or another, placed outside the system. He must attend a special (read *inferior*) school for dropouts and other deviants.

Given the extraordinary range of human diversity, the conception of a common school mold for each child strikes us as being, at best, completely unjustified. If a physician ordered all his patients to have the same operation, take the same medicine, and pay the same amount, regardless of their ailment, we would think his performance outrageous and probably illegal. If an attorney filed the same plea for each of his clients, he would very shortly find himself devoid of business. Similarly, an architect who designed the same structure for each customer regardless of the intended function would shortly go bankrupt. However, little thought is given to the fact that each child, despite the wide variations in background, ability, interests, and ambition, as he enters into and progresses through school is treated in a substantially similar fashion. Whatever adjustments are made, he must almost always make himself. The bell rings, the teacher goes on, and the examinations take place in a highly standardized fashion. The child's idiosyncrasies are seldom considered; more usually they are discouraged. The operation of schools appears to be geared primarily to administrative efficiency rather than educational proficiency.

In our view, the only feasible alternative is to find a means by which the schooling of a child can be tailored to his particular needs and abilities. Rather than requiring that he shape himself to fit the pattern of existing services, the pattern of those services should be fitted to him. This view calls for a vastly different conception of what constitutes a *school.* A means must be found whereby the desired outcomes of schooling can be better specified than is currently the case. With such specified outcomes, it would be possible to view schooling somewhat as a diagnostic and treatment process in which individual deficiencies and abilities of students were assessed and their paths through the learning process plotted accordingly.[14] An individually tailored path periodically might lead to classrooms filled with thirty other students, but it just as frequently might lead to museums, seashores, individual tutorial sessions with teachers, an eye doctor, the city hall, an auto assembly line, and so on. The first contact a child has with "school" probably should not be with a four-walled, fenced fortress, but rather a small office in which a battery of diagnostic procedures is pursued. This process might well last for days or even weeks. In any event, it should be sufficiently thorough so as to be able to prescribe for a child a host of educational experiences tailored to his particular capabilities and deficiencies.

The process should probably begin with any treatment needed to prepare the child physically for school. Good physical condition is not sufficient in itself to guarantee learning, but physical handicaps can block learning. Consequently, children must be made healthy and this may very well mean extensive medical treatment. Following this stage, steps need to be taken to gear the processes of formal education to the child's abilities and interests. As we have said, this might very well lead to many different learning paths, but periodically the child should return to the "clinic" where the diagnosis must be repeated in order to assess progress and prescribe the next steps.

As the child becomes older, he should be able to assume a greater role in prescribing his own educational experiences. Moreover, if the early steps were completed successfully, there should be less need for school experiences prescribed in accord with social standing. Instead, the child's individually developed interests and innate abilities should play a larger role in determining the nature of his schooling. And, as we have held as an objective from the beginning, at least by completion of the twelfth grade, children of various social groupings should be in an equal stance ready to pursue whatever postschool paths they choose with equal chances of success. Only when this condition has been achieved will equality of opportunity be a reality.

As we have stated previously, this approach will require greater educa-

[14] For another view of how the pedagogical process might be decentralized, see H. Thomas James, "Schools and Their Leaders" (The Alfred Dexter Simpson Lecture delivered at Harvard University Graduate School of Education on May 15, 1969).

tional services the lower the SES of the child. The learning performance of the low SES child is impeded by factors that vary from malnutrition and undiagnosed medical problems to the emotional damage that often accompanies a broken home. The learning environment is further handicapped by a lack of school-related educational reinforcement in the home. Under these circumstances the diagnostic and rehabilitative educational services required for lower SES children are likely to be exceedingly more costly than those needed by their higher SES counterparts.

IMPLICATIONS FOR SCHOOL FINANCE

Before outlining specific approaches for financing schools for equal opportunity, it is useful to make some general statements. Most important, we wish to emphasize that there are many possible ways of implementing true equality of educational opportunity. The actual choice of a plan is as much a function of taste and judgment as it is of technical public finance. Administrative criteria, political expediency, tradition, and other factors must all be taken into account in identifying specific arrangements for guaranteeing to all children what the law and cultural ideals have promised. The purpose of this preliminary comment is to make the reader aware, explicitly, that the following are but illustrations of means for modifying financial arrangements. They are not presented as the only approaches nor as optima. Rather they are suggested as points of departure along which change might be initiated.

AN ILLUSTRATIVE APPROACH

The ability of a local school district to generate revenue from property taxes should not be allowed to serve as the primary determinant of the quality of school services it offers to children. However, the property tax is not totally devoid of merit.[15] Indeed, some experts believe " . . . that it would be far better to strengthen this levy than to plan for its eradication."[16] In keeping with this view, our prescription is to employ a uniform and relatively low statewide property tax as a *partial* means for financing schools. In this form, most of the disadvantages of the property tax are eliminated while retaining the practical advantage of being able to tap a commercial source of revenue that might be left substantially un-

[15] For a detailed discussion of the advantages and disadvantages of the property tax, see Dick Netzer, *Economics of the Property Tax* (Washington, D. C.: Brookings Institution, 1966), Chap. VII.

[16] Jesse Burkhead, *State and Local Taxes for Public Education* (Syracuse: Syracuse University Press, 1963), p. 105.

touched under other forms of taxation.[17] The revenues needed in excess of those generated from the application of a minimum statewide property tax levy would come from state general funds to be raised through means such as income taxes, sales tax, and the like. Because of the substantial equities associated with the income tax as a revenue-raising procedure, we are predisposed toward a heavy reliance upon it as the primary means for generating the state's direct dollar contribution for education.

The state would determine the per-pupil school service expenditure requirement for children at each level on the SES spectrum. In general, the per-pupil requirement would vary inversely with the SES level of the students being served. Table 12–3 displays a hypothetical index of per-

Table 12–3 HYPOTHETICAL EXPENDITURE INDEX FOR EQUALITY OF EDUCATIONAL OPPORTUNITY

	SCHOOL LEVEL		
SES Level	*Preschool*	*Elementary*	*Secondary*
High	–	1.50	2.00
Medium	1.00	2.25	3.00
Low	2.00	3.00	4.00

pupil expenditure requirement by SES level. In this table, each number represents the multiple of some arbitrary dollar amount. For example, if 1 is equal to $400, 2 is equivalent to $800, and so on. Exact dollar amounts are not represented for two reasons. First, dollar requirements fluctuate over time with shifts in educational priorities and changes in price levels. Second, exact dollar figures in such a table might lend the impression that expenditure requirements are easily fixed. The truth is that these dollar relationships should be estimated initially and might have to be altered over the long run to approximate the differential costs of schooling different populations. Thus, Table 12–3 depicts a general pattern where units of expenditure and their multiples are presented as the appropriate heuristic model. Of course figures in this table are suggestive rather than ones based on precise estimates of need. However, the pattern of dollar requirements is meant to represent one which would more nearly approach equality of educational opportunity than does the present scheme.

Because high SES children tend to receive such a high educational en-

[17] Admittedly, this is a matter of practicality. If business firms are to be taxed to support local or state government, it is more reasonable and theoretically more efficient to tax them on the basis of their output as measured by value-added than to tax them on the basis of their real property, equipment, and inventories. On a practical basis, it is probably easier to levy and administer a property tax than to determine what is owed on value-added. See Harvey E. Brazer, "The Value of Industrial Property as a Subject of Taxation," *Canadian Public Administration,* Vol. 55 (June 1961), 137-47.

dowment in their homes, the scheme in Table 12–3 suggests that no public preschool provision is necessary in order to fill their needs. On the other hand, the preschool period represents an ideal time for disproportionate investment to begin for lower SES children. The efficacy of preschool investment has been widely noted in both the child development literature and in practice.[18] Indeed, some particularly productive preschool programs, such as the one in Ypsilanti, Michigan, have produced substantial and long-lasting gains in achievement.[19] Accordingly, Table 12–3 suggests that medium SES children be provided with one-half day of preschool instruction at 1 unit per child and lower SES children receive a full day of preschool education at 2 units per student. Alternatively, the state could choose to enroll lower SES students on a half-day basis for two years while medium SES children would attend for only one year. That is, the lower SES child would begin his preschool experience at the age of three while the middle SES child would start at age four.

Expenditures at the elementary and secondary level, as presented in Table 12–3 also reflect the pattern required for an equal opportunity approach. The higher expenditures for all groups at the secondary level are based upon the necessity for greater specialization (and thus higher qualifications for and larger numbers of personnel) at that level. Many states already take these differences into consideration when apportioning aid to local school districts. The salient characteristics of the requirements at all levels of the matrix is that the schools must expend greater dollars on lower SES groups in order to close the "opportunity gap."

One necessary adjustment in a SES expenditure matrix such as that presented in Table 12–3 would be for differential costs. The dollars available to a school district should be weighted so as to balance dollar differences in items such as land prices, labor costs, and salary level differentials between rural, urban, and suburban areas.

Once the state's expenditure requirements are established, the task becomes that of financing those requirements. The following method, or a variant of it, could be used to generate the required financial support. First, the state would require every local school district to levy a property tax at some uniform and relatively low rate. For example, a rate of 10 mills might be appropriate. The dollar difference between what this levy raised for the students in each school district and the state requirements

18 For some of the research basis supporting formal educational preschool experiences for lower SES children, see Benjamin S. Bloom, *Stability and Change in Human Characteristics* (New York: John Wiley, 1964).

19 For a description of the Ypsilanti program, see David P. Weikart, *Preschool Intervention: A Preliminary Report of the Perry Preschool Project* (Ann Arbor: Campus Publishers, 1967). For an evaluation of the Ypsilanti program and other programs for disadvantaged children, see D. Hawkridge, A. Chalupsky, and A. O. H. Roberts, "A Study of Selected Exemplary Programs for the Education of Disadvantaged Children," Final Report, U. S. Office of Education Project No. 089013 by American Institute of Research, Contract No. OEC-0-8-089013-3515 (010) (September 1968).

for equal opportunity for those students would be allocated from state funds to each local school district. These revenues would be derived from general state sources with heavy reliance upon state income and sales taxes.

Obviously the equal educational opportunity requirement for a school district would be based upon a weighting scheme, where the dollar amounts required for each district were tied to the relative number of students in each SES group and distribution of these across each schooling level. Now having presented the overall plan, it is useful to provide an example of how it might operate. In order to simplify the illustration, we will use the hypothetical unit requirements for elementary children suggested in Table 12–3, and we will let each unit of expenditure be equivalent to $400.

Table 12–4 displays the proposed financing arrangement for two school districts, A and B. District A is assumed to contain all low SES children

Table 12–4 AN ILLUSTRATION OF PROPOSED FINANCING ARRANGEMENTS FOR ACHIEVING EQUALITY OF EDUCATIONAL OPPORTUNITY

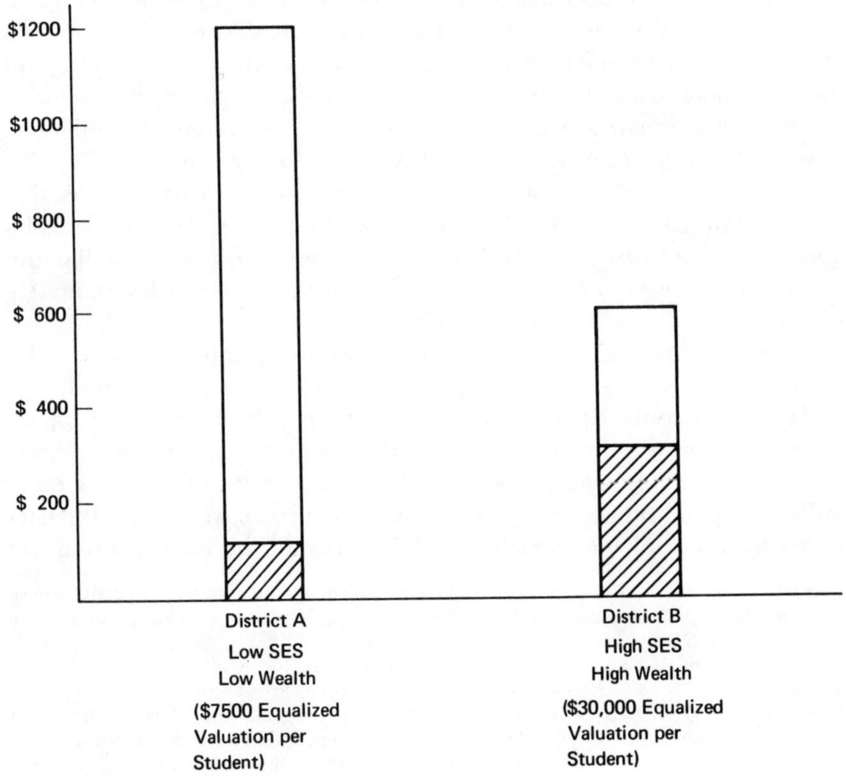

of elementary school age. It is also a relatively low wealth district with only $7500 of equalized assessed valuation (of the property tax base) for each student. On the other hand, District B is inhabited by upper SES residents, and its property tax base is substantial, $30,000 of equalized assessed valuation per pupil.

Applying the uniform tax rate of 10 mills to both districts yields $300 per student in District B and only $75 per student in A. But the state requirement for low SES elementary school students (taken from Table 12–3) is $1200 per student and for high SES students the requirement is $600 per pupil. Therefore the state would grant $1125 per pupil to District A and $300 per pupil to B. In this way the state would fill the gap between the local contribution where uniform tax effort is mandatory and the state requirement for equal educational opportunity. This approach might be termed a "variable level" foundation program since the state requirements represent expenditure foundations below which support cannot fall.

Any suggested changes in financing the schools will be characterized by transitional problems. In such a complex area as education and its financial foundations, utopia can be approached, but it is not likely to be attained. Yet, we believe that the obstacles surrounding effective financing for equal educational opportunity are indeed surmountable. The point is that great strides forward are not costless, but they are nevertheless worthwhile if the benefits sufficiently exceed the costs, as we believe that they do in the present instance.

IMPLEMENTING FINANCIAL ARRANGEMENTS

Any alternative financial arrangement that strives for equality not only must be theoretically sound, but also must lend itself to the realities of implementation. The financing model we have described appears to meet both these criteria. It is particularly important, however, to suggest guidelines for implementation.

Perhaps the most important change required in financial arrangements is for state support to be based upon individual schools as units of expenditure rather than school districts. That is, the state should provide assistance to local school districts on the basis of school-by-school calculations; school districts should spend those dollars accordingly. The reason for focusing on and emphasizing individual schools is that there frequently are enormous differences in SES levels between schools within single districts. If funds are provided to school districts on the basis of district average SES, there is too little assurance that the money will be distributed to individual schools on the basis of school SES. Indeed, where school districts have been examined on a school-by-school basis within large cities, it has been demonstrated that poor and black children attend schools which are considerably less endowed than those attended by their white, middle class counterparts. Dollar expenditures tend to be lower; and, in some cases, even compensatory monies allocated specifically for schools serving children from low income families have been siphoned off to support general school services throughout the districts.[20]

One obvious means by which funds can be conveyed directly to the schools for which they are intended, while retaining present school district boundaries, is (1) to allocate locally generated revenues from the state's mandatory millage levy to all schools within the district on a per-student basis. (2) From the state requirements matrix (Table 12.3), compute the dollar amount per student needed in each school to attain equality of opportunity. (3) Grant local school districts financial support equal to the differences between the amount raised by mandatory millage and the state requirements computed for all schools in the district. (4) Require a school-by-school financial accounting each year to ensure that monies intended for particular schools were, in fact, expended in those schools. That is, unlike the present line-item accounting system, in which expenditures are reported only for the district, the state must require information on a school-by-school basis in order to guarantee equity among schools. Otherwise the leakages which presently deprive low SES students of additional state and federal resources will persist. A mandatory school-by-school accounting system is necessary if the conduits between state coffers and low SES schools are efficiently to convey resources to the schools for which they are intended.

One further point in favor of using the school rather than a school district as a unit of financial analysis is that it is probably easier to obtain accurate SES information on a regular basis for the smaller units. In a study conducted for New York State, Walter I. Garms and Mark

[20] For evidence of within-district financial discrimination, see Henry M. Levin, "Decentralization and the Finance of Inner-City Schools," mimeographed, Stanford Center for Research and Development in Teaching, R & D Memo No. 50 (May 1969); to be published in *Fiscal Planning for Schools in Transition: Restructure, Reform, or Revolt* (Washington, D. C.: NEA, in press). Poignant evidence of misallocation of funds intended for low SES schools is found in a California State Department of Education report for the City of Oakland. Oakland had received $10 million in federal funds to aid some 12,000 ghetto youngsters. Instead, much of the money was spent for services throughout the district. Thus, while financing was provided to give all ghetto elementary school children additional reading and language arts instruction, only two out of five actually received such assistance. Of 477 staff positions approved for the "target" schools, only 276 employees could be accounted for (the funds for the other positions presumably were financing personnel at other schools). Further, one-third of the total budget for instruction supported administrators working in the district's central office. This resulted in a severe understaffing of schools for which the federal and state governments had designed the grants. See the review of the report in "This World," *San Francisco Sunday Examiner and Chronicle* (August 3, 1969), pp. 5 and 6. Also, for evidence of widescale misuses, see *Title I of ESEA: Is it Helping Poor Children?* (New York: NAACP Legal Defense and Education Fund, Inc., 1969).

C. Smith demonstrate that it is feasible to develop an SES-related measure of educational need from information which can be provided readily by school principals.[21] They suggest that an index of resource need be computed from information such as the percentages of various specified racial and ethnic minority group students, the percentage of children from broken homes, the average number of schools attended by pupils in the last three years, and the average number of years of schooling of the father, if present, otherwise the mother. These variables in linear combination predict approximately 70 percent of the school-to-school variation in reading and mathematics achievement.[22] Other measures might be developed at the individual school level which are also easily compiled and which are more appropriate for discerning differences in SES in rural areas. Garms and Smith also suggest ways in which the measure of school resource need can be woven into a state school finance formula.

FINANCING FOR EQUALITY AND SCHOOL ADMINISTRATION

The state must necessarily assume the dominant role in financing schools for equality, and this poses a provocative question. Under the present system of school finance in most states, the state decides many of the regulations and policies relevant to local school district operation. Personnel licensing, curriculum requirements, staffing ratios, and mandatory expenditure levels are but a few of the areas in which states typically dictate educational practices. Given these procedures, it is entirely possible that if the state increases its level of financial support to schools, it will also attempt to increase its operational influence over schools.

Greater central administration from the state with its almost inevitable imposition of greater operational uniformity would be exceedingly counterproductive for two reasons. First, the variety of educational needs that confront particular schools and school districts cannot be met by increased standardization among schools. Good education is individualized, meaning that decisions affecting each child's instruction should be made as close to that child as possible. The state is clearly an inappropriate level upon which to make such decisions.

A second reason for resisting increased state operation is the sheer technical difficulty in administering large numbers of schools. Schooling is an activity characterized by substantial inefficiencies once a critical threshold of individual school or school district enrollment is exceeded. The nature of schooling is such that large-scale bureaucracy appears incapable of managing by any but the most mummified means. Instructional

21 See "Development of a Measure of Educational Need and its Use in a State School Support Formula," Report on the Study of the New York State School Support Formula, Staff Study No. 4 (Albany: New York State Conference Board, June 1969).

22 "Development of a Measure of Educational Need," p. 47.

innovation and personal flexibility both seem to disappear in large school districts. With the exception of school districts to small that they cannot provide a reasonable range of services, large operational units appear to be a deterrent to good education.[23] An extensive survey of the related literature suggests that diseconomies of scale (inefficiencies and higher costs) are characteristic of school districts with enrollments in excess of 10,000 students in average daily attendance.[24] It is little wonder, then, that many school districts throughout the nation either already have or are under pressure to decentralize their operations.

In short, there are sound reasons for allowing most local school districts to continue to administer their schools without additional state regulations encumbering them. Indeed, a far better case can probably be made for decentralizing decision making for the schools beyond the degree to which it presently exists[25] (see Chapter Nine).

SUMMARY

Persons suffering from educational handicaps are caught in a downward spiraling cycle of despair. On one hand they are tempted on almost every side by the advantages that can be achieved with the assistance of good schooling. On the other hand, their own pursuit of such objectives is frequently brought to an abrupt halt by the inadequacy of their education. For them as individuals the goals of our society become relatively meaningless. At best they are left to experience frustration and defeat. At worst, they may be propelled into a life of crime and decadence. From the prespective of the entire society, this human wastage is a double burden. The undereducated do not contribute their share, and everyone else is deprived of the benefits of those individuals who, if properly schooled, could have contributed more than their share. We have long since passed the point in our development where we can tolerate vast numbers of unskilled and underdeveloped individuals.

In this chapter we have set forth a new conception of equality of educational opportunity and described new means for pursuing that goal. We are not wedded to the specifics of our proposed approach, but we are wedded to the general need for change. The gravity of the present inequitable situation is immense, yet it is difficult to motivate concern among those who possess the greatest ability to remedy the situation. If

23 See Robert G. Barker and Paul V. Gump, *Big School, Small School* (Stanford: Stanford University Press, 1964).

24 See H. Thomas James and Henry M. Levin, "Financing Community Schools," presented at The Brookings Institution conference on the community school, December 12-13, 1968; published in Henry M. Levin, ed., *Community Control of Schools* (Washington, D. C.: Brookings Institution, 1970).

25 James and Levin, "Financing Community Schools."

allowed to persist, present disparities in school services will almost inevitably undermine our society.

Societies which have persisted longest throughout history appear to be those which have avoided vast social and economic differences among major segments of their populations. Clearly, the relative success of the United States in avoiding such extremes has been fostered significantly by the past successes of our schools. Today, however, because of a shortage of resources and an inappropriate distribution of the resources which are available, schools are no longer so successful. The preservation of equal opportunity and the reality of an open society, wherein individuals rise or fall in accord with their interests and abilities, demands a restructuring of present arrangements for the support and provision of school services.

thirteen

A New Model for Educational Decisions

Plenary authority for the provision of public schooling is held by state legislatures. Other school officials, including local school board members and school administrators, may also make decisions about schools, but when they do they are operating in the capacity of a state officer. Thus, legally speaking, many significant decisions about education are presently outside the hands of parents. The rationale for this arrangement has traditionally been that the education of a child in a democratic society is too important to leave totally to the discretion or whimsy of his parents. If the society is to sustain itself, then children must be educated in a fashion which is consistent with the society's values, and they must acquire minimal knowledge consistent with performance as "good citizens." In order to ensure the inculcation of such values and the acquisition of such minimal levels of knowledge, states have assumed responsibility for the schooling of children.

The continuation of the state as the primary locus of decisions about children's education is usually assumed by most educational reformers, even the most radical among them. However, the authors of the following article, John E. Coons, William H. Clune III, and Stephen D. Sugarman, are sufficiently heretical to question even this assumption. They imply that parents, as well as the state, have an interest in the education of children. They proceed to recommend that the governance and financing of schools should be rearranged in a manner which would allow parents to assert a substantial degree of decision-making discretion in keeping with this interest.

They recommend a system of family grants as a mechanism by which families could be provided with educational decision power.

Moreover, they contend that under their system grants could be structured so as to achieve a number of added benefits, benefits not readily attainable under the present system of state and local level decision making. These added benefits include reestablishment of competition between schools, added attention to the learning problems of children from lower socioeconomic strata, and the attainment of more significant levels of racial integration.

The reader might well consider this proposal one of the most radical contained in this book. However, is there anything about it which should automatically preclude its trial on a limited basis? Might not such an experiment provide us with an opportunity to assess its advantages and disadvantages without running unthinkable risks to our present education system and to our society? As the authors themselves recognize, one of the advantages of this model would appear to be the degree to which it is amenable to implementation on a number of levels, a local district, a county, a state, or a nation. Also, it appears particularly compatible with some of the other proposals contained in this book. For example, family grants, community control, and accountability might all be tied together into one integral reform package.

RECREATING THE FAMILY'S ROLE IN EDUCATION

John E. Coons/William H. Clune III/Stephen D. Sugarman

> At common law the principal duty of parents to their legitimate children consisted in their maintenance, their protection, and their education. These duties were imposed upon principles of natural law and affection laid on them not only by Nature herself, but by their own proper act of bringing them into the world. It is true that the municipal law took care to enforce these duties, though Providence has done it more effectively than any law by implanting in the breast of every parent that natural insuperable degree of affection which not even the deformity of person or mind, not even the wickedness, ingratitude, and rebellion of children, can totally suppress, or extinguish.—*1 Blackstone Sec. 447*

The power to fix the number of dollars spent on any particular child's education in the public schools presently lies almost entirely with the apparatus of government. The interest in the quality of that child's education lies in significant measure with his family. Under the present system of educational finance and control, there are few exceptions to the rule that the family must accept whatever education is delivered by the district in which it lives. In the volume *Private Wealth and Public Education,* we have suggested a scheme which would permit the family to become a primary locus of decision within a publicly financed system of education.[1] The concept is called "family power equalizing," and we offer it as one among several equitable models for the reform of education. The model is now sufficiently developed in the form of draft legis-

An earlier version of this chapter appeared in *Inequality of Education,* Vol. 1. Cambridge, Mass.: Harvard Center for Law & Education, 1969.

[1] John E. Coons, William H. Clune III, and Stephen D. Sugarman, *Private Wealth and Public Education* (Cambridge: Harvard University Press, 1970). The book first analyzes the existing state structures, suggesting a model for testing the extent to which such systems permit variations in wealth to affect per pupil expenditure; next it pro-

lation[2] to justify the brief general description that follows. This is not to suggest that its probable effects are sufficiently understood or that its form is final.

THE MODEL'S VALUE CHOICES

State governments enjoy plenary constitutional power over educational spending in public schools, but most states have chosen to share this power in a complex manner with local political units, typically school districts and counties empowered to levy taxes upon local property and to spend locally whatever they raise. This balkanization of the states' tax resources produces the wild variations in property taxes and spending levels which have driven outraged pupils and taxpayers in poorer districts to the courts. (See Chapter One.) Here, however, we will be concerned exclusively with a legislated cure, one which is simultaneously radical and conservative in form.

The family power equalizing model would eliminate local political units altogether. In their place the family would, in effect, become the school district for two crucial purposes: It would assign pupils to particular schools, and it would fix the level of "local" taxation and spending through its choice of rate under a variable self-selected tax on the family's income. Each level of that tax would trigger a different level of state-guaranteed educational spending for the family's children. Henceforward, educational decisions requiring political consensus would be rendered exclusively at the state level; but, within a range of per-pupil spending politically established, the decisions fixing the number of public dollars available to a particular child for education would be made exclusively by the child's family.

Superficially there is a resemblance here to the rash of "family grant" proposals which have surfaced in recent years.[3] These have generally appeared in one of two forms. The first is the uniform grant, a device which would grossly disadvantage the children of poor families, ensur-

---

poses a "wealth free" system of decentralized funding called "power equalizing"; finally, it suggests an approach to the judiciary designed to invalidate the existing dispensations under the Equal Protection Clause. See also Coons, Clune, and Sugarman, "Educational Opportunity: A Workable Constitutional Test for State Financial Structures," 57 *Calif. L. Rev.* 305 (1969).

2 The model statute is entitled "The Family Choice in Education Act" and has been drafted to be adaptable specifically to the economic and educational context of California. Although the statute is in third draft, it will receive substantial additional revision. It is highly detailed and likely to become more so.

3 James A. Bensfield, "School Financing and the Fourteenth Amendment," *Inequality in Education,* Vol. 1 (1969); Henry M. Levin, "The Failure of the Public Schools and The Free Market Remedy," *Urban Review* (June 1968); and Rey A. Carr and Gerald C. Hayward, "Education by Chit," *Education and Urban Society,* Vol. II, No. 2 (February 1970), 179-91.

ing their isolation in schools charging no more than the amount of the grant; [4] the second would avoid this injustice by employing compensatory grants for the disadvantaged in amounts fixed by some governmental body, still giving the family itself no voice in determining the level of spending for its children.[5] A recent refinement of this latter system is considered at the end of this chapter. The family power equalizing model rejects both approaches for a system of variable grants based upon the family's demonstrated interest in education.

A number of value choices inform the system. Two are fundamental:

I

The quality of public education may not be a function of wealth other than the wealth of the state as a whole.

We would elevate this principle to constitutional dignity as an aspect of equal protection; it would invalidate the state systems currently employed to apportion educational resources at the primary and secondary level.

II

Above an adequate minimum expenditure per pupil required by law, one sound policy alternative is to permit families to choose among dollar levels of educational offering, each of which levels is made purchasable for an economic sacrifice equalized for families at all income levels.

The model aims, therefore, to eliminate, insofar as possible, the influence of wealth variation upon publicly financed education, while, at the same time locating in the family the responsibility and the freedom not only to choose among schools but also to fix its own order of preference between education and all the other opportunities for consumption that compete with education for the family dollar.

In addition to these two basic aims, there are nine related purposes which the model is designed to advance: efficiency in educational spending; accountability; independence of spending from local tax referenda; variety in style and content; increased experimentation; community control; racial integration; compensatory education; political feasibility.

Consideration of the extent to which these various purposes might be served by the proposed scheme will be reserved until the mechanism has been described in greater detail.

[4] Milton Friedman, "The Role of Government in Education," in Robert A. Solo, ed., *Economics and the Public Interest* (New Brunswick, N. J.: Rutgers University Press, 1955).

[5] Theodore Sizer and Phillip Whitten, "A Proposal for a Poor Children's Bill of Rights," *Psychology Today*, Vol. II, No. 3 (August 1968).

OUTLINE OF THE MODEL MECHANISM

Basically, the model would create an educational market offering products (schools) at several distinct levels of per pupil cost. At each of these levels within the market, proprietors, public and private (the system could be made exclusively public or private), would compete for the custom of buyers (parents) all of whom have been made substantially equal in their power to purchase admission. To establish that equality the model would condition access to any school upon an equivalence of economic sacrifice for every family choosing that school, irrespective of family income. Accordingly, each family's selection of a school from among schools of varying per pupil costs would represent also a choice among varying rates of a special tax to be levied upon the family's income; but the tax burden on families of different incomes choosing schools of the same per pupil cost would, in economic terms, be rendered equivalent by means of a progressive rate structure.

For example, upon enrolling its children in a school costing the minimum of $500 per pupil, a family with an income of $5000 would become subject to a levy of, say, $25 (.5 percent). Access to a $1000 school might cost that same family $60 (1.2 percent). Enrollment in these same two schools by children of a family with a $20,000 income might cost that family $200 (1%) and $700 (3.5%) respectively. The tax would be more than proportionately larger for wealthier families.

In absolute terms the family's yearly educational tax liability (as the model now is conceived) could range from nearly zero up to a ceiling of $3400 for the costliest high school. A welfare family choosing the cheapest class of school would pay perhaps $5; a very wealthy family choosing the most expensive class would pay the maximum. The total tax would not vary by the size of the family; thus the hypothetical wealthy family with two children attending a high school spending $1700 per pupil would "break even" in the sense that it would receive a dollar equivalent in education ($3400) for its tax contribution ($3400).

The question of imposing a ceiling on the wealthy family's tax burden is vexing. Currently, we conclude that no family should be required to pay under the special tax more than twice the cost of the education received by its children. Hence the $3400 limit for the most expensive high school and proportionately lower limits for the schools in lower spending categories. But the imposition of such a ceiling, or any ceiling, on the tax raises an issue of principle. The effect of a ceiling would be that, above a particular level of wealth, families would make no greater dollar contribution than relatively poorer families below that level. A family income of a million dollars might be taxed at the rate of .34 of 1 percent, while one of $10,000 might pay as much as 4 or 5 percent. Obviously this violates the principle of equality of economic sacrifice for all families however that concept might be defined. The justification for the departure is purely pragmatic; it is a concession designed to assure that the richest families would not automatically desert the system for purely independent private schools. No one is likely to be willing to pay $50,000 for a $3400 education. The number of families wealthy enough to be above the breakeven line can be made very small (even for families with only one school age child); however, there is little to be gained by driving them from the system for the sheer sake of consistency.

There is a slightly different form of the system which would permit somewhat higher exactions from the rich. This is the "preemptive" model in which all schools would be required to operate within the publicly financed structure, leaving the rich no choice. Although such a scheme might be constitutional if it were sufficiently tolerant of ideological differences, it is not one we prefer. It would be likely to prove too confining for certain forms of experimentation, and, in any event, for political reasons would still be unlikely to include a fully progressive tax rate operating without a ceiling at all levels of wealth.

Schools within the system are classified in two ways: (1) a division is made between schools which are public (categories "A" through "D") and private (categories "E" through "H"); (2) all schools, public and private, are divided into four per pupil cost levels (four each for K-8 grades and high school grades respectively). As currently envisioned (much depends upon the wealth of the state), the schools would be permitted to spend the following amounts per pupil:

	A and E Schools	*B and F Schools*	*C and G Schools*	*D and H Schools*
K-8	$500	$ 800	$1100	$1400
High School	$800	$1100	$1400	$1700

Public schools in the area affected by the system would be administered by a state superintendent and board (county and district authorities in these areas would cease) with authority to unify or decentralize that administration for some purposes, but with general protections for academic freedom of public school teachers and with a detailed requirement of financial decentralization, as we shall see. Private schools would qualify to enter the system essentially by meeting the minimum standards imposed upon those private schools outside the system that satisfy the truancy laws. Each private school would decide for itself under which one of the four proposed levels of cost it would operate; this decision would also fix the rate of the family tax imposed on parents for attendance of their children at that school. For each public school that choice would be made by the state superintendent, based largely upon demand in the area for each level of per pupil cost with its accompanying tax. For every school, public and private, the superintendent would maintain a drawing account containing the number of dollars appropriate to schools of that class for each student enrolled. The dollars would be earmarked by student and a prorated share would move with the student from school to school, if he transferred during the year. The system thus skirts the church-state problems in private schools by treating the child as the recipient.[6]

The funding of the total system would be based primarily upon statewide sources such as a state income tax. The special family tax described above is designed principally as a vehicle for measuring and distinguishing family interest in education. Clearly it would not fund the bulk of the total cost of the system. This means that the cost of education would be broadly distributed, but also that the primary beneficiaries would pay an additional cost representing a very rough estimate of the value to them of the purely private benefit.

At a point in time well before the opening of school (for example, January 15), each family would select a particular school (and alternates) based upon its personal choice, including such matters as a school's cost category and certain other information concerning each school (for example, curriculum, test scores, and religious affiliation) that the state superintendent would be required to supply each parent. *All* schools (public and private) would be required to admit applicants without selection—by lot—up to the limit of the schools' preannounced capacity.[7] (Academic and disciplinary standards for staying in school have yet to be drafted.) Transportation would be essential to such a system, and would be financially supported by the state up to a reasonable distance to be fixed by regulation.

Because of its commitment to the market mechanism, the family power equalizing model would financially isolate each school (public and pri-

[6] See *Board of Education of Central School District No. 1* v. *Allen,* 392 U. S. 236 (1968); *Walz* v. *New York,* 397 U. S. 664 (1970).

[7] Thus suggesting limits on indoctrination, e.g. as follows: the form of the rule we have chosen is the following: "No child . . . shall be required to engage in any act or ceremony with religious significance or to attend any class or course of instruction devoted primarily to the teaching of religion." The precaution may be unnecessary, since the school would be self-chosen and the constitutional objection possibly waived. The whole question deserves considerable reflection, at least if it is the state's policy to attract many existing private schools into the system. However, it may be necessary in any event under the Establishment Clause to separate clearly the financial support for religious instruction from the state's input. If that is so, the same administrative devices of separation might be designed to serve the purposes of both clauses of the First Amendment.

vate), limiting its income (with certain exceptions outside the regular program) to the amount fixed per pupil by statute for its class. This limitation is a guarantee of equality in competitive position. If the state were permitted to pour additional money into a public school that was failing to attract students, the market stimulus to excellence would be diluted, and families in the nonfavored schools would be unfairly treated; the same would be true if private charitable sources sought to shore up a failing private school. Further, such a limitation is important to prevent affluent religious and ideological factions from using public funds as a base upon which to build the most prestigious schools. A refinement of this principle incorporated in the model would require an accounting for the fair market value of services that are effectively donated, as in the case of teaching nuns.[8]

On the other hand, certain kinds of necessary or desirable school activities (for example, preschool programs) might not, or legally could not, be carried on within the competitive system as structured. The cost of these activities should be borne by other sources, public or private. Provision is made in the statute for distinguishing and encouraging such special services, the cost of which could be reimbursed by state or private sources. Also, it may be sound policy that every child should have the opportunity, if he prefers, to attend a publicly owned and operated school; the model could include a guarantee that such a school will be available.

Entry to the market for new private entrepreneurs is encouraged by a guaranteed loan program similar to the FHA structure. Again, however, access to credit is to be substantially equalized for all schools within the system (public and private) and detailed provisions are included to ensure this result.

The family power equalizing model is intended to apply initially only to selected urban areas. This reflects both an estimate of the difficulties in supplying adequate transportation and a conviction that the system should begin upon an experimental basis. However, where applicable, it would be the exclusive public system except for special provisions for handicapped and other special students and such special, experimental, or compensatory programs as the legislature would permit or prefer to be operated separately.

[8] Article 15, Section 3, of the draft handles the problem in the following manner: "Section 3. Services performed on a regular basis for schools under this act at less than fair market value shall be reported to the Superintendent in such form as he shall direct. The amount by which the market value of such services exceeds wages paid therefore shall be deducted from the tuition account maintained for the children of such school. No person with authority over an employee of any school under this act shall use such authority directly or indirectly to influence or persuade such employee to assign or otherwise transfer directly or indirectly to any person or organization all or any portion of the consideration paid for the services of such employee."

PREDICTING THE CONSEQUENCES

This very generalized description of the stucture permits us to ask whether the family power equalizing model would serve the objectives identified in the introductory paragraphs:

1. *Neutralization of the Effects of Varying Wealth.* For constitutional, political, and practical purposes, we think that the rates of the family tax can be adjusted so as to equalize realistically the burden upon families at all levels of income. Of course, any particular formula can be challenged, and there can even be disagreement concerning the proper criteria for expressing equality of sacrifice. Our own preference is for a behaviorally oriented approach seeking a random distribution of rich and poor among the available tax choices open to families. Of course, under such a standard the determination of equality of sacrifice could only be made after the model had been in experimental operation for a substantial period. The rates in the initial legislated experiments should be adopted with this standard as an ideal, but, until a fair test has been conducted, we are, to a considerable extent, guessing about the attitudes which would determine the behavior of various income classes.

2. *The Vesting of Decisional Power in the Family Unit.* By definition the mechanism achieves its purpose of placing power and responsibility for choice in the family. Depending upon his philosophy about human freedom and parental rights, the critic may inquire how well that choice would be exercised. This is answerable in part in terms of the effectiveness of elaborate information requirements in the model which will not be discussed here; in part, it depends upon one's estimate of the good judgment and good intentions of parents. Also one's attitude is affected by his opinion of the probable relative success of competing alternatives for disposing the fates of children.

Of course, the question itself is quite unclear. If the issue here is defined to be whether the "right" children will be sent to the "right" schools, our equally ambiguous response is that a family's choices for its children on the whole would be no less appropriate than those presently dictated by a statutory or administrative formula. In fact, what this question often is intended to suggest is that the poor will "undervalue" education in the sense of choosing the cheaper schools more frequently than the rich. Obviously this is possible. The opposite is also possible. There is simply no experience upon which to draw, since the poor have never been in a position of parity with the nonpoor in manifesting their interest in education. The only evidence we have is that poor districts today frequently tax themselves more heavily than rich. To the extent that personal poverty and district poverty coincide (a difficult correspondence to demonstrate as statistics now are reported), one might conclude that the poor value education more than the rich and would thus tend to choose the most expensive categories. This, however, is as much a non sequitur as the conventional wisdom that high spending districts value education more. In any view of the matter, the adoption of a family power equalizing model would represent a challenge to the leaders of the poor to assure that their clientele understood both the opportunity and the responsibility at stake. The options that the family would have to exercise do not seem so involved as to elude the understanding of ordinary men.

A fundamental feature of the model is that it permits families to place a value upon education which differs from the value that would be chosen for them by the bureaucracy. Unquestionably, under the model, some families would decide that their personal objectives are satisfied by a choice to spend less for education and, therefore, more for TV, cars, travel, or other proletarian pleasures. This freedom is a bone in the throat of some critics, a point of basic principle to which we shall return.

3. *Efficiency.* Too much can be made of this point; it is enough for present purposes that the purchasing of educational goods and services plausibly could be accomplished with greater efficiency within a competitive system than under current institutional arrangements.

4. *Accountability.* Permitting midyear transfer to another school with space and providing the economic resources including transportation to support that transfer, the model would replicate for all parents the experience of fate control now reserved to the rich who use private schools. This power would be supported in its exercise by a system of information disclosure and dissemination sufficient to expose educational swindlers.

5. *Independence of Spending from Local Tax Referenda.* As noted, the cost of the system would be borne in largest part by general taxes at the state level. The relative invisibility of such levies renders them a vastly more dependable source than the highly erratic local property tax from which the schools would be liberated. Statewide support also guarantees a measure of "equality" among the children of the state that may put at rest the objections of critics to a "district power equalizing" system with its geographical disparities in spending.[9] As we have observed, it invites the cognate objection that the child is unprotected from his parents.

6. *Variety in Style and Content.* The stimulus to private action justifies a prediction of significant diversification, especially in states where "private school" heretofore has meant almost exclusively the Catholic

[9] See Michelman, "The Supreme Court, 1968 Term—Foreword: On Protecting the Poor through the Fourteenth Amendment," 83 *Harv. L. Rev.* 7 (1969). Michelman should be consulted for his splendid insights into many of the problems dealt with in this model. His work also represents a pioneering probe into the hitherto murky distinction between minimum protection and equal protection.

parochial school. A wide range of ideological and curricular responses seems likely among private groups. Indeed, since the economic control of formerly parish schools would now pass to the parents, it is probable that a broad spectrum of choices would become available even within nominally "Catholic" education. It is significant that most bishops who thus far have engaged in the debate have favored purchase of services directly from private schools by the state, a distinctly "Establishment" approach.

7. *Experimentation.* The threat to survival from competitive pressures ought to stimulate vastly increased experimentation even within the limits of the resources available to each school for its regular program. Provisions encouraging cooperative programs among the schools on a contract basis and the reimbursement of the costs of special programs by the state should be strong additional incentives to experiment.

8. *"Community Control."* Many of the current decentralization proposals (see Chapter Nine) appear to be hypocritical for at least two reasons. First, authentic community self-determination can only be a function of financial autonomy, and few of the proposals so far seriously advanced would yield power over the budget to the local board; second, any proposal based upon a geographically defined unit must tolerate domination of minorities within the unit; the "community" is that group of residents which successfully imposes its programs on all the children of the district. Shifting to a family base would permit organization of nongeographical communities of interest which can be freely chosen and freely abandoned. Family power equalizing would permit each "community" to operate with financial independence.

9. *Racial Integration.* Our present judgment is that the system here proposed would increase racial integration in metropolitan areas in the medium and long run (perhaps beginning within two to three years of adoption) with accelerating effect thereafter, and with some differential burden imposed upon minority group children in terms of travel time. In the initial operation of the system, the opportunity to attend any system school within a large area should cause at least some middle-class minority students to attend putatively superior schools in white areas. Thereafter, as performance scores on standard tests became better known through the mandatory publicity provisions (see Chapter Three on accountability) a larger emigration of students could be expected from schools with lower performance to those with better. Ultimately, the shifts and countershifts of this movement should manifest three effects. First, they would tend to depopulate schools in the ghettos; second, they would tend to diversify social classes and races within the formerly white schools; third, they would tend to level out the overall test performances among the most elite of the formerly all-white schools. The magnitude of these movements would be modest, but, over the long haul, the

consequences would probably be more *stably* integrative for densely populated areas than any of the administrative proposals with which the authors have been associated or are familiar.

10. *Compensatory Education.* Whether the effect of the model could fairly be called "compensatory" is largely a problem of definition. Providing access to excellent schools on the basis of equal family sacrifice seems to the authors a plausible approach to ameliorating the special burdens of the disadvantaged. It would be surprising if certain high spending schools did not specialize in a curriculum designed for such children. Of course, such schools would have to be chosen by the parents, and some whose children need them would not choose them. Would the total effect be less compensatory? It is impossible to say unless we could accurately predict both the numbers of such "bad" choices and the alternative systems of compensation foreclosed by the adoption of the proposed system. It should be added that there is nothing in the model which would foreclose other compensatory efforts outside the regular school programs.

11. *Political Feasibility.* The authors' judgment is that the proposal, properly lobbied, could produce nice combinations of bedfellows. It should be attractive to Black Panthers, John Birchers, Muslims, Catholics (laymen, not the hierarchy), classical liberals, educational experimenters, property owners, residents of poor districts, and other disparate and overlapping cadres. It will threaten school administrators, residents of socially tight and very rich suburban districts, philosophical centralizers, those who for various reasons would discourage social diversity, and the multitude who fear all change. It would probably be opposed at first by conservative teachers' unions, although the opportunities for industry-wide bargaining and potential increase in the total pie ultimately should open their eyes to wider horizons. The total prospect seems problematic, but in an era of extreme frustration over property tax absurdities, it would be a hardy prophet who would dismiss it as political nonsense.

A CONTRASTING MODEL

The Harvard Center for the Study of Public Policy, working under a grant from the Office of Economic Opportunity, has proposed the rough outlines of an experimental voucher system which provides a useful contrast to the model we have described.[10] The Harvard proposal is a refinement of schemes for compensatory vouchers for the poor. In geographical areas selected for experimentation, children would receive a basic

[10] *Education Vouchers, A Preliminary Report on Financing Education by Payments to Parents* (Cambridge: Center for the Study of Public Policy, 1970). The Harvard system is entitled the "Regulated Compensatory Model."

voucher worth a minimum of, say, $750. Vouchers for the poor would be augmented in value in inverse proportion to the family wealth, up to a maximum voucher of perhaps $1500. Admissions to each school would be in part by lottery among applicants; the balance of admissions (one-half is suggested as a maximum) could be picked by the school, at least in the case of private schools.

The current form of the Harvard model runs the risk of producing highly undesirable effects. The nonrandom admission program is but the least of a nest of problems. The proposal would even permit private groups such as religious bodies to supplement the income that their schools receive from vouchers, thereby bestowing an advantage upon wealthy sponsors over poor and of private schools over public. This and many similar lacunae render the model as drafted unacceptable. However, the proposal seems to be far from its final form and will only be fully and fairly judged when viewed as a whole after the difficult work of drafting specific provisions is completed. What can be said at this point in time is that, if properly implemented, the Harvard model would appear plausible and attractive to many critics of the present system. It poses a nice contrast in its fundamental philosophy to the voucher structure we have described and proposed above.

Though ambiguous and contradictory in some respects, the basic goal of the Harvard model seems to be to provide the variety and freedom associated with vouchers while simultaneously equalizing the quality of schools within the system. This equality would be achieved by a trade-off of two basic inputs, money and good students. The more low performing children (using family poverty as the sole criterion) in the school, the more dollars; the more high achieving children, the fewer the dollars. ". . .The price of choosing more advantaged classmates would be that the school had less economic resources." [11] While children would be free to shop for differences in style, curriculum, or social mix, all would receive an education equal in quality. At least this would be so, if we are willing to assume that the specific relations fixed by the experts between the ability of the students and the value of their vouchers are the right ones.

The basic conflict between the models is obvious. Above an adequate minimum spending level for education, the model we have proposed would permit families to implement their private judgments about the value of education compared to other purchasable goods and services. The Harvard model, on the other hand, would constrain all voucher recipients from poor families to accept a uniform political decision on that question. It would permit wide choice among quality levels (except to the extent that quality differences were to arise from sources such as teacher

[11] *Education Vouchers,* p. 55.

quality which are outside the reach of the voucher system as proposed). The family could choose between a public and a private school, a progressive or a traditional school, a Catholic school or a Lutheran school, a red school or a blue school; but it could not choose between better schooling and better housing. The Harvard model would set an absolute value upon education; or, more accurately, it would permit experts and legislators to set an absolute value upon education. Their decision would fix the level of educational quality for all children whose parents could not afford private schools outside the system.

There is, of course, much to recommend such a system. It has many of the virtues of equality while eluding at least some of the vices of uniformity. Children could have equality of opportunity while remaining free to be different. This seems worthy of support as an experiment, or even more. Nonetheless, some cautious observations are in order. First, if equality is to be a decisive or at least significant value here, it is not clear that one model is on this ground to be preferred over the other. Each model can claim its own kind of equality—the one an equality of input, the other an equality of power to control that input. It would be difficult to say which is the more "democratic." Yet there is a significant difference, though not a simple one to describe. At first what seems to be at stake in the choice between these two forms of equality is the radically differing effects upon freedom of choice, the other value besides equality which dominates the voucher rhetoric. Clearly the Harvard model is much more restrictive in this regard. Is that, then, an end to the debate? Not so, for the freedom that is at stake here is primarily that of the parents; any freedom of the child is, at best, derivative. Indeed, if the child and the parent could be viewed analytically as independent of one another, the question might be posed pejoratively: Should we trade off the child's equality for the parents' freedom?

Of course the matter is not so simple, and few would suggest such a polarity in the child-parent relation. However, the point is that there is a fair question concerning the degree to which it is appropriate to invoke the increase of parental freedom as a basis for the preference between these two models. In the end, one's judgment on this will depend largely upon his view of the reasons for permitting families to have any choice in the first place. Is the preference of family over bureaucrat merely instrumental; does the family simply make better choices? Or does that preference spring from some deeper perception of the nature and proper prerogatives of the fundamental social unit? Or both? Or neither? We confess that a good deal more reflection will be necessary before we are prepared to commit ourselves on what is a major philosophical issue.

However, it is fair to make one final observation of a more terrestrial order about the role of the family within the Harvard model. That system would tolerate, indeed encourage, the family to make decisions of the most sophisticated character. Parents could choose between and among a variety of curricula and pedagogical approaches. We concede to the Harvard proponents the capacity of parents to make judgments on these matters, judgments which on the whole would be as reasonable as those of the experts. But, if so, why are parents unqualified to make what are the much less sophisticated choices between and among spending levels? If parents can evaluate the nuances among academic programs, would they be insensitive to the value of $300 extra in spending? Is the parent competent to determine only the kind of education and the state to determine how much education?

Presumably, this anomaly in attitude is not explained by any concern that each child receive an adequate minimum education. If the present minimum in our model were insufficient for that purpose, obviously it could be raised. Rather, there is operating here an unexplained disrelish for implementing the educational aspirations of poor parents who are willing to make an extra effort. The most that one can conclude is that the Harvard group do not wish to see children segregated according to parental attitudes toward education. Their report to the OEO describes such separation as "cultural" [12] and, though the intendment is ambiguous, perhaps it is a reasonable description of the probable empirical result. Persons who, after any given level of educational quality is reached, prefer to consume other goods can fairly be said to share a "culture." What is not plain is the ground of objection to their choice. Why should a system which permits and encourages families to separate for education on the basis of religion and ideology balk at separation on the basis of culture? In the light of the professed market orientation of the authors of the Harvard model, the enforced homogenization of quality for the poor stands in need of a rationale.

12 *Education Vouchers,* p. 38.

fourteen

A New Model for Learning Away from Schools

Somewhere in America's history we began to think of education as something that happened only in school. Important benefits developed from this perspective. If persons learn only in school, it justifies placing great emphasis on the school experience, and perhaps our society has placed more emphasis on formal schooling as a means for achieving social progress than has any other major society in history. As a result, we probably have the most elaborate and effective school system.

Still, we would all grant our approach involves an oversimplification: we must admit that only a part of our learning really takes place in school. Once we are reminded of this, we might consider other questions such as: what is the appropriate division of "instructional responsibilities" between schools and other sources? Is this division recognized in practice by schools? By students? By parents and other facets of our society? What are the implications if we agree that inadequate attention is being given to this division of responsibility? What harm can occur? What will be poorly "taught"? What may not be taught at all? How important is this ignorance of nonschool knowledge? How would such ignorance manifest itself?

Edward Wynne has attempted to approach these questions from a historical perspective to see how youths were raised in our past, and how changes in school modes have necessarily introduced both additional knowledge and ignorance for modern youths. He also traces efforts of Dewey and other reformers to prevent the artificiality of formal education from producing artificial adults. Unquestionably, Wynne's approach is affected not only by his academic research, but also by his experience in affairs as a labor lawyer and government administrator. His analysis suggests that modern youth unrest may be an inadvertent by-product of an education system that gives excessive emphasis to school knowledge and that discourages youths from acquiring maturing nonschool experiences.

The analysis includes a prescription for change, aimed at permitting youths to acquire more life experiences before completing school. Thus, this proposed educational model suggests that a recognition of the larger definition of education is, in itself, a model; such recognition will inevitably lead to the pattern of discussion followed in this chapter. While the prescription proffered in the chapter is surely debatable, any debate framed about a broader definition of education will lead us to see the role of schools in a new light.

ON MENTORSHIP

Edward Wynne

One of the weightiest problems with which the philosophy of education has to cope is the method of keeping a proper balance between the informal and the formal, the incidental and the intentional modes of education.—John Dewey, *Democracy and Education* [1]

Most of the education models considered in this book are concerned with alternative ways in which education can be conducted *in school.* In this chapter we have a concern for what youth learn away from school. We frequently expect schools to teach things which cannot be well learned in classrooms. This presumption usually precludes students from learning this information elsewhere. This mistaken policy may be a major cause, perhaps *the cause,* of the student unrest we see about us in universities and high schools. In sum, students revolt because we have kept them ignorant. However, first let me propose a remedy and then explain its rationale.

A PROPOSAL

I propose that every adult with a modicum of energy, vision, and flexibility should assume that within his lifetime he will act as mentor or advisor-counselor for five to fifteen youths (for about a year each). This *mentorship* might well take place at the conclusion of high school. As I will explain later, school systems, as well as other institutions, might play important roles in promoting the spread of mentorship. During mentorship, the youth should maintain an intimate and continuous association with the mentor, and probably work on the job with him. If the mentor is a doctor, he should be with him while he talks to a terminal cancer patient; if he's a lawyer, he should sit in while a witness is prepared for trial; the youth should listen as a salesman and his

[1] John Dewey, *Democracy and Education* (New York: Macmillan, 1916), p. 10.

boss develop a selling strategy; watch a foreman break in a young worker; follow a union business agent as he processes a grievance; walk the beat with a policeman; assist the man who manages the service station; or listen while a faculty committee decides who will get tenure.

Undoubtedly my examples may cause some readers to wince—do we have to let "outsiders" or "children" see that? Yes, we do, because we have to bring them in from the outside. Only if we bring youth into life, "warts and all," can we achieve the goals of this proposal. While the youth might acquire some useful vocational skills, this would not be our prime goal. The goal would be to develop an association in which the major values of informal education could be transmitted to the youth, and one in which the mentor could enjoy the challenging experience of assisting an informed and maturing young adult move into the world. The job would be a vehicle for structured interaction.

What would we hope to achieve by this process? To give the youth an appreciation of the controlling role of nonacademic values in the world. (Even where mentors have professional and "bookish" jobs, the youth will see that human interaction is properly the major concern in the life of most men.) To suggest to the youth the subtle, implicit, moral, and personal concerns that must govern the control and assessment of personal conduct. To give him the background to absorb better the extensive book learning that may lie before him in school and life. To permit him better to estimate how he will fit into the adult world, and, thus, to be more patient about the (apparent) irrelevancies of formal education that may lie ahead. To give him some grasp of adult negotiating skills, so he can more effectively (and less destructively) alter any irrelevancies he perceives in the system. To stimulate some institutions into reconsidering their existing policies of requiring college degrees where academic knowledge is irrelevant to the job. To permit adults to recognize the right of youth to help manage our society, and to restructure our institutions to permit such engagement. To force the most able adults in our society to increase their ties with formal education through their contact with these youths so they are better informed about these institutions, their conduct, and their products.

No doubt many of the objectives of this proposal are akin to the responsibilities of parenthood. But there are important distinctions. First, there is the matter of perspective—a mentor will bring to his engagement a perspective new to the youth. If, as Dewey once suggested,[2] a good learning situation requires the learner to adapt to some situations beyond his control, as well as modifying other conditions to serve his ends, then a stranger-mentor will give the youth such an opportunity.

Second, the knowledge explosion has placed excessive demands on

2 Dewey, *Democracy and Education.*

parents as guardians, as well as contributing to the strains on youth. The explosion has increased the amount that most youths learn in a year of schooling and increased the length of schooling they receive. These effects, together with the emphasis on formal education, have diminished the prestige (or adequacy) of their guardians. The relationship frequently becomes strained as the youth perceives that he's better informed than his guardian. Mentorship, by concentrating the responsibilities upon the more open and better informed citizens, would diminish the intensity of such tensions.

Finally, focusing the attention of the best of our society on the process of maturation would provide youths with the best models, and engage the attention of our most productive persons with the issues of education and socialization.

Anyone who reflects on his own maturation process, or observes the maturing youth about him, will recognize that this proposal is a codification of an existing informal practice. Almost any person who attains adequate growth has, at some stage, associated with effective adults, and learned from them. This means the conscious recognition and encouragement of an implicit practice: the acknowledgment that the matter is too important to be left to coincidence, the personnel department, or chance; that it should occur at an appropriate time; that the current process is too effervescent and often too brief; that it is considerably hampered by "modern," and thus obsolete, job structures; that our mores are usually unsympathetic to adults or youths who engage in this process; and that "credentialism" aggravates the process by foolishly grounding many job distinctions on book learning or narrowly defined experience. Today, revolution is the only means for youth to be sure of obtaining the engagement of competent adults. Only our explicit attack on the problem can produce the revamping of priorities that is essential.

There are diverse internship programs that exist in society today, and undoubtedly some of them are akin to the process of mentorship I advocate. Where they exist, they should be expanded. But in many cases, it appears the function of the process is to transmit job information rather than attitudes, and thus the most desirable part of the process is explicitly ignored or undervalued. Sometimes the programs attempt to give youths experience by assigning them to jobs conceived especially for youth. Unfortunately, such assignments are often designed to salve the conscience of adults, but still keep the youth out of the adults' hair. Under these conditions, the intergenerational engagement that should be the first purpose of such activities is prevented. Many other programs are for persons at the postgraduate level, while I contend that the engagement should occur earlier (which does not preclude a later internship for other purposes). Finally, my suggestion emphasizes that the relation between the youth and one significant adult should persist for about a year. I doubt that most internships have this kind of attention span. A year suggests the intensity of relationship that should be generated; even persons without great natural affinity may develop important personal ties during a year's commitment to common tasks. One test of the intensity is whether or not the youth and adult might stay in communication with each other after the internship ended. (Such a continuing tie could enable both to receive sustained benefits from the exposure.)

This proposal is grounded on a rather complex analysis of important dysfunctions that have evolved within our educational system. To justify the proposal, let us first consider some important data and then the history of the system. We will then see how these perspectives tie to mentorship.

THE DATA

The pattern of schools, colleges, and other learning institutions that has evolved in our nation is without parallel in human history. This formal education system serves as a model for numerous other societies. Peculiarly, many Americans are insensitive to the most unique characteristic of this system: an enormous and growing proportion of our populace spends the greater part of its youth in school. As the chart suggests (Figure 14–1), this trend is a comparatively recent development in our history and shows every sign of following its present direction. At this moment, we are far ahead of every other modern society in the amount of school exposure our youth receive. (Although some of them are attempting to follow our example.) In fact, *no other major society in human history has come near giving all its youth the amount of formal schooling presently provided in America.*

DESIGNING AND BUILDING THE SYSTEM

But where does this information lead us? We cannot adopt the overly simple proposition that schooling is bad. No, but we can reflect on the more subtle implications of these data. First, consider the contrast between formal and informal education. It is notorious that schools and books are not the only source of human wisdom and that education must cover far more than formal knowledge. For instance, Emile Durkheim, a sociologist, wrote:

> Education is the influence exercised by adult generations on those that are not yet ready for social life. Its object is to arouse and develop in the child a certain number of physical, intellectual and moral states which are de-

FIGURE 14–1 *Amounts of Formal Education Being Received by Youths*

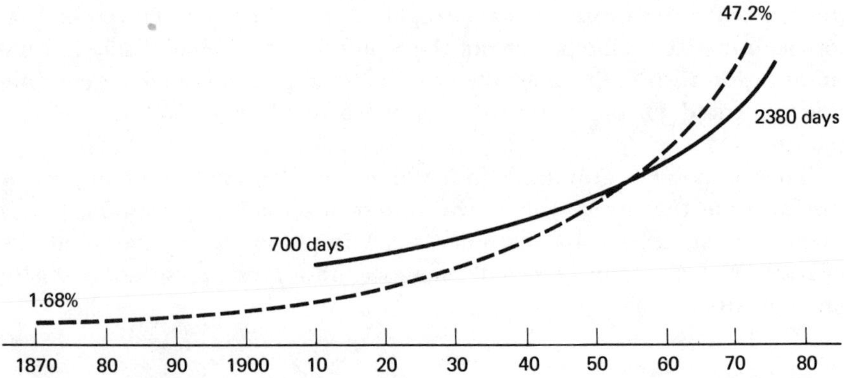

Solid line—Average amount of total days of formal schooling received by male labor force member, 1910-1980. Data after 1955 are projections.*

Dotted line—Percentage of youths 18-21 attending institutions of higher education.†

* E. F. Denison, *The Sources of Economic Growth in the United States and the Alternatives Before Us* (New York: Committee for Economic Development, 1962), pp. 72, 73; U. S. Bureau of the Census, *Historical Statistics of the United States, Colonial Times to 1957* (Washington, D. C.: U. S. Government Printing Office, 1960), p. 113.

† U. S. Bureau of the Census, *Historical Statistics of the United States,* p. 210; U. S. Bureau of the Census, *Statistical Abstract of the United States,* 89th edition (Washington, D. C.: U. S. Government Printing Office, 1968), p. 126.

manded of him by both the political society as a whole and the special milieu for which he is specifically destined.[3]

Other reflective persons have arrived at similar conclusions. The philosopher, R. S. Peters,[4] emphasized that education was a process of "initiation into modes of thought and experience." Its aim is to develop:

> Judgment, . . . the final flower of much experience. But such experience has usually to be acquired in the company of a man who already has judgment . . . , subtleties in an educational situation are usually caught rather than taught . . . , those who acquire them are drawn by some sort of attraction towards a particular practitioner of an art or a mode of thought, who functions as an exemplar to them. And so skill and judgment are handed on from generation to generation, each master contributing his individual increment to the common stock.[5]

What these writers are suggesting is simply what our common sense tells us—that many important things are learned out of school. As a simple instance, many of the major designers of our current educational

[3] Emile Durkheim, *Education and Sociology,* translated by S. D. Fox (Glencoe: Free Press, 1956), p. 71.

[4] R. S. Peters, *Ethics and Education* (London: George Allen and Unwin, 1956).

[5] Peters, *Ethics and Education,* p. 60.

system, men such as Benjamin Franklin and Horace Mann, were persons who acquired the bulk of their intellectual seasoning in the world of events. Franklin was working as an apprentice in his early teens, and Horace Mann, the major leader in the founding of our present public school system, experienced approximately ten weeks of formal schooling before beginning college at age sixteen. Mann later observed that, before college, his youth was composed principally of "work and church going." Even leaders with a comparatively extensive formal education, such as Thomas Jefferson, had their schooling interposed with "the society of horse racers, card players, fox hunters, scientific and professional men." In almost every instance, it is possible to identify significant adults, outside of their family, who had an important impact on the young lives of these leaders.

Ironically, these early designers could not conceive of an education which would separate maturing youth from the bustling, untidy, frustrating real world of their times. In their view, adults and youths worked and strove together, sometimes succeeding, sometimes failing, but usually enjoying the satisfaction of a common effort at a real task. Unquestionably, their experience convinced them that more isolation from this real world was appropriate to permit the transmission of finer formal knowledge. Essentially, what they envisioned was a more structured education process, which would prevent the recurrence of the educational deficiencies that had been seen about them. Such an improved system would (1) be widespread, (2) be responsible for reaching every student, and (3) permit every student to receive adequate exposure to formal learning. By definition, it would be a powerful and efficient bureaucracy, with all the characteristics carefully catalogued by the sociologist, Weber:

1. Division of responsibility.
2. Review of subordinate conduct by the hierarchy.
3. Formalization and precise definition of job qualification and responsibilities.
4. Specialization and routinization of tasks.
5. Provision for planning.
6. Emphasis on adequate records and files.
7. Routines for determination of leadership succession.[6]

Such a system would establish its legitimacy by stressing its development from charismatic, nonbureaucratic founders and designers such as Mann. By doing honor to vital leaders, the system would increase the prestige of their creations.

To Weber the word "bureaucratic" was not inherently pejorative. It described an institutional form that was appropriate for certain tasks

[6] Max Weber, *On Charisma and Institution Building,* S. N. Eisenstadt, ed. (Chicago: University of Chicago Press, 1968).

that arise in modern civilization. In such societies, large, complex organizations are often the way of accomplishing important jobs. One cannot have small, effective postal systems, weather bureaus, computer shared time arrangements, oil pipelines, pollution control plans, or airline flight pattern structures. Yet such systems inevitably diminish the independence of their participants. This is so because each actor must follow a predictable course in order for the other actors to coordinate their performance with his. In sum, such bureaucracies, whatever their contributions, sap some of the personal vigor of their employees. Demands placed on the developing formal education system caused it to evolve into perhaps the most restricted large bureaucracy in America. But those demands could not have been met without such an evolution. The system had to accommodate itself to (1) an immense increase in the number of students, (2) a continuous lengthening of the span of education, and (3) a tremendous explosion in the amount of knowledge that the system has to transmit to students. Only a vast bureaucracy could manage the planning and coordination that have been required to stay abreast of this tide.

(It is correct to say that American formal education is not integrated into one tight structure, as are the education systems in some other western nations. However, the operation of the total system, universal compulsory schooling, common patterns of college entrance requirements, the comparatively uniform training and certification requirements of teachers, the mobility of pupils which has compelled a common curriculum, has had much the same effect. The integrated national communication structure has also given citizens a common body of expectations about their schools.)

A conspicuous consequence of this bureaucratization has been a society that has come close to meeting the goals of its founders. Economists have concluded that it is not irrelevant that the society with the longest established, most intensive, and most widespread free public education system has developed the highest living standard in the world. Only one other large country, Great Britain (with 60 percent smaller population), has a longer tradition of continuous, freely elected government. In view of the continuing increase in (1) the number and proportion of students receiving college education, and (2) the invention of new knowledge, the growth pressures for the continuation of bureaucratic modes will remain. While some humanizing improvements are possible, it seems unlikely that we can anticipate the elimination of bureaucratic education. As Warren Bennis observed, "universities surpass business in subterfuge [against concern for] the common life." [7]

[7] Warren A. Bennis, "Post Bureaucratic Leadership," *Trans-Action,* Vol. 6, No. 9 (July/August 1969), 49.

DEWEY'S CRITICISM

John Dewey was a sensitive analyst of these bureaucratizing tendencies. On one hand, he recognized them as the inevitable effects of a widespread education system. He observed that: "The task of teaching certain things is delegated to a special group of persons. Without such formal education, it is not possible to transmit all the resources and achievements of a complex society." [8] "First a complex civilization is too complex to be assimilated *in toto.* It has to be broken up into portions, as it were, and assimilated piecemeal in a gradual and graded way. . . . The first office of the social organ we call the school is to provide a *simplified* environment." [9] He saw the schools' emphasis on knowledge transmission as a natural concommitant to their development in a pioneer society. "Books and everything concerned with them were, on the other hand, rare and difficult of access; they were the only means of outlet from a narrow and crude society. Whenever such conditions obtain, much may be said in favor of concentrating school activity upon books." [10]

On the other hand, Dewey was conscious of the inherent shortcomings of formal education. He said, "Schools are, indeed, one important method of transmission which forms the disposition of the immature; but it is only one means, and, compared with other agencies, a relatively superficial means." [11]

To compensate for the artificiality of the bureaucratic formal system, Dewey proposed to tie schools more closely to the nonbookish business of life. He recognized that our society was far removed from the predominantly agricultural world of the early 19th century, where the labors of childhood slid imperceptibly into those of the adult society. In earlier days, even when fortunate children were exempted from agricultural labor, their work and social obligations merged them smoothly into the adult world. They often received their education from tutors, and the lack of credentialism in the society and the comparatively unsophisticated nature of the skills required permitted significant responsibilities to be given to the young. Even in higher education, the first emphasis was on human interaction, moral philosophy and Sunday evenings in the college president's parlor. The system was "blessed" with a shortage of formal information to transmit, and so concerned itself with informal education.

[8] Dewey, *Democracy and Education,* p. 9.
[9] *Ibid.,* p. 23.
[10] *Ibid.,* p. 229.
[11] *Ibid.,* p. 4.

Dewey's prescription was "The Transformation of the School"—to apply the title of Lawrence Cremin's famous work about the progressive education effort. The object: to reform the school into

> . . . a miniature social group on which study and growth are incidents of present shared experience. Playgrounds, shops, workrooms and laboratories not only direct the natural active tendencies of youth, but they involve intercourse, communication, and cooperation . . . all extending the perception of connections.[12]

Dewey's vision became the goal of the progressive education movement.

The most significant aspect of this reforming approach was its tacit acceptance of formal education as the medium for the transmission of diverse types of educational experiences. While Dewey appreciated the importance of informal education, his goal was reformation of the education bureaucracy; to correct the bureaucracy by "informalizing" it. However, the massive knowledge transmission responsibilities of schools were not diminished during this period. This is understandable. But as Toynbee observed, "When a separate formal kind of education makes its appearance, it brings into existence a new class of professional teachers who work, like other professional men and women, for pay." [13] "Formalism is psychically cheap," [14] and we cannot expect informal, personal interaction from a class of professional knowledge transmitters. Cremin pointed out that:

> What the progressives did prescribe made inordinate demands on the teachers' time and ability. "Integrated studies" required familiarity with a fantastic range of knowledge and teaching materials; while the commitment to build up student needs and interests demanded extraordinary feats of pedagogical ingenuity. In the hands of first-rate instructors, the innovations worked wonders; in the hands of too many average teachers, however, they led to chaos.[15]

Viewing the matter simply as a problem of economics and organizational restructuring, we could probably achieve the pattern of breadth and intensity prescribed by Dewey if:

1. We increased the proportion of the nation's GNP invested in education by perhaps 500 percent. Only such a shift could attract into education (a) the number of persons needed to permit the intense interpersonal engagement prescribed by Dewey, and (b) the types of people (now in other careers) whose abilities and personal styles are consider-

[12] *Ibid.*, p. 416.

[13] Edward D. Meyers, *Education in the Perspective of History* (New York: Harper & Row, 1960), p. 286.

[14] Williard Waller, *The Sociology of Teaching* (New York: Russell & Russell, 1932), p. 433.

[15] Lawrence A. Cremin, *The Transformation of the School* (New York: Random House—Vintage Books, 1961), p. 348.

ably broader than those of typical teachers and who currently find teaching either too low paying or too filled with trivial, hyperbureaucratic chores.

2. We made formal learning so akin to the larger society that students' tasks put them in touch with the same rewards and frustrations that exist in the outer world: the pain of failure, the challenge of limited time and resources, the satisfaction of having overcome disinterest and hostility, the stress of competition, *the rewards of having improved or changed a real thing,* the need to relate to many persons of other ages, with other values. But if all these things occur, in what sense will the restructured institution be a "school"? Would not it simply be a firm, a factory, a garage, a politician's office?

Finally, one might raise the question of whether or not our new and "better teachers" would stay better teachers if they came into education on a prolonged, full-time basis. While worldly adults should have more engagement with youths, it is not clear that the engagement should exclude such adults from all their ties with the larger world. The ties are part of what makes the adults' contributions so valuable. In other words, prolonged, exclusive exposure to youth may be dangerous to the perspective of adults, just as I am suggesting that it is dangerous to youth. Indeed, one of the weaknesses I perceive in our current education system is that it has excessively insulated many of its instructors from the world.

THE PERSPECTIVE OF HISTORY

But how important is this separation of students from the world of interaction and unbookish life? There is no simple answer, but we can engage in productive speculation. Considered in a historical light, our current formal education system is a radical experiment. This is not to contend it is a failure, but to urge more sensitivity to the novel implications of what we have evolved. The uniqueness of our venture is best seen in the work of Edward Meyers [16] who summarized the available information about education systems found in the fifteen diverse societies described in Toynbee's *Study of History*. While there can be differences about minor judgments made by Meyers, the major weight of his work appears indisputable.

Our formal education system is unique in world history. The educational systems that existed in the great "(Chinese), Indic and Hellenic civilizations saw education as primarily the development of character, though this was not inconsistent with knowledge transmission, since the

16 Meyers, *Education in Perspective.*

moral man was informed." Such systems gave emphasis to "the relationship that existed between the tutor and pupil: it was one of friendship and love, close and intimate and personal as the relations between members of the family." "The pupil associated constantly with his tutor, and observed his speech, his manners, his social and moral attitudes, and so, little by little, learned all these things from his tutor and his tutor's associates." "The tutors were those . . . who had proved themselves to be among the ablest and wisest not only of the people as a whole but even of their much smaller social group." [17]

Another historian, Phillippe Aires, studied the evolution of the concept of childhood in western society from about the tenth century onward.[18] His central conclusion was that the evolving concepts persistently moved toward promoting greater isolation of young persons from the adult world, on the plea that healthy maturation can best occur in a more child-centered environment. Separation has been the continuing trend. Although Aires did not explicitly concern himself with the current American education system, he would unquestionably conclude that it is the apotheosis of the trend he has perceived.

Interestingly enough, Peter Drucker, whom one might term an economist-technocrat, reached a conclusion approximating that of the historians and philosophers. In his recent book, *The Age of Discontinuity*, Drucker observes:

> To keep everyone in school until the age of eighteen or twenty greatly extends the years of adolescence. Adolescence is not a natural state. It is a man-made, cultural condition. The adolescent lives simultaneously in two age levels; his "cultural age" is lower than his chronological age . . . the young man of twenty-five is expected (by the institutions about him) to seem younger and to be emotionally immature.[19]

Drucker proposed getting most youths out into life sooner, and making formal education more available to people thirty and beyond rather than administering it all in one dose.

THE SYSTEM'S ESCAPE FROM FEEDBACK

Designers such as Thomas Jefferson, Benjamin Franklin, and Horace Mann based their educational plans essentially on intuition—there had never been historical experience with an educational effort of the type and scope they proposed. On the other hand, the concepts of political democracy they supported had undergone developmental work in other

[17] *Ibid.*, pp. 254, 256.
[18] Phillippe Aries, *Centuries of Childhood* (New York: Knopf, 1962).
[19] Peter F. Drucker, *The Age of Discontinuity* (New York: Harper & Row, 1969), p. 325.

countries and societies before our constitutional convention. Still, the founders, in drafting the Constitution, consciously designed a self-correcting system for their political model, one that left room for experiment, further development, and revision. The operation of that system, too, has heavily engaged the continuous attention of the larger society, and so it has benefited from persistent analysis and change pressures. Conversely, the schools, as Cremin observed in *The Wonderful World of Elwood Patterson Cubberley,* generated the myth that they are matured organizations, and that school management can best be left in the hands of "professionals." [20] Furthermore, despite Dewey's efforts, assessment of the system has largely focused on its formal aspect: is Johnny learning to read? How competent are our scientists? It is precisely here that the system is at its comparative best, and where "technical" questions play the largest role in debates that arise. We have forgotten the question of whether any "system" can teach Johnny to live, and whether some systems may make him more or less equipped for "life."

Educators have thus successfully co-opted their own history, and currently laymen have forgotten, or never learned, that the system's visionary inventors were principally laymen, not professional educators. This ignorance has inhibited public feedback and isolated the system from dynamic change. Even where there has been change, the essential pattern has been mere enlargement: the end has been to prolong schooling further and make school systems bigger.

Thus, the idea of a major political leader making original proposals about the conduct of education might seem abnormal to us. However, since much of the talent and change affecting skills of the society drift onto the stage of politics, the lack of such proposals means schools are deprived of the stimulating criticism of our more effective spokesmen. The controversy in 1969 regarding Mayor Lindsay's engagement in the New York City school decentralization debate confirms this observation. Lindsay's strategic premises, that schools were not meeting important needs of many pupils, that major changes were needed, and that one could not expect schools to attempt such changes within the current framework, were clearly correct. His bull-in-a-china-shop tactics were undoubtedly open to criticism; decentralization, if well presented, need not divide racial groups, religious denominations, or political parties. However, Lindsay's errors are of a type that we might well expect to result from lack of experience in school problems, a result of the divorce of education policy from politics. Consider also the obvious indecision of the Nixon administration about college unrest—again, lack of experience; hopefully, they would have known better how to handle a missile crisis. When schools are well run, such inhibitions upon politicians are

20 Lawrence A. Cremin, *The Wonderful World of Elwood Patterson Cubberley* (New York: Teachers College, 1965).

ideal—"overdoses" of public scrutiny, that is, political criticism, can clearly be detrimental. However, this extended isolation of formal education from the feedback generated by the give and take of politics or other competitive forces suggests that serious dysfunctions may have evolved.

Historically speaking, our education system is a great new ship that has been sent on a dangerous voyage by brilliant designers, but with passengers and a crew that are not adept or unaware of the dangers of the voyage. On such a voyage, broad-visioned helmsmen should replace seasoned careerists.

STUDENTS ASSESS THE SYSTEM

These abstract considerations lead us to a more complete perception of the unrest that arises in education today. One observer said that "denial of pertinent information to participants prevents a cognitive structuring of events and results in emotionalism, lack of direction, alienation and conflict. When the subordinate is denied information, he is prevented from seeing the relationship between his immediate activities and the larger group of objectives." [21] The essential cause for the current student unrest can be seen as a product of the denial of information: the crucial information and perspectives that can flow to youth from intimate intergenerational engagement.

Strident student demands for "relevance" and increasing pressures for institutional change can all be seen as evidence of the failure of the institutions to "teach" life adjustment. Of course, the concept of "teaching" such values is a solecism, as long as we think of teaching as restricted to formal education. But the way things are now, if something is not taught via formal education, it is not taught at all. We are creating generations of youths who have lived principally on the vicarious nurture of book learning. Why should we assume they know anything about life, if we remember the real definitions of education? Why should we be appalled when their change strategy is confrontation which is unconcerned with the effect of the crisis they generate, and a philosophy which refuses to decide or describe the kind of improved world they want? Is it surprising they have a special sense of identification with the blacks and poor, the other classes that have been systematically excluded from the informal education processes of the larger society? Is it not also significant that many youths from bookish family environments, whose parents also, perhaps, received excessively formal educations, are among the more alienated; is it not plausible that the deficiencies in their parents' education are being magnified in their children?

[21] K. Lewin, *Resolving Social Conflicts* (New York: Harper Bros., 1948), p. 157.

These youthful protestors seem to see all intergenerational differences as the product of conspiracy, and they exhibit a cynicism which would make a hardened machine politician uneasy. With their entire lives ahead of them, they are tormented at the idea of evolutionary change. In a society which has moved more persons out of poverty in the past ten years than any comparable time in human history, they demand immediate elimination of problems that have baffled mankind for thousands of years. When all other great nations have sometimes become ensnared in unsound and immoral foreign wars, they view our current mistake as unique in human history. On one hand, they propose instant engagement of youth in correcting society; on the other hand, drugs and mysticism are proffered as remedies. Perhaps worst of all, they appear determined to win themselves a voice in the shaping of events, and they are insistent that their voice should override when there is a conflict between their concerns and the aspirations of other citizens.

Students may be wiser than even they realize. There is something terribly wrong: a society which has allowed the formalities of education to absorb the elements of initiation and intergenerational exchange may be approaching its day of reckoning. The current system has won us great benefits, far more informed students, the relief of adults from "baby-sitting," and the development of a job structure which leaves to schools the responsibility for late adolescent maturation. But I suggest the price is too high: the tensions resulting from such continuing unrest will (1) increase the school-based frustrations of even the most scholastically oriented students, (2) further increase intergeneration polarization and diminish the likelihood of useful dialogues (unless our perspectives change), (3) stimulate universities and faculty members into a frantic search to achieve an unattainable degree of rapport with their students (some increases in openness are possible and desirable, but the large degree of change necessary to do the job is beyond the responsibility of the university; it should not be mother to us all) (4) deprive society of the counsel of a valuable institution, that fulfills a unique need, and (5) eventually produce an adult generation whose immature values and petulant frustrations will endanger our society.

America is not immediately threatened with violent overthrow, but there are other dangers. For instance, ten to fifteen years ago, adolescent gang war was rampant in the New York slums. Finally, the police decided to adopt ruthless repression as their tactic. After intense oppression, fighting gangs were broken up. Frustrated, alienated ex-gang members, no longer supported by the social ties of their gangs, turned to dope (and individual thievery to buy dope). Self-destruction and terror as described in *Manchild in the Promised Land* [22] increasingly swept the

[22] Claude Brown, *Manchild in the Promised Land* (New York: Signet, 1965).

slums. Repression is not synonymous with the long-range solution of important social problems. The deep scars that the current system inflicts on our youth will haunt us all as they grow older and acquire real power.

MENTORSHIP

This presentation urges all of us as "passengers" to concern ourselves again with the direction of the ship. There must be a widescale public involvement in the conduct and assessment of our education systems, formal and informal. I propose a return to mentorship to achieve this effect. However, it is possible to accept the principles outlined in this chapter, and differ on the remedy. Acceptance of the principles is of larger importance, since other remedies might serve. For instance, Drucker's suggestion for postponing much of formal education until later in life may provide a solution. However, let us complete our exploration of the possibilities of mentorship.

Is not arrogance one of its major flaws; how can we reshape the priorities of a whole society? The lovely thing about mentorship is that it can be attempted on any scale. On a small scale, it can be integrated into our existing institutions and structures without radical revisions. You and I could explore exchange of mentorships for our children. While there might be many advantages of involving a number of people in the effort—not in the least to permit these late adolescents to feel that there were some peers engaged in the project—the commitment of one-half of 1 percent of our society, 500,000 persons, would provide a magnificent pool. It would be valuable to establish a clearing-house unit, to bring interested youths and adults together and to collect information about the results of different modes. Of course, there is research in psychology and sociology which would be of some use, and new research concerns can be developed. The whole proposal must win the attention of reflective citizens and concerned late adolescents and students, but it is not an effort that needs to be analyzed definitively and researched before it is attempted. If it succeeds on a small scale, then it can grow.

It is true that the proposal conflicts with the bureaucratic modes of work that have evolved from our reliance upon credentialism, and changing these modes will not be easy. However, it may be possible to make some institutions work for this change, since some institutional leaders may realize the survival of institutions depends on the health of our society. Colleges, universities, high schools, business corporations, foundations, alumni associations, professional groups, local, state, and federal governments could all assist. Schools could promote mentorships for their recent graduates (with their alumni?) or for students seeking admission. Businesses could revise personnel practices to permit employees at all levels to act as mentors. Government could change its civil service rules, or fund research.

It may be contended that the mentors, or their organizers, might exploit the youths. This could happen and undoubtedly would in some places, if we have mentorship on a large scale. However, we might ask: is not there some "exploitation" in our current formal education systems? Is it not true that many of the policies they follow are more in the interest of the institutions than the students? Is not this exploitation? This does not justify exploitation, but suggests that no system, unless we isolate youths from all adult contacts, will completely eliminate exploitation. I contend that the "exploitation" practiced by the current formal system is worse than that which may spring from the change I propose. At least mentorship offers, in exchange for possible exploitation, a chance to relate to human beings rather than to an institution. Indeed, some novelists have portrayed the "corruption" of youth by worldly men as a rewarding learning experience. Remember, we are not going to send six year olds into the Manchester mills; we are only saying youths who are old enough to be effective soldiers can generally take care of themselves on a job. If they do not like it, they can quit, find another mentor, go home, or go back to school.

But can we assume youths are interested in such involvement? Is not their present posture hostile to such efforts? Presumably we cannot draft them into mentorship, and extensive youth resistance may kill the idea. However, we may predict the course of events if we consider a pattern that sometimes arises even among extreme youth activists: the presentation of so-called "nonnegotiable demands," and subsequently the discussion (negotiation) of these demands if any responsible adult becomes seriously engaged. This pattern suggests that youth can be opened to engagement, *if* they are convinced, by words and conduct, that adults are concurrently open too. It is distressing that our future mentors may, in some cases, need to attempt discussions with youths who cannot say simply that they would like to have a talk. However, adults must recognize that the institutions they have permitted to evolve are a primary cause for this intergenerational inarticulateness; thus, it may only be fair that they accept the cost of this barrier.

In some ways, I worry more about adult fear of engagement with youth. The fear may be twofold: the potential discomfort of facing their judgmental attitudes and the concern that youth engagement will distract them from their business needs. As for the potential discomfort, either we adults are grossly immoral, and should have our styles moderated, or we are not as far away from our children as we fear, and both we and the youths should recognize this proximity. In any case, society cannot persist on a continuing basis of intergenerational schizophrenia; there must be a resolution.

I suspect distraction from business is the more grave problem. (I am really suggesting that the generation gap is not due to differing moralities, but to poor communication.) Unquestionably, in the short run, mentorship will use up adult time and energy that might ordinarily go into "work" affairs (though eventually, the youth contribution might materially increase the work output). If you expose youths to real experiences, questions, explanations, and dialogues will be inevitable. That is exactly the goal—to establish the principle that education is part of the work of all of us. We need to realize that society cannot designate a group of persons as teachers, pay them salaries, and assume the responsibilities for education are lifted from society's shoulders. That is the current state of affairs, and that is why things are going wrong; that is what must change! It would be surprising if some adults did not find this painful, and want to escape to the shelter of "work." But change usually is painful, and that is perhaps why we prescribe it for youths, rather than ourselves. Can we take our own medicine?

The concept of mentorship is not new. It has been routine in other civilizations. Even in recent western soceity, it is the premise underlying the work of Dewey and his associates. Others have raised the matter in slightly different forms. For instance, in 1934 Willard Waller proposed:

> The cause of education in personal development would be greatly furthered if students could be brought into intimate contact, if possible daily contact, with the leaders of the outside world, the leaders of business and society, of sport and of the intellect. One can imagine a great draft system like compulsory military service, but unlike it in that the inclusion in the draft is a special honor, that reaches out and drags in the great men and the great women of the community and forces them to do their bit for the young. . . . What we have in mind is that it is necessary to provide a channel for personal interchange between children and the outstanding men and women of the community, and that possibly the school can reorganize its curriculum in such a way as to bring this about.[23]

This essay is an emphatic criticism of American education. But the criticism is not so much aimed at the formal system, as at a society that looks to schools instead of to itself to correct learning shortcomings. That approach may well have reached a dead end. Dewey's great efforts at reform in the system failed. Waller's proposal, to bring in outsiders, is more than 35 years old; it has not caught on. These failures are, in the main, due to the assumptions of society that (1) the schools must transmit substantial formal knowledge, and (2) that formal knowledge is the main tool for satisfactory maturation. As long as society con-

[23] Waller, *The Sociology of Teaching,* p. 454.

currently applies these premises, we are probably scheduled for serious trouble. Schools will not go out of the formal education business; therefore, society must reshoulder its responsibility for transmitting informal knowledge.

Epilogue

It would be inappropriate for us to suggest preferences among the models and reforms our proponents have set before you. However, a few summarizing observations appear to be in order. As we observed at the outset, the proposals presented here deal both with models and modules. Some few chapters imply exclusive remedies, but the larger proportion propose concepts that may be combined in various ways. The appropriate mix must be determined by the persons and institutions that are actually on the scene.

A larger matter is the question of how to achieve any effective and substantial school change. It is evident that the models proposed are generally not ideas that can be simply picked up and adopted without controversy or effort by an interested school or district. In fact, this is one of their attractions; one can be deservedly suspicious of any "innovation" that lends itself to easy integration into the existing system. Is it possible for such an innovation to be noteworthy? At this stage of the game, are there any fast, cheap, pleasant-tasting medicines? But if the models will engender controversy and take time to perfect or put into effect, what are the prospects for reform? What strategy will win the day? A glance at the history of educational change in America provides some clues.

Perhaps the first important theme that arises in considering that history is the rediscovery that "public schools" were not only developed for the public, but also they were developed *by the public*. Moreover, public leadership, and nonschool institutions, have played the major role in initiating, supporting, and implementing the larger reforms that have since taken place in the public school system. Robert Coram, with whose words we opened Chapter One, was an 18th century journalist. Jefferson and Franklin stimulated important education development. Indeed, perhaps the clearest example of public leadership is found in the early 19th century "common school movement." The movement transformed the then existing system of fragmented and limited schools into organizations which made free, public elementary education available to most every child, and thus formed the base for our present pattern of universal education. The common school movement won its goals through public agitation, political propaganda, widespread lobbying, venturesome legislation, and the high quality of its personal leadership.

Horace Mann, the prime promoter of the common school movement, was a politician and lawyer before accepting the post of Secretary to the Massachusetts State Board of Education in 1849. Governor DeWitt Clinton of New York was founder of the Public School Society in 1805, and was an active officer for 23 years. Thaddeus Stevens, as a member of the Pennsylvania State Legislature in 1834, presented a lengthy defense against efforts to repeal the State's recently passed common school law. He contended that:

> If an elected Republic is to endure, every elector must have sufficient information not only to accumulate wealth and to take care of his pecuniary concerns, but to direct wisely the legislature, the ambassadors, and the Executive of the Nation—for some part of all of these things, some agency in approving or disapproving them, falls to every freeman. If then, the permanency of our Government depends upon such knowledge, it is the duty of the government to see that the means of information be diffused to every citizen.[1]

A writer on the common school movement observed that of 14 important promoters, many of whom obtained positions as school leaders, 11 had at some time held elective offices, such as state legislators. Nine of the 14 were former lawyers; only one had been a teacher. The efforts of these leaders were supplemented by the agitation and petitions of workingmen's societies, whose members wished to ensure that adequate schools were made available to their children and that schools were not simply preserves for the privileged.[2]

Many educators were sympathetic to the common school movement, but the major burden of reform was borne by laymen. In addition, certain antieducator themes evolved. Powerful, effective personalities like Mann inevitably developed competencies and knowledge that gave them broader perspectives on pedagogical problems than those held by many of their contemporary schoolmen. Mann aired these views in his *Seventh Annual Report on School Conditions in Massachusetts,* and became engaged in a prolonged public controversy with the school masters of the existing Boston schools. They took his sympathetic observations on

[1] Elwood P. Cubberley, *Public Education in the United States* (Boston: Houghton Mifflin, 1934), p. 155.

[2] David B. Tyack, *Turning Point in American Educational History* (Waltham, Mass.: Blaisdell, 1967), p. 125.

European educational practices (which included a deemphasis of "birching") to be a criticism of their own methods. Mann was a tenacious fighter, and a lengthy, published exchange arose. The exchange terminated with Mann's rebuttal to their critique and this seemed to carry the day. Also, in other parts of the nation, the common school literature frequently included a criticism of the free schooling then being provided to the children of paupers; the criticism inevitably reflected unfavorably upon the performance of educators.

Similar noneducator themes have underlain other important reform efforts. For example, John Dewey, a philosopher (in inspiring the progressive education movement); the Supreme Court (in school desegregation); Admiral Rickover (in his criticism of school curriculum); James Coleman, a sociologist (principal author of the Coleman Report); the Congress (in its attempts to compel effective evaluations of programs under Title I of the Elementary and Secondary Education Act); the United States Commission on Civil Rights (in school desegregation); and, apparently with increasing frequency, the students themselves (in their protests and demonstrations) are all typical instances of such intervention. The efforts have met with mixed success, but this is not surprising (remember Mann's *answer* to a *response* to a *rebuttal* of a *critique*?). The instances we offer are almost all comparatively "new."

Of course, "lay control" has not always fostered healthy developments. For example, in southern communities, educational administrators may sometimes be "ahead of their constituencies" on the issue of school desegregation. However, in some senses, this exception still illustrates the rule—neither desegregation nor segregation have been initiated or aggressively promoted by educators, but rather by courts, civil rights activists, legislatures, White Citizens Councils, governors, and presidential commissions. The major arguments over this issue have not been between educators, and desegregation will probably only take place when a clear majority of laymen take a definitive, affirmative position. Until that day, educators probably will play a relatively subordinate role. This concept of lay control suggests that lay involvement (plus educator support) will be a key to the successful implementation of new models. In fact, the change-oriented perspective the outsider can bring is exemplified in the previously presented writings. The designers of the models include social psychologists, lawyers, sociologists, and economists, as well as activist educators. Let us hope that equally diversified alliances, plus parents, students, and politicians, arise to move us from analysis to action.

Index